Spirituality
and the
Awakening Self

Books by David G. Benner

Soulful Spirituality (2011)

Opening to God: Lectio Divina and Life as Prayer (2010)

Desiring God's Will: Aligning Our Hearts with the Heart of God (2005)

The Gift of Being Yourself: The Sacred Call to Self-Discovery (2004)

Surrender to Love: Discovering the Heart of Christian Spirituality (2003)

Strategic Pastoral Counseling: A Short-Term Structured Model, 2nd ed. (2003)

Sacred Companions: The Gift of Spiritual Friendship and Direction (2002)

Free at Last: Breaking the Bondage of Guilt and Emotional Wounds (1998)

Care of Souls: Revisioning Christian Nurture and Counsel (1998)

Money Madness and Financial Freedom: The Psychology of Money Meanings and Management (1996)

Choosing the Gift of Forgiveness: How to Overcome Hurts and Brokenness, with Robert Harvey (1996)

Understanding and Facilitating Forgiveness, with Robert Harvey (1996)

Counseling as a Spiritual Process (1991)

Healing Emotional Wounds (1990)

Psychotherapy and the Spiritual Quest (1988)

Therapeutic Love: An Incarnational Interpretation of Counseling (1985)

Books Edited by David G. Benner

Spiritual Direction and the Care of Souls: A Guide to Christian Approaches and Practices, with Gary Moon (2004)

Baker Encyclopedia of Psychology and Counseling, 2nd ed., with Peter Hill (1999)

Christian Perspectives on Human Development, with LeRoy Aden and J. Harold Ellens (1992)

Counseling and the Human Predicament: A Study of Sin, Guilt, and Forgiveness, with LeRoy Aden (1989)

Psychology and Religion (1988)

Psychotherapy in Christian Perspective (1987)

Christian Counseling and Psychotherapy (1987)

Spirituality
and the
Awakening Self

THE SACRED JOURNEY *of* TRANSFORMATION

David G. Benner, PhD

BrazosPress

a division of Baker Publishing Group
Grand Rapids, Michigan

To Ed Plantinga,
for helping me stay awake

© 2012 by David G. Benner

Published by Brazos Press
a division of Baker Publishing Group
P.O. Box 6287, Grand Rapids, MI 49516-6287
www.brazospress.com

Printed in the United States of America

Library of Congress Cataloging-in-Publication Data
Benner, David G.
    Spirituality and the awakening self : the sacred journey of transformation / David G. Benner.
        p.   cm.
    Includes bibliographical references (p.   ) and index.
    ISBN 978-1-58743-296-5 (pbk.)
    1. Self-actualization (Psychology)—Religious aspects—Christianity. 2. Maturation (Psychology)—Religious aspects—Christianity. 3. Self—Religious aspects—Christianity. 4. Spirituality. I. Title.
    BV4598.2.B46 2012
    248—dc23   2011036998

12   13   14   15   16   17   18   7   6   5   4   3   2   1

Contents

Preface

The Journey of Human Becoming

Being human is a journey of becoming. At birth we humans are not yet what we have the capacity to fully become. Newborns may contain the possibilities for mature personhood, but they do not show any of the characteristics that psychologists have identified as markers of fully actualized humanity. Never present in childhood are such things as the capacity for nonpossessive love, a spirituality that makes life meaningful and suffering sufferable, and an identification with all humans, not simply those of one's own tribe. Many other things could be specified and will be identified as we proceed, but even this partial list shows the magnitude of the task of achieving full-orbed personhood.

Although the journey of human becoming is lifelong, it is not simply a result of the passage of time. Time is necessary but not sufficient. Maturation may make human actualization possible, but full personhood comes only from a lifelong journey of becoming that, as we shall see, must be lived in a posture of openness, trust, willingness, and surrender.

Glimpses of the Evolving Self

Watch as the young child learns to trust that her mother is still there even though she may be out of sight. Piaget called this developmental accomplishment the achievement of object constancy. It is a moment to celebrate, and parents usually do. But then watch as the cognitive skills of this same little girl continue to develop, and notice now how she suddenly seems secure within a first-person perspective on her world. She speaks as an "I" and organizes her experience around this "I." The result is something that we could call an egocentric perspective on the world: this is a tremendously important moment of human becoming.

But the journey is far from over—even if we continue to follow just this single line of cognitive development and the way in which it provides a perspective from which the person views and relates to the world. Notice how a few years later she has hopefully added a second-person perspective to this egocentric way of relating to that which is beyond her own self. What we might call a sociocentric worldview now allows her to see things from the perspectives of others. A developing capacity for empathy allows her to adopt an alternate perspective and no longer be limited to the first-person point of view that earlier was such a developmental triumph.

The subsequent development of the capacity for reason ushers in another stage as, in adolescence, she now adds third-person perspectives and is capable of adopting a more truly world-centric orientation to that which is beyond her. And because we can only identify with what we can see in relationship to self, she is now able to feel herself to be integrally connected to the world, not just to her social or religious group or to her family or herself. Through this process her self is unfolding. The same is true for all of us. By a sequence of ever-expanding identifications, we become what we identify with, and if we trust the flow of this process, our small self becomes a larger and truer self.

There are other important steps in this cognitive and perspective-taking line, and many other important lines of development also shape the journey of the developing self. But let us look at just one more image from later in the journey of this hypothetical young woman. Suppose that she remains open to life and that this openness includes openness toward God. It may well be that when we next look into her life, we recognize something that others around her may not see, or at least not understand. They may notice her equanimity and nonjudgmental openness, and they may even describe her as a very spiritual woman. But if we take the time to get to know her, we may begin to notice how deeply her identity and consciousness are grounded in her relationship to God. Yet relationship may not be exactly the right word because she might talk more of an abiding sense of being in God and God's being in her. She might also talk about this leading to a sense of being at one within herself and within God. Although we may not understand exactly what she means, we might begin to suspect that she is something of a mystic. In response to this suggestion, she might laugh and say that she is no mystic. But when asked more about her life, she might tell you, as the woman I am thinking about recently told me, "It's true: there is nothing I want more than to know God deeply. But it's also true that I am less and less clear about where the boundaries between God and me—or God and anyone—begin or end. Increasingly I see God in all people and all things—not contained in any of these people or things but expressed in and through them all. And increasingly I feel one with God and one with life—really, one with all that is."

This journey into a deeper consciousness of our being in God will be our focus in this book. We can describe it as a journey of the evolving or unfolding self because the self that begins this journey is never the self that ends it. But we could also call it a journey of an awakening self because awakening is the central dynamic of the unfolding and evolving. The self that emerges during this journey is larger, more enlightened, and more whole. This journey is one that all humans are invited to make. It is the journey that defines our humanity, for it is a journey toward our source and toward our fulfillment. It is a journey into what Christian theology has traditionally described as union with God.

A Theology of Becoming

The source and ground of all existence lies in the constantly outpouring life of God. Moment by moment all creation is sustained by God. Creation is not just something that happened in the past. Though there may have been a beginning point, it was the beginning of an active relationship that never stops—a relationship that exists between God and every person and thing that exists. If this relationship were suddenly to stop, we and everything else that is would instantly cease to exist.

But it is not just all being that is grounded in God: so too is all becoming. The universe is a place of creativity, becoming, and transformation because these are fundamental properties of the God who sustains it. All things are not only sustained by God; but all things are also being made new in Christ. All things are being liberated and restored—becoming more than they are, becoming all they were intended to be in their fullness in Christ.

The Spirit of God—the source of all generativity, all creativity, and all life—invites us to participate in the grand adventure of human becoming. Openness to becoming is openness to God. This is why the Christian mystics have so much to teach us. They show us that longing for the fullness of God demands openness to a radical form of transformation that we cannot control. It is something we can neither engineer nor accomplish. But it is something we can experience.

It is, however, alarmingly easy to fail to discern the ever-present nudges of the Spirit to become all we are meant to be. The culture of family and society and the rhythms of our lives lull us into a sleep of complacency within the small, safe places we have arranged for ourselves. Seekers settle for being finders, even when what is found is so much less than what their spirits call them toward. Being and becoming are both routinely sacrificed on the altar of doing. The gentle but persistent heartbeat of our deep longings to find our true place in God is gradually drowned out by the cacophony of superficial desires, and we are left with a small ego-self rather than an awakening self that is ever becoming in the Spirit.

Being Realistic about Deep Personal Change

There are many possible metaphors for this journey of becoming. I have already introduced the concepts of awakening, unfolding, and evolving. Other possible metaphors include rebirth (from death to life), integration (from fragmentation to wholeness), liberation (from captivity to freedom), unification (from separation to oneness), enlightenment (from blindness to seeing), and homecoming (returning from exile). All of these help us identify elements of the transformation of the self that are involved in this journey, and I will draw on each of them as we proceed.

Nevertheless, given how hard change of any sort is, we need to be realistic about these grand ideals of becoming, awakening, enlightenment, and transformation. Becoming is a luxury that evades those whose lives are preoccupied with survival or basic coping. Until lower-level needs are dependably being met, talk of human unfolding remains nothing but meaningless chatter on the part of those who have the luxury of full bellies, a reasonable base of personal security, and idle time.

I am also quite aware of how easy it is to be cynical about the possibilities of deep personal change. After all, anyone who has ever tried to keep even the simplest New Year's resolution knows the limits of self-improvement projects. If such things as stopping smoking, eating less, or exercising more are as notoriously difficult as most of us recognize them to be, what hope could there ever be for the sort of quantum leap in change that is implied by the concept of transformation?

Recall the familiar story of the frog and the scorpion. One day a scorpion decided it wanted to cross a river. The problem was that he couldn't swim. Seeing a frog sitting on the bank, he asked the frog to carry him across the river on his back. The frog refused. "I don't trust you," he said. "I know how dangerous scorpions are. If I let you get on my back, you'll sting me and kill me." The scorpion answered, "But why would I do that? That would be stupid because if I sting you, then we'll both drown." "But how do I know you won't just wait until we get to the other side and then kill me?" asked the frog. The scorpion had an answer for this question as well: "I would never do that because when we get to the other side, I will be so grateful for your help that I could never sting you." The frog thought about these answers for a while and finally agreed to let the scorpion get on his back. He began swimming, gradually feeling safer and safer, and starting to even think that he had been foolish to have ever worried about the scorpion. But half way across the river, suddenly the scorpion stung the frog. "You fool," croaked the frog, "now we will both die! Why did you do that?" The scorpion answered, "Because I'm a scorpion. It is in my nature to sting."

Personality is, by definition, highly stable, and profound changes in the organization and orientation of the self are quite rare. Most alterations are cosmetic and contextual. They are much more likely to involve dressing the scorpion up in some more fashionable clothes than changing its nature. Changes that we see are usually not much more than accommodations to tribal and cultural expectations, not radical reorganizations of the self from the inside out. Although we can see evolution of human consciousness over large periods of human history, it is rarer to see genuine and significant changes in consciousness, identity, values, and ways of relating to self, others, and life after late adolescence or early adulthood.

However, after three decades of providing psychoanalytic psychotherapy and one decade of working with people who seek personal transformation through spiritual openness, contemplative stillness, and awareness, I would have to say that while deep and really meaningful changes in people are relatively rare, they are very possible. It is possible to experience a profound reorganization of the very foundations of our identity, values, meaning, and consciousness. It is possible for our whole perspective on life—on our self, on others, on the world, and on God—to shift dramatically. It is possible to awaken and move from blindness to seeing, from captivity to freedom, and from separation to oneness. It is possible for us to experience the emergence of our larger, truer self that we in reality are. These sorts of quantum shifts in the organization of our being are never something that simply result from things that happen to us. Nor are they simply the cumulative result of the small incremental steps of growth associated with our efforts at spiritual or psychological self-improvement. But when we respond to life and the continuous invitations of the Spirit to become more than we presently are, with consent and openness of heart and mind, it can be our experience—with or without external triggers.

These sorts of changes are deeply spiritual. Our spirituality either keeps us safely immune to such changes or facilitates them. But genuine transformation never happens without profound spiritual implications. Although personal transformation will be my primary focus, we will also see that ultimately transformation is not just a personal matter. Genuine transformation occurs only within a communal and interpersonal context. Often those communal contexts inhibit transformation, but they can facilitate it and always mediate it. We either open each other up to the transformational possibilities that we encounter in life or close each other down. Sadly, it seems to me that much of the emphasis on spiritual formation and transformation that exists in Christianity does the latter, as do the ways we relate to each other in Christian communities and churches. But I am convinced that we can experience transformational awakenings much more frequently and fully if our families, churches, and communities can learn to support them rather than fear or resist them.

Anyone who has influence over the lives of others is in a position to help make this happen—particularly those of us who are involved in any aspect of the nurture, care, formation, or reformation of others. Therapists, spiritual directors, clergy, religious workers and educators, parents, mentors, coaches, and others who are involved with the nurture of the inner life of persons—all these can do much more to help those they are encouraging to truly become all they can be. We can help people notice and respond to the moments in their journey that are pregnant with transformational possibilities. And we can help them attend and respond to their deep spiritual longings, longings that always point us beyond the safe way stations where we settle, onward to those places and ways of being that hold genuinely transformational possibilities for us and for the world.

Becoming All We Can Be

My interest in these possibilities of becoming all we can be has been at the center of my life's work in psychology and spirituality. This was the interest that originally led me into training in clinical psychology and later in spiritual direction. I wrote an outline of this book in 1974, but I was far from ready to write it or, much more importantly, to experience it. The ground on which I stood was too small—theologically, spiritually, and psychologically. Of course, it was me who was too small. I was far too invested in the life of the mind and soul to make the journey of spirit for which I longed. I flirted with ideas but was not ready to respond to the deep call of the Spirit to my spirit that drove my interest in human unfolding and awakening. Over that time I wrote a number of books on psychology and spirituality in which transformation organized my approach to both but remained a secondary focus. In this book *transformation* moves from the background to the foreground.

This book also moves something else from the back stage of recent books to center stage: *mysticism*. This, I am convinced, is the branch of spirituality that has the most to contribute to an understanding and experience of transformation, awakening, and human becoming. All major religions have a mystical tradition, and if we are to experience the fullest unfolding of our self, it is essential that we learn to listen to what the mystics have to teach us. Mysticism uniquely supports the integration of insights of psychology and spirituality into a framework for both understanding and nurturing the unfolding self. Without mysticism I am convinced that neither psychology nor spirituality have much worth saying about personal transformation or the further reaches of human becoming.

Psychology and spirituality are not, however, the only fields of study that offer important potential contributions to understanding human unfolding. In what follows, I will draw on insights from Perennial Philosophy; evolutionary theology; cultural anthropology; comparative spirituality; and clinical, developmental, and transpersonal psychology—placing all of this back within a Christian understanding. But before your eyes begin to glaze over, I should make clear that this will not be a dry academic exercise. The map I will be sketching of the awakening self is complex, and the ideas are big, but I will be repeatedly pausing to step back from these ideas so we can examine the difference they actually make in real life. My primary interest is in the spirituality of this unfolding, not the theory of it. Although I will have to lay out a fairly complex conceptual foundation for us to understand that spirituality, we will keep returning to the lived difference it can actually make.

It is the Christian mystics who will provide the overall framework for the synthesis I will offer and—although this might surprise you—it is they who will help us keep this practical. Mystics are interested in experience, not in theories. They are aware of a profound truth that most of the rest of us fail to appreciate. Mystics know that all of life is flowing toward God, and they have learned how to open themselves to this flow and participate in it. Life has a direction. It is returning to its source. The outflowing vitality and love of God that is life itself leads back toward God. This is the key to understanding the human journey and the key to understanding the transformational journey of human becoming. Transformation is not simply change. Nor is it reducible to maturation or self-improvement. Transformation is movement toward wholeness. It is an unfolding of the self that moves us toward being at one within our self and with God.

Christians affirm that everything that exists is being held this very moment in Christ, and that everything that exists is being made new in Christ. These mystical truths may be beyond our comprehension, but they are not beyond our potential experience. We may not understand these things, but we can know them. To that end I have written this book. I have written it with the Collect of the Fourth Sunday after Epiphany as my prayer:[1]

Living God, in Christ you make all things new.

Transform the poverty of our nature by the riches of your grace, and in the renewal of our lives make known your glory; through Jesus Christ our Lord, who is alive and reigns with you and the Holy Spirit, one God, now and for ever.

Amen.

D. G. B.
Holy Cross Day
Victoria, British Columbia, Canada

1

Human Awakening

Many things keep us content with our small selves and block us from becoming all we can be. None, however, is more important than the fact that most of us go through life as sleepwalkers and, even after a moment of awakening, tend to quickly drift off once again into a sleep of self-preoccupied oblivion and of a mindless robot shuffling through a somnambulistic fog. This is the reason spiritual teachers have always taught the importance of awareness. Hasidic Jews tell a story of a young man who approached Reb Yerachmiel ben Yisrael one afternoon. "Rebbe," the young man asked with great seriousness, "what is the way to God?" The rebbe looked up from his work and answered: "There is no way to God, for God is not other than here and now. The truth you seek is not hidden from you; you simply do not notice it. It is here for you if you will only awake."

This is the truth that has been proclaimed by all the great Christian mystics across Christian history. And it is the truth taught from cover to cover of the Bible. In his Areopagus sermon, Paul declares that God "is not far from any of us, since it is in him that we live and move and exist" (Acts 17:27–28). God is closer than our next breath. Job even reminds us that not only is God the source of each breath, but each breath also is God's breath (Job 27:3). How much more intimate could our relationship with God be? God is not absent. It is we who fail to notice divine presence. It's all a matter of awareness.

Jesus also often urged his followers to awaken from their stupor and be attentive (Matt. 25:13; Luke 12:37). And he used the most dramatic of all possible metaphors to describe this ascent from unconsciousness. He described it as being "born again" (John 3:3–8 KJV).

A Fresh Start

All of us know something of the desire to wake up in the morning and be able to start the new day as a new person. We want to believe in the possibility of change—real change. We want a fresh start for our personal lives, and many wish it were possible for our communities, nations, the world, and the cosmos.

Saul undoubtedly started the day that was to be his fresh start without any idea of what awaited him as he headed off for Damascus. As the story is told in the Acts of the Apostles (Acts 9:1–19), Saul was a well-known and particularly aggressive persecutor of first-century Christians. The account of his spiritual awakening is immediately preceded by reference to his supportive presence at the stoning of Stephen, a Christian whose dedication to Jesus matched the opposition of Saul. Christians were living in fear of this man, who was famous for his hatred of them. What happened next was, therefore, as much a surprise to others as it was to Saul.

The details of the story are quite simple and straightforward. On the day in question, while going to Damascus to pick up authorization from the high priest for further arrests of any Christians he could find, Saul suddenly and inexplicably found himself surrounded by a heavenly light. Blinded, he fell to the ground. He then heard a voice addressing him, "Saul, Saul, why are you persecuting me?" Asking who addressed him, the voice answered: "I am Jesus, and you are persecuting me. Get up now and go into the city, and you will be told what you have to do." Saul did just as he was told. He got up—still seeing nothing—and allowed himself to be led to Damascus by hand. There he waited for three days, eating and drinking nothing and still blind, until Ananias came to him and said, "Brother Saul, I have been sent by the Lord Jesus, who appeared to you on your way here so that you might recover your sight and be filled with the Holy Spirit." Immediately, as though scales fell away from his eyes, he could see.

In that moment Saul ceased to exist and a new man, Paul, was born. The new man was as radically committed to the promotion of the church as the old man had once been committed to its destruction. The man who had come to the city to arrest Christians was transformed into a man who was to spend the rest of his life as the early church's most tireless and fearless advocate.

I have worked on the reduction of ethnic hatred in the war zones associated with the collapse of the former Yugoslavia and know how difficult it is to make even small dents in entrenched patterns of prejudice and hostility, especially once they become established parts of identity. But this was no small dent. This was a dramatic re-formation of attitudes, values, character, and behavior. Obviously Saul needed a new name to accommodate the magnitude of these changes. He was a new man. Nothing less than the metaphor of being born again could adequately describe the significance of Saul's awakening.

Christians have usually referred to this awakening as conversion. Although this is certainly an appropriate term, it casts the change in overly narrow religious terms. It implies that what is involved is essentially a change of religions, or the adoption of the beliefs and practices of a particular religion. Saul's change involved much more than this. The biblical account of the story points us to the broader implications of the transformation by its focus on seeing. At the core of the experience was his movement from blindness to sight. But his blindness was far deeper than the temporary three-day absence of sight. What he had been blind to was the reality of and his relationship to Christ. When the scales fell off his eyes, what he saw was not just his surroundings but also the truth behind the words of those he had sought to silence—that Jesus was indeed the Light of the world.

Saul's personal encounter with the Light was the core of his awakening, and his subsequent enlightenment was the central dynamic of the new man that he became. New life began to surge through parts of his self that had shriveled under the weight of hate and murderous zeal. Love began to seep into his soul. He didn't simply switch causes and retain the same self: his mind and his heart were transformed, his spirit realigned, and his life reorganized.

Awakenings are not always this dramatic, nor do they always involve a recognizable encounter with the Divine. But when we offer our consent to the awakening that either external or internal circumstances may provide, those circumstances can be a gateway to a rebirth—not just in a theological sense but also in a psychological and spiritual one. They can lead to dramatic new life that is grounded in profound changes in the self.

Losing Our Mind and Coming to Our Senses

We have recognized that Paul's awakening was more a matter of seeing than simply a change of beliefs. But it is not just seeing that is involved in awakening. Awakening can come through any of the senses.

Gestalt therapy is built entirely on this power of awakening. Fritz Perls, the founder of this approach to psychotherapy, calls it "awareness" and describes the way in which awareness draws us back into our bodies, in touch with our senses, and mobilizes us for action.[1] He argues that in order to be truly alive, we must be aware of our impulses and yearnings, of the here and now, of our sensory experience, and of what he calls our unfinished business. Then and only then is real change possible.

Perls describes three levels of awareness: awareness of the self, awareness of the world, and awareness of the intervening fantasy between the self and the world. This intermediate world contains our prejudices and prejudgments through which we view our experiences of everything beyond us. Here we see the world through the labels we give things and the categories into which we jam them. But experiencing the world through categorization, bias, and prejudgment is not experiencing things as they actually are. It is experiencing our thoughts about the world rather than directly experiencing the world. The distance this provides from the raw reality of things as they truly are keeps us comfortable but out of touch with reality and unaware.

Anthony De Mello, the twentieth-century Christian mystic who has done so much to bring together the spiritual wisdom of East and West, describes this lack of awareness by means of a pithy aphorism. "Life," he suggests, "is like heady wine. Everyone reads the label on the bottle. Hardly anyone tastes the wine."[2] Confusing the reading of labels with tasting and drinking the wine is responding to the world through this intermediate zone of thoughts, judgments, biases, and preconceptions. It is mistaking this comfortable place within our self for an authentic encounter with external reality. It is failing to recognize the difference between fantasy and raw experience.

Becoming aware of this intermediate zone empties it by drawing us into the present moment. Suddenly the world is present to us and we are present to it. Suddenly we have moved from our mind to our senses, and through them, we are in more immediate and direct contact with what truly is. This is what Eckhart Tolle calls the power of the now.[3] An embrace of the present moment can do something that nothing else can do: it can bring us into the only place where we truly are, the only place we can truly be alive, and the only place where we can truly meet God.

Sometimes, however, we choose to withdraw our attention from the present moment because it is unpleasant or threatening. We have two major options for this form of escape: we can escape to the past through nostalgic remembering and compulsive review, or to the future through anxious anticipation and obsessive rehearsals. Both involve an escape into the safety of our minds. They are, therefore, ways of staying asleep, or if we have had a momentary awakening, of quickly returning to sleep.

This is the reason why awakening and awareness are so vital to the spiritual life. From time to time we may awaken for brief moments of intense emotional experience, but then we quickly slip back into a tangled dreamworld of the intermediate zone between genuine awareness of our self and genuine awareness of the world. The invitation of the present moment is always to awaken, to respond rather than simply react, and to become full participants in our lives.

The Context of Awakenings and Awareness

Each moment of awareness is a small awakening, and each awakening—no matter how insignificant it might seem—can be a doorway to becoming. As an object of awareness, nothing is too small to empower such an awakening. Awareness of anything opens us to the transcendent. This is why awareness is so central to prayer. Douglas Steere describes prayer as "awakeness, attention, intense inward openness." In his view, sin is anything that destroys this attentive wakefulness.[4]

Let us look more closely at this sequence of events that surround awakening. Awareness is always preceded by a sensation. Sensations are invitations to engage with something in the present moment, something either in our inner world or in the external world. The traditional five senses—sight, hearing, touch, smell, and taste—are the most familiar to us and are the most regular doorways to the present moment that we encounter. Each invites us to notice something. Each is, therefore, an invitation to awareness. Awareness begins, therefore, as a response to a sensation.

The act of responding to the invitation of a sensation by noticing it (awareness) immediately sets in motion a chain of events and possibilities. The first is that it brings us back from our heads (where we escape whenever we are not present to the moment) to our bodies and to our vital energies that are grounded in them. We can only be alive in our bodies through our senses. And conversely, we cannot be engaged with our senses without being in touch with our bodies. However, as soon as we attend to a sensation—any sensation—we immediately experience the gift of mobilized energy. This energy will not always feel positive. But awareness always mobilizes energy that prepares us to respond to whatever we now notice. If we back away from this energy out of fear, we shut it down, cut off our access to our vitality, and go back to sleep. However, if we respond to whatever our attention has engaged, we allow the energy to awaken us.

Returning to the awakening of Paul, the sensations that invited attention were the blinding light and the voice addressing him. Even such a dramatic encounter as Paul experienced could have been easily ignored and regularly is ignored. But Paul responded to the sensation by offering attention rather than resistance. From a more theological perspective, we can say that he opened himself to God. He did this by submitting to those who told him where to go and waiting until God revealed what he should do next. This waiting was preparation

FIGURE 1.1
The Context of Awakenings

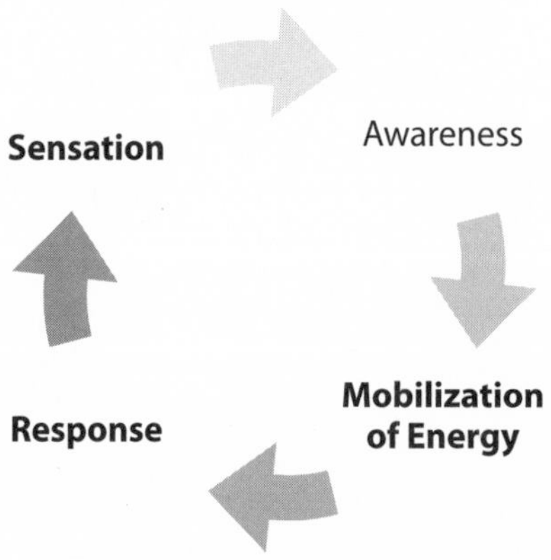

Sensation   Awareness

Response   **Mobilization of Energy**

for response; the immediacy and lifelong persistence of his response attests to the magnitude of the vitalization that was associated with his awakening.

Invitations to Awaken

A great variety of experiences can serve as the messenger that brings us an invitation to awareness and offers us the potential of an awakening. Unfortunately, however, we usually evaluate these events negatively and, instead of welcoming them, do everything we can to ignore, minimize, or avoid them. In general, anything that produces significant internal conflict, a disruption of meaning and self-coherence, or a sense that our way of being in the world needs to change—any such thing has this potential to awaken us. Some of these emerge from the circumstances of our life. A divorce, major financial reversal, death of a spouse or child, natural catastrophe, or a business failure can all contain a hidden gift of a potential awakening. Many people speak of a significant and valued change to the course of their life following such unwelcome events. Sometimes these changes are limited to behavior or lifestyle, but deeper transformations of self are also possible when one moves beyond simply trying to get back to how things were before the crisis.

Near-Death Experiences

Near-death experiences have particular potency as a context for potential awakenings. Keith's experience illustrates many of the common features of this phenomenon, including the spiritual awakening that sometimes accompanies it.

Keith was an experienced thirty-eight-year-old scuba diver when, on one fateful dive, he became separated from his dive buddy and trapped in a narrow passage of a network of caves they had been exploring. Already very low on air, his panicked thrashing and squirming quickly depleted his remaining air, and he soon lost consciousness and stopped breathing. Not long after this, his friend found him, immediately brought him to the surface, got him onto the dive boat, and began mouth-to-mouth resuscitation. After what seemed like an eternity but was probably only a few minutes, Keith suddenly began coughing, sputtering, and eventually breathing. His report of the experience emerged much more slowly.

At first he said nothing about it. Words seemed totally inadequate to describe what had happened in those few moments, and in a strange way he felt that it was too sacred to share with someone he knew could never understand it. This was an odd thought for him because he had no religious background and certainly did not think of himself as spiritual. However, as he began to talk about it with his wife, he told her that he felt like he was living in the first days of a brand new life. He told her that after immediate panic, he felt very calm as he drew what he knew would be his last few breaths. He noticed that he was viewing himself from some point outside his body. Slowly he noticed that the darkness of the underwater tomb in which he was trapped began to be filled with light and that he was passing through the darkness and rising toward this light. Watching from this vantage point outside his body, he saw his friend pulling him out of the cave and up toward the surface of the water. He wanted to tell him that it was OK, that everything was fine—actually, much better than fine. He felt total peace and was, therefore, somewhat annoyed by his friend's efforts to resuscitate him. But he also knew that he faced a choice: he could return to life or stay in the place of bliss. It was, he said, very tempting to stay, but, thinking of his wife and young family, he chose life and began to breathe.

The Keith who walked away from that experience was indeed quite different from the Keith who went diving that morning. His wife expected the changes to fade when he returned to work. But even his coworkers noticed that he had changed. His greatly enhanced appreciation for life was understandable. Even Keith was surprised by his deeper compassion for others and the way this began to change his sense of purpose and meaning in life. He had experienced an awakening. It might not be enough to stay awake for the rest of his life, but he knew that he was a new person, and he knew that the trajectory of his life had changed.

Experiences such as Keith's have been well documented and researched. Long-term spiritual changes often accompany near-death encounters such as Keith's, and when they do, rather than diminish over time, they often increase.[5] It seems that they are self-reinforcing. But this is just what you would expect with an awakening. One awakening invites openness and responsiveness to others. Nevertheless, just as an encounter with the Divine on a trip to Damascus did not guarantee awakening but simply provided an invitation to it, the same is true of near-death experiences. I have talked with people who have had a significant near-death experience that left them shaken but unchanged. But this shouldn't surprise us because just as we can sleep through an alarm clock or an earthquake, so too can we respond to any sort of crisis by ignoring the invitation to awaken that the moment may contain.

Psychological Symptoms

Invitations of another category are those annoying and always unwelcome psychological symptoms that most of us experience from time to time, things like depression, anxiety, or unusually high levels of anger or irritation. These symptoms can have a physiological basis, and this possibility should never be ignored. However, as existential, psychoanalytic, archetypal, and analytical therapists remind us, this does not mean that they do not *also* serve as the voice of the soul. Once again, therefore, they can function as messengers that carry an invitation to awaken from our somnambulistic state.

Although we are tempted to believe otherwise, ultimately there is no way to avoid the realities of the inner self. Eventually they will catch up with us. The truths of our inner life that we seek to ignore lurk on the edges of consciousness like troublesome dogs nipping at our heels. They also seep into relationships and behavior, dragging issues that remain unfinished from the past into the present and keeping us on an eternal treadmill of reacting to the unresolved aspects of our history. This may sound like bad news. Yet it also contains good news since this means that we regularly are afforded opportunities to deal with these internal saboteurs that sap our vitality and compromise our presence. Unfortunately, however, because those opportunities come to us in the form of symptoms and crises, only rarely do we offer them the hospitality that is necessary if we are to use them as an opportunity to awaken.

In addition to whatever other functions psychological symptoms may serve, they do bring us information about the state of our inner self. That nagging depression or low-level anxiety, or the ease with which we lose our temper or are tempted to despair—these are all messengers from our depths that have been sent into consciousness to tell each of us that all is not well in our soul. However, if we ignore or silence the messenger, or refuse to open the letter they bring and attend to the issue they are pointing us toward, we are doomed to allow the inner problem to worsen and simply postpone the crisis that is eventually awaiting each of us.

If we return to the invitation to awaken that Saul encountered that day on his way to Damascus, we likely first notice external circumstances that invite his awakening: the blinding light and voice. But a closer look at his story suggests the possibility of an inner struggle that may have been preparing him for this day. Let me paint a picture of what might well have been the inner world of Saul as he headed off to Damascus that day.[6]

Since Augustine of Hippo, theologians have generally assumed that Saul suffered from a guilty conscience. Later describing himself as "chief among sinners" (1 Tim. 1:15), Paul was undoubtedly referring primarily to his preconversion behavior, which went as far as offering his supportive presence at the stoning of at least one Christian: Stephen. On the road to Damascus, the words addressed to Saul in his encounter with Jesus point to his inner conflict. This is particularly clear in the language of the King James Version where, after Saul asks who is addressing him, the text reads: "And the Lord said, I am Jesus whom thou persecutest: it is hard for thee to kick against the pricks" (Acts 9:5). Without owning up to this inner conflict of kicking against pricks, it would have been impossible for Saul to respond to this moment's invitation by awakening. And apparently that is just what he did. We hear no words of protest or self-defense. We see no expressions of anger. Instead, we see a remarkable period of quiet self-reflection as he spends the next several days in fasting and undoubtedly reflecting on his life while waiting for God's further words to him.

Saul's readiness to attend to rather than ignore this sense of guilt made his awakening possible. It was not enough for him to focus on the external events to which his physical senses drew his attention. Paying attention to his inner conflict engaged the depths of his soul, and this was essential if this encounter was to be an encounter of his spirit and the Spirit of God.

Dreams

But there is another very important and even more common place where we encounter the voice of the soul: in our dreams. Dreams form a part of the life of all of us, even a much larger part than most of us realize. Whether we feel that our nights are filled with dreams or that we never dream, we all spend approximately one-quarter of each night dreaming, thus an average of two hours of dreaming for every eight hours of sleep.

However, if the default response to symptoms is to repress them rather than listen to the message they bring from our depths, it is even easier to ignore and dismiss dreams as an important voice of the soul. After all, we are often told that dreams are simply random neurological activity that occurs when we are asleep—quite irrelevant to the daily life of nonsuperstitious modern and postmodern individuals. Yet this is far from the way premoderns viewed dreams. Before the eighteenth century, virtually everyone assumed that dreams had spiritual significance. The traditional Jewish understanding, for example, was that all dreams are given by God as a gift to the dreamer for the well-being of oneself or related others. This implies a relationship between the dreamer and God, but it also implies that the gift must be opened if it is to be of value. This is why the Jewish rabbis often compared dreams to a letter, maintaining that if it is to be of any value, it must, like a letter, be opened and read.

In appendix 1, I offer a more detailed discussion of how one can work with dreams to discern their spiritual and psychological significance as voices of the soul. Here let me simply say that if you are interested in receiving a dream with hospitality and opening it with prayerful attentiveness to the gift that it might contain, the most important principle in doing so is to avoid analyzing it. Rather, listen to it as you would listen to a story or a parable, asking, "What could this be telling me about the state of my inner world?" The assumption behind this question is that our dreams are usually about us, not about the other characters who may populate our dreams as stand-ins for parts of ourselves. So do not try to analyze the meaning of the story. Just listen to it with prayerful attention and ask, "Lord, what might you want to draw to my attention through this dream?"

To illustrate this, let me share the dream of a thirty-six-year-old single woman at a transitional point in her life. Anna was a librarian at a major research university and described herself as having a fulfilling life and a rich network of friends. However, over the past several years she said that she had become less satisfied with her work and increasingly wondered if she had settled for too small and comfortable a place for herself. She said that she had been wondering if she should go back to school and try something different. After beginning to explore several potential directions that attracted her, she sought help in reflecting on the decisions she faced. The night before our first meeting she had a dream. This is how she reported it to me:

Last night I had a dream that was a variation on one I have had several times over the last couple of years. I was a waitress in a wild-West saloon. The place was full of rough-living, foul-mouthed males. I was quite surprised to notice how comfortable I was with them because it is so unlike how I usually am and was certainly unlike the sort of life I actually live. But then I noticed how good so many of them were to me. Although they didn't let each other see it, they were actually quite tender to me. But they liked it when I treated them rudely, and so that's what I did. I was quite shocked to see how I was in the dream: I swore at them, I ignored the insults they hurled at me in good fun, and I dished insults back to them in a rather shocking form. Watching myself, I could see that I really liked the interaction. But it was so strange to be watching someone who looked like me and felt like me but was so different from me. The scene changes in each dream, but the basic elements remain the same.

I did not tell Anna what her dream meant. That is not something I would ever do. The dreamer is in the best position to discern any possible meaning that the dream may have. The job of anyone else who is listening in is simply to help maintain a reflective space that is safe, open, and free from reductionistic attempts to find the one true meaning of the dream. I encouraged her to simply listen to it as a story that might just have something to say to her about her life; I asked her what most struck her about the dream. She told me that it was herself—or better, the woman who looked like her and with whom she identified in the dream but who behaved very differently from her. After talking for a while about what differences she noticed and how she reacted to this woman, I asked her if she felt that there might be any invitations for her in the dream. After a few moments of reflection, she said, "I don't think I want to be a bartender, but I wonder if the dream might point toward a less passive and less safe way of living." I then asked her what this way of living might look like. She responded by telling me about a colleague at work whom she admired, a woman who seemed full of vitality and passion and who was prepared to take risks and live spontaneously. As she talked about this, I noticed how much more animated she became. The dream wasn't about jobs: it was about her. It was an invitation to consider more vital and authentic ways of living her life.

Attending to dreams involves the same process as attending to psychological symptoms, to surprisingly strong reactions to a person or situation, or to anything else arising from within one's self. It involves receiving the experience with hospitality, not judgment, analysis, or an attempt to fix yourself or the experience. Offer the experience a reflective space and listen, watch, and be open to what emerges in that space and within you. This is the process of attending to a dream. It expresses your openness to fresh gifts of awareness and to the experience of an awakening. And because, from my perspective, all awareness and awakening is a gift of God, it is a brush with the Divine—an encounter of the same sort Saul experienced on his way to Damascus.

Listening to Our Body

For those who have eyes to see and ears to hear, our bodies offer us a continuous stream of invitations to awaken. This is why body awareness forms the foundation of all awareness. You can be no more aware of anything than you are of your body—and in case you are wondering, I am convinced that this limit on your awareness includes your awareness of God.

Every breath can be a doorway to awareness and awakening. This is why attending to one's breath is such a foundational practice in all spiritual traditions. Its important place in Christian spirituality has often been overlooked; yet the foundation of breath prayer as a Christian practice is grounded in the creation story, which speaks of God forming humans from the dust of the earth but animating them with God's own breath.[7] Each breath we receive is a gift of God, drawing God into our very being. Attending to our breathing is, therefore, a prayerful way of opening our selves to God—an opening that can be an awakening.

Aging is another important source of body-based invitations to awakening. Because most people fear death and resist giving in to any signs of diminishment, we tend to view aging as the enemy of the vital life. Western culture strongly reinforces that message. However, aging is not the same as dying, nor is aging reducible to decay. George MacDonald reminds us that aging can be "the ripening, the swelling, of the fresh life within that withers and bursts the husk."[8] It always invites us to come alive in new ways. It invites us to let go of the life we had or might have hoped for so we can have the life that is awaiting us with new possibilities. It invites us to age well—to live well and to be well—so that others whose paths cross ours may have the courage to do the same. It invites us to live as full participants in our life, not as spectators who unconsciously drift along. It invites us, therefore, to awaken.

Aging offers rich possibilities for transformation to those who are willing to receive each stage of life—really, each day of life—as a fresh gift of new possibilities of being. Paradoxically, aging offers the gift of well-being in our spirit and soul, even if that well-being is less and less present in our bodies. It is an invitation to learn that being well does not depend on physical realities. It is an invitation to a self that is at one in relation to itself and in relation to life, God, and the world. Receiving this gift is never the result of a single moment of awakening. But it is a gift that will never be received unless we learn to respond to aging with acceptance of life as it comes to us, not as we might arrange it if we were God.

Conscious Love

One final and immensely valuable source of continual invitations to awakening comes from journeying with other people in relationships of intentional love. Rather than regarding love as a feeling, John Welwood suggests that we should think of love as an action. He calls a commitment to love "conscious love" because it is something that we consciously choose to express and to which we open ourselves.[9] What such love opens us to is awakening, because a commitment to journey with another in such a way calls forth who we really are. The more intimate the relationship, the more it will inevitably present us with opportunities to awaken. The most important of these invitations to awaken are associated with the tensions that necessarily form a part of any relationship. Our default response to these tensions is annoyance (fight) or defensiveness (flight). Awakening demands quite a different posture. It demands hospitality to the tension or conflict and presence to your self and the other.

Welwood suggests that conscious love also involves an expectation. Instead of looking to the relationship primarily for either gratification or shelter, "we would welcome its power to wake us up in the areas of life where we are asleep and where we avoid naked, direct contact with life. This approach puts us on a path. It commits us to movement and change, providing forward direction by showing us where we most need to grow. Embracing relationship as a path also gives us practice: learning to use each difficulty along the way as an opportunity to go further, to connect more deeply, not just with a partner, but with your own aliveness as well."[10]

Conscious love is probably the most accessible of all means of awakening. It is available to anyone who is in any form of relationship. Such relationships do not need to be romantic or even ongoing—although the more ongoing and the more intense, the more opportunities for awakening the relationship will present. Cynthia Bourgeault suggests: "The bottom line is not the 'who' but the 'how': the direction of the energy flow. On a path of conscious love the energy is always radiating outward; it is never self-defended or congealed."[11] The how is a path of love. It is love that allows one to move from defensiveness to openness, and it is love that allows people in a relationship to stay present and open to each other when they otherwise would want to either attack or run and hide. It is love that allows partners to work their way through inner logjams that would otherwise normally take much longer to resolve.

Ken Wilber describes this sort of shared journey of intentional love when he writes of his relationship with his wife, Treya, as they approach the end of her five-year ordeal with cancer. He says, "We simply and directly served each other, exchanging self for the other and therefore glimpsing that eternal Spirit which transcends both self and the other, both 'me' and 'mine.'"[12] On this path, love is in the service of awakening, and awakening is in the service of love. The two become almost indistinguishable.

Dialogue and Reflection

"Awakening" is what I call this first stage of transformation. But naming this moment doesn't really explain what happens, why it happens some times and not others, or why we seem to resist it and fall back asleep so easily after a momentary awakening. It also positions the act of awakening solely within the individual and doesn't help us understand the communal context in which awakening—and staying awake—happens. These and many other related questions will be answered as we explore the big picture of the unfolding of the human self. But be prepared: the picture I will be presenting is big, and the concepts are big. However, I am convinced that nothing less can adequately frame the possibilities for the awakening and unfolding of the self that the mystics describe.

Before we get to that big picture, let us pause for a moment to consider some questions that I hope will help you reflect on the things we have discussed in this chapter. I draw these questions—and those with which I will end each of the following chapters—from ones asked when I have presented these ideas to colleagues or in public lectures.[13] As you listen in on our interaction, perhaps you will hear some of your own questions and thoughts. Hopefully these little slices of conversation will help you open up reflective space and aid your engagement with what we are discussing.

1. **I was interested to see how much emphasis you place on the body and the senses in awakening. Often awakening is presented primarily in terms of consciousness, and that is presented in more mental terms. Can you say anything more about this?**

    I am glad that you noticed this because I think it is very important that we do not reduce awakening to a change of beliefs. Such changes can be evidence of an awakening but can easily occur in its absence. If awakening is to have the psychospiritual potency that is needed to change us in our totality, it cannot be simply a mental change. It must involve something deeper and broader than this. Spiritual awakening always involves the senses, and this leads us to our body and to the world beyond. Awakening moves us from the intermediate zone of thoughts, judgments, opinions, beliefs, and classification and slowly introduces us to a more direct and immediate encounter with that which is transcendent to us and exposes the small, comfortable realm in which we so comfortably live and sleep away our existence.

2. **You said that any experience that produces significant internal turmoil, disruption of meaning and self-coherence, or a sense that your way of being in the world needs to change—any such experience has potential to awaken us. But I gather that the key word is "potential" because you then go on to illustrate how experience is not enough to guarantee awakening. What makes a person ready to awaken?**

    In general terms, what makes us ready to awaken is sufficient openness in either mind or heart to allow our attention to be drawn to something we would normally dismiss. I describe this as an openness of either mind or heart because either can express the necessary soul hospitality to pay attention and subsequently receive the gift of awakening. In upcoming chapters I will have much more to say about the dynamics of this awakening and the unfolding of the self that results, so hang on to those questions since they are important.

3. **You also said something about every breath being a potential doorway to awareness, and every moment of awareness a doorway to awakening. Can it really be that simple?**

Let me first say that awakening isn't simple. What is simple is our part in it. Our role, as I have said, is more one of consent and willingness than striving to awaken or stay awake. You are not responsible for your own awakening. It isn't something you need to achieve. But it is a gift that you can receive, and there are things you can do to increase that possibility. In any moment you can choose to pay attention. Paying attention to anything is a potential doorway to awakening because paying attention to anything is a doorway to the transcendent. This is why, over and over again, Jesus urged people to watch and to listen—in short, to pay attention. Once we pay attention to something, we are ready to be gripped by it and drawn into awareness and wakefulness. It can start right now. In fact, there is no time other than the present moment in which it can happen. All that is required is to be present to yourself in this moment, and as you do so, your wakefulness will increase. That is your part in the process, and that is why spiritual practices that center on awareness are so foundational to any genuine awakening and subsequent becoming.

4. **Maybe I missed something, but I can't help but wonder where Jesus is in all of this.**

I believe that Jesus both reveals and leads us to the one he called Father, and through him, his Father can be known as our Father. So Jesus is tremendously relevant to this journey into God because Jesus shows us what is possible and leads us to the One who makes it possible. The way he shows us is reflected in his teachings but never reducible to a set of propositions. His way was a way of turning in openness and trust to the One who is continuously present to us even though we are generally unaware of that reality. The kingdom of God, he taught, is within (Luke 17:21). God, he implied, is not to be encountered through belief in propositions or certainty of convictions but in our depths as the One who is, everywhere and at all times, calling all people and all of creation to be more than it is in and through Christ. This God whom we encounter in Jesus is the source of all genuine human awakening and becoming. That may not satisfy you, but stay tuned, and let's see if the role of God in all of this awakening and becoming doesn't begin to become clearer as we proceed.

2

Mapping the Unfolding Self

Questions of how people change, develop, evolve, devolve, re-form, and transform are among the most important that we face as a human community. Clearly change is needed—at both individual and collective levels. The Age of Aquarius did not usher in the promised new era of peace, love, and happiness. Particularly in periods of economic stress such as we have witnessed in the early years of this new millennium, deep and persistent patterns of ethnocentrism, xenophobia, and racism reveal the presence of a dark, unacknowledged shadow in the soul of individuals and our societies. Yet the situation is always mixed. When looking at a long span of human history, it is usually possible to identify signs of both social evolution and devolution. But it is always hard to put the present into a bigger framework that lets us know where we are and where we are headed. And this is just as true for individuals as it is for human society.

This is the reason we need maps of the territory we pass through as we awaken and begin to unfold. Without such maps, it is almost inevitable that we limit the possibilities of human transformation, and when we do this, we settle for far too little. This is easy to do when our sense of developmental possibilities is limited by our own experience. The mystics may talk about union with God and being at one with everything, but this can't help but sound utterly irrelevant to

19

life as we know it when we lack a large-enough framework to connect our experience to theirs.

In cartography, the bigger the area covered by a map, the smaller the scale and less the detail. Small-scale maps give us the big picture with few details, but we also need large-scale maps since they provide us with a more molecular level of analysis. I am a sailor, and like any prudent mariner, I never leave shore without bringing along both small-scale and large-scale maps (known in a nautical context as charts). The fine-detail charts help me stay off underwater rocks or other dangers when I am close to shore. But the big-picture ones keep me oriented to the whole scope of the trip; they help me know where I am when the shore is nowhere to be seen and allow me to make course corrections to get where I want to go.

In this chapter, we are going to look at two big-picture maps of human unfolding, both of which use very broad brushstrokes to paint a picture of the contours of the journey. We begin with an ancient map emerging from the world's wisdom traditions, a map that is often called the Great Chain of Being. Following this we will then take a brief look at a more modern map offered by cultural historians and anthropologists who track evolving worldviews.

The Great Chain of Being

Millennia before modern psychology first began to investigate human development, philosophers, theologians, and spiritual teachers were hard at work in mapping the possibilities of the unfolding self. Given that these people were drawn from the ranks of all major world religions, the striking thing about what they offered was how congruent these various visions often were with each other. There certainly were differences among the various maps, but the same deep truths about the nature of the self, the world, ultimate reality, and God appeared over and over again, regardless of the culture, religion, or belief system that was involved. Noting this, people like Gottfried Leibniz, Aldous Huxley, Huston Smith, and others began to describe this core of understandings as Perennial Philosophy—what they took to be timeless truths that lie at the basis of the world's wisdom traditions.

The Great Chain of Being was one of these insights. Arising out of ideas developed by Plato and Aristotle but heavily influenced by Augustinian and Thomistic Christian theology, the notion of a great chain of being was a way of understanding the relationship of matter to God, breaking this down into a hierarchically ordered range of forms or levels of reality between what Ken Wilber calls dust and divinity. Its roots go back to ancient Egyptian and Greek civilizations, although it runs continuously through ancient Chinese thought, Hinduism, Judaism, Buddhism, Christianity, and Islam. The number of levels and the names assigned to each of these varies across these traditions. However, the names and exact number of levels are not important for the point I want to make in this chapter. Rather, I draw attention to the framework for the unfolding self that the Great Chain of Being offers. Think of it as a big picture of developmental possibilities. If it helps us envisage the contours of the journey of human unfolding, we can then fill in the details later.

Traditionally the Great Chain of Being is organized around five levels of existence: matter, life, mind, soul, and spirit. Ken Wilber points to the interesting fact that each of these states has its own attendant academic discipline specializing in its study.[1] Physics studies matter, biology looks at life, psychology at the mind, theology at the soul, and mysticism at the spirit. Wilber thinks this suggests that each level of existence is somewhat independent from the others.

The most basic level of existence is matter. Think, for example, of the Christian creation story and the sequence of the early "days" of this metaphorical "week" of creation. Day one begins with God's creating earth. Everything else must emerge out of matter—even humans, who in this account arise from God's animating action of taking the dust of the earth and breathing into it the divine breath.

The second level of existence is life. But notice that life comes to matter: life doesn't stand independent of it. Matter is enlivened. Higher levels contain lower levels but are not reducible to them. This is extremely important and is something to which we will return when we consider the transformational dynamics of human unfolding. Matter includes only itself, but each of the higher levels includes all lower levels while at the same time transcending them. Thus life transcends matter, includes it, and is not reducible to it. Life contains possibilities and expressions that cannot be reduced to matter alone. Vitality, for example, is expressed through matter but represents something transcendent to matter alone.

The third level, mind, operates the same way. Mind includes life and matter but is neither reducible to nor explainable by either. It transcends both and can never be accounted for strictly in terms of the lower levels that it subsumes. Within such a view, mind is more than brain. It has its own emergent properties that transcend mere vitalized matter. Consciousness, thought, memory, will, imagination, and emotion are all mental processes that illustrate the way in which mind is grounded in matter (brain) but transcends it.

In the same ways, soul, the fourth level, contains and transcends everything below it. Understandings of soul have been famously varied. As recorded in the Hebrew Bible, God is described as having fashioned Adam from the dust of the earth, into which God then breathed the breath of life, and "man became a living soul" (Gen. 2:7 KJV). In most general terms, Christians have often understood this to suggest that the soul is the innermost aspect of humans—that which is of greatest value in humanity, sometimes that which is eternal. My own understanding of soul is a bit more metaphorical than this. Drawing on archetypal and analytical psychology, I suggest that soul be understood as the womb of experience—a middle ground between spirit and matter, constituting the reflective space between us and the events of our lives.[2] It is not a part of self but a way of living—a way of living with fuller consciousness, which brings depth and vitality to life.

Christians have sometimes been divided on the matter of whether or not soul can be distinguished from spirit—the fifth level of existence suggested by the Great Chain of Being. But this disagreement has arisen when the question is approached more ontologically than metaphorically. Rather than considering spirit to be a part of self, I suggest that we again think of it more metaphorically. Viewed in such a light, we can think of spirit as the fire in our belly. Spirit is dynamic, energizing, vitalizing, and enriching. Like fire and wind, spirit ignites, moves, and animates us. It gives us the energy to live life to the full. But it also always calls us beyond our self, orienting us toward a self-transcendent reference point. Soul pulls us down and into our experience, encouraging us to find meaning there; spirit points us beyond ourselves, to that within which we fit as a hand within a glove. Spirit points us toward our source and our destiny, toward the place wherein we most deeply belong. It is expansive, always questing, always driven by deep longings that point us toward Absolute Spirit.

As seen in figure 2.1, these levels of existence can be regarded as a series of concentric circles. Each level holds and contains the lower levels. Viewed in this way, we see why some have suggested that the Great Chain is really a Great Nest. This image of a nest is more organic and therefore seems to be a more suitable way to describe how higher levels of being enfold lower ones. Plotinus, a major contributor to the development of Perennial Philosophy, described the nesting as "development that is envelopment."[3] What he meant by this was that forward movement (development) was not based on moving beyond a lower level but by integrating it within the self (envelopment). Anticipating modern psychological understandings of human development by seventeen hundred years, what he correctly noted was that human unfolding does not mean abandoning lower levels of existence but no longer being limited to them. I will be returning to this important notion later because it is the key to understanding transformation.

FIGURE 2.1
Levels of Existence

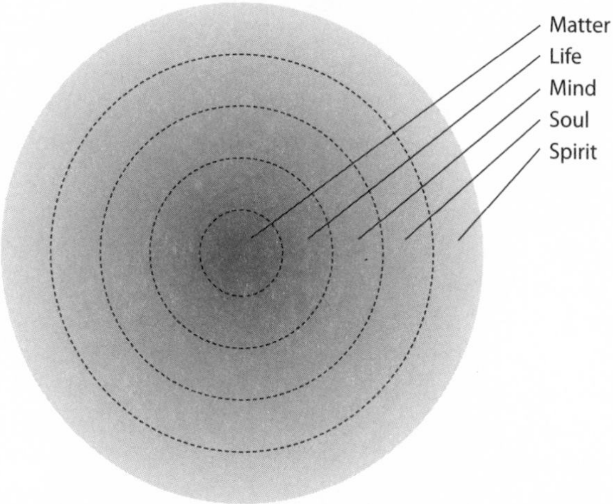

Matter
Life
Mind
Soul
Spirit

Dynamic Possibilities

This map (fig. 2.1) depicts the nesting of the levels of existence; one important implication of it is that the direction of human unfolding involves movement from matter to life to mind to soul and finally to spirit. Spirit is the goal of the entire sequence. But Absolute Spirit—God—is also the ground of the whole process. In truth, the nest is not a static entity but is evolving, not a two-dimensional set of flat circles but a three-dimensional dynamic cradle of all levels of existence. In Christian terms we can say that God holds, directs, and energizes the dynamism of this cradle of existence. As expressed by the sixth-century BCE Greek philosopher and poet Epimenides—quoted appreciatively by the apostle Paul (showing his own willingness to draw on the fruits of Perennial Philosophy and use the insights of the world's wisdom traditions to help unpack Christian thought)—it is in God that we all live and move and exist, for we are all God's children (Acts 17:28). The source and fulfillment of all existence is God. God is the Alpha and the Omega of all that is. God is in all that is because everything that exists is held in existence in Christ. Behind and beneath all of existence is the outpouring life of God.

This understanding that all of life flows from and back toward our Source is very clear in Plotinus, and it comes to us as a Christian understanding through the mediating influence of such prominent theologians as Augustine, Thomas Aquinas, and Gregory of Nyssa—all of whom were heavily influenced by the writings of Plotinus. We have already encountered this third-century Egyptian philosopher, but to better understand the nature of the flow of existence, we should perhaps pause for a moment and review what he actually had to say about the dynamics of this Great Nest of being. Although his language may seem somewhat esoteric and his map rather complex, his ideas have enormous potential to help us understand the transformational journey of awakening.

The name that Plotinus gave to what Christians call God was "the One."[4] He taught that this supreme, totally transcendent One contains no division, multiplicity, or distinction and is beyond all categories and objects. The One is not simply the sum of all things but is prior to everything and the source of everything that exists. The One contains everything that exists, just as white light contains the entire spectrum of light that we witness in the rainbow. All things that exist emanate from the One. This emanation *ex deo* ("out of God") confirms the absolute transcendence of the One and makes the unfolding of the cosmos a consequence of the existence of the One.

Just as the sun emanates light without appearing to diminish itself, or a mirror produces reflections of objects that in no way diminish or alter the mirror, so too the emanations from the One in no way diminish or alter the One. Plotinus suggested that these emanations can be thought of as stepped-down, or less perfect, expressions of the One. The image in the mirror contains something of that which it reflects, but it is a less perfect presentation of that which it reflects. Plotinus argued that the stepped-down or more-limited emanations cannot exist without the perfection and singularity of the One. The less perfect must, of necessity, issue forth from the perfect or more perfect. Thus everything that is emanates from the One in succeeding stages of lesser and lesser perfection. Lower dimensions of existence always contain traces of higher ones. And because all emanate from the One, being and life are characterized by a dialectical return to origins, a process that Plotinus described as a return to unity and singularity.

Translating these abstractions back into the more concrete terms of the Great Nest, what this means is that the Spirit—or the One—is singular but that traces of spirit are found in the increasingly less singular emanations of spirit that we encounter in soul, life, mind, and matter. The inner rings of figure 2.1 represent levels of existence that have their origin in God and are always in movement back toward God. None of them can exist apart from God. They are held in God, and their fulfillment and perfection are found in their movement back toward God.

The central claim of the Perennial Philosophy is that humans can move all the way up the hierarchy from matter to spirit itself. This might sound like heresy, but recall the assertion of Christian mystical theology—the oneness with Christ that can be our experience, not merely a theological proposition. This union with God is clearly set forth as the end point of the spiritual journey by Christian mystics and is also clearly the trajectory of the Great Chain of Being. God is our source and our destiny, the One who holds us, and all that is, in existence. All of life flows outward from God and seeks to return to God. This is the essential dynamic of the Great Nest of Existence.

But this dynamic nesting of existence holds another important implication. Ken Wilber suggests that infolding must always precede unfolding. Evolution is only possible because there has been a prior process of involution.[5] If, as suggested by Plotinus, lower dimensions of existence contain traces of higher ones, from a Christian viewpoint this is because everything that is has come from God and is held in God. Nothing exists that has not come from God, and nothing exists that is not in God and God in it. Though God is beyond the material world and not reducible to it, the divine life interpenetrates every atom of the created order.

Human unfolding does not mean moving away from lower levels of existence but moving beyond being limited by them. The possibility of the unfolding of a human self (that is, the possibility of higher levels of consciousness or being emerging out of lower ones) lies in

the fact that the higher (Absolute Spirit) has already come and en-
folded into the lower (the material world). Without this there would
be no possibility of human growth or development. Wilber describes
this great unfolding as "Spirit's creative play in the fields of its own
manifestation."[6] In this creative play, Spirit throws itself outward in
self-emptying kenosis, to create a manifest universe. Spirit creates soul,
"which is a stepped-down and diluted reflection of Spirit; soul then
steps down into mind, a paler reflection yet of Spirit's radiant glory;
mind then steps down into life, and life steps down into matter, which
is the densest, lowest, least conscious form of Spirit. . . . These levels
in the Great Nest are all forms of Spirit, but the forms become less
and less conscious, less and less aware of their Source and Suchness,
less and less alive to their ever-present Ground, even though they are
all nevertheless nothing but Spirit-at-play."[7]

Although Wilber is not a Christian, this is a profoundly Christian way of understanding creation as materiality that has emerged
from the Spirit of God. Creation (including humans) represents the
stepped-down forms described by Wilber and the emanations of
the One described by Plotinus. We see the same truth expressed in
the Christian theology of the incarnation, which again reminds us
of the indissoluble relationship between God and humans, between
Spirit and matter. Wilber speaks of this relationship when he suggests
that lower dimensions of existence contain traces of higher ones. The
possibility of us becoming more than we are lies in the fact that we
emerged from more and are, we might say, a stepped-down version
of that more. What he calls our "Source and Suchness" is God, and
this is why we are moving toward God. If every atom of the universe
were not in God, nothing would be. Because we exist and are held in
God, we can both be and we can become more than we are.

The Great Nest of Existence reminds us of the enormous potential of human becoming. It points toward possibilities that are seldom named in discussions of Christian spiritual formation. Only
the mystics dare to speak this language of becoming one with God:
speaking thus frightens the rest of us too much. And yet the truth
that is represented in these ancient sources of perennial wisdom is
echoed by Christian Scriptures and embraced boldly by its most radical
daughters and sons—the mystics—who dare to take seriously such
biblical teachings as Christ's living in us and our living in Christ and
the possibility and promise of our participation in the divine nature
(Gal. 2:20; 2 Pet. 1:4). The Great Nest reminds us of our home and

calls us to become who we most deeply and truly are—children of the God in whom we live and move and have our being (Acts 17:28).

Evolving Worldviews

We get another big-picture map of human developmental possibilities from cultural historians and anthropologists, particularly those who focus on the evolution of worldviews and the states of consciousness that seem to be associated with them. To put our own Western worldview in perspective, listen to a story told by Leo Frobenius in his book *Unknown Africa*, describing a rite that he observed in the Congo jungle in the early 1930s.[8]

> Members of the hunting tribe of Pygmies (three men and a woman) drew a picture of an antelope in the sand before they started out at dawn to hunt antelopes. With the first ray of sunlight that fell on the sand, they intended to "kill" the antelope. Their first arrow hit the drawing unerringly in the neck. Then they went out to hunt and returned with a slain antelope. Their death-dealing arrow hit the animal in exactly the same spot where, hours before, the other arrow had hit the drawing. . . . Having fulfilled its magic purpose, . . . this arrow was then removed from the drawing with an accompanying ritual designed to ward off any evil consequences of the murder from the hunters. After that was done, the drawing itself was erased.

Some people in the twenty-first century still relate to the world in the magical way seen in this group of people. But the vast majority do not. Those who do not hold this sort of worldview suggest that this sort of thinking contains an important logical fallacy. At the core of what we might call a magical worldview is the association of things that look alike or that appear together, and the assumption of a causal connection between things that are temporally related. With the exception of very young children or those suffering from a major mental illness, most people do not believe that shooting an arrow into a picture of an antelope can kill the antelope. Similarly, most of us do not accept other standard parts of a magical worldview; we do not believe that private, noncommunicated thoughts can change external realities in the world, nor do we believe that naming or capturing an image of something gives us power over it. These changes are not simply based on the fact that we know certain things that these Congolese tribespeople did not. They are based on a significant change in how we structure our relationship to our self, to others, and to the world. They represent a changed worldview and a different level of consciousness.

Worldviews are so basic and reside so deep in the background of consciousness that most of us never stop to notice that we have one. Yet we all do have a framework for relating to life. This framework is our own. It may be different from that held by most others in our culture or subculture, but at any point in time there will be a dominant worldview within a culture. It is these dominant worldviews of cultures, or even epochs of human history, that cultural historians track. Doing so, they suggest that over the course of the last several million years of human history, three major ways of organizing experience and thinking about self, others, and the world can be identified. We might call them magic, mythic, and modern worldviews. If our goal were to develop a more detailed map of the development of worldviews, it would certainly be possible to identify more than these three, but let us content ourselves for the moment with the big picture and consider how these three ways of organizing one's self in relation to that which is beyond the self might help us understand the human journey of unfolding.[9]

A magical worldview is characterized, as we saw, by such things as the confusion of apparent or imagined events and real events, the equation of symbols and their referents, the belief that the world can be modified and controlled by thoughts, and the inability to see the difference between contiguity (or coincidence) and causality. In hunter-gatherer cultures—approximately 300,000 BCE (the beginnings of the Old Stone Age) to 8,000 BCE (the rise of agriculture and movement from migrant foraging to village life)—life was tribal, religion was largely animistic, and thinking was predominantly egocentric and preconceptual. Life within a magical worldview has a quality of being boundless—in space and in time. Everything intertwines, and this is the reason for the interchangeability of the concrete and the symbolic. Self, others, and the world all run together in an undifferentiated way. This worldview might seem strange to us, but it can still be encountered in present-day indigenous populations that have resisted contact with the outside world. So, just because it is no longer the dominant way of relating to the world does not mean that it is not still alive and well in our day. Remember that the dominant worldview is not necessarily the worldview held by all individuals at any point in time, even all individuals within a given society.

With the emergence of the mythical worldview in the Neolithic period (running from approximately 9,500 BCE to 3,500 BCE) humans began to differentiate themselves from nature. This disengagement led to an awareness of the boundary between the internal and external worlds. In other words, it led to the discovery of the internal world of imagination and, soon after this, to a broad range of expressions of human creativity. The worldview associated with this period takes its common name from the rise of interest in religion and the pantheon of mythic gods that soon populated the world of the day. Here we encounter the beginnings of self-definition based on beliefs. In contrast to the more egocentric world associated with the magical worldview, we might describe the communities that developed around a mythical worldview as mythocentric. Now, rather than living simply in tribal communities, individuals of different tribes discovered that when they believed in the same god, they could live peaceably together within rules and belief systems associated with that god. Rules and belief systems became, therefore, central to the mythic worldview. And a strong identification with the community provided a sense of belonging, safety, and identity.

The modern, Western worldview arose during the sixteenth and seventeenth centuries (CE) and represents a radical change in how humans understand the world and their place within it. The rise of science shattered the premodern understanding of both the world and humans as a unified living organism. As described by the seventeenth-century French mathematician René Descartes, the world is simply a giant clock—fully comprehensible through study of its parts. In such a view humans, if not the clockmaker, could become the ones who would finally be capable of controlling what had previously been thought to be beyond control and worthy, therefore, of worship. The age of reason had dawned. Not everyone may have believed that the world was fully comprehensible or capable of human control, but the dualistic vision of humans over against nature quickly and insidiously changed human consciousness. Cutting across tribes and beliefs, this is the first worldview to apply to all humans. It is thus the first world-centric (as opposed to egocentric or mythocentric) worldview. While the mythic framework is more conservative and conventional, the modern worldview is postconventional. Beliefs are now passed through a filter of reason to determine suitability. The fact that they were good enough for my tribe or family does not mean that they are good enough for me; consequently, beliefs now must be personalized. Within a modern worldview, one first and foremost belongs to the world, just as one's identity is most fundamentally that of being human. Though there is certainly room for personal beliefs and religious faith, they do not eliminate this fundamental identification of one's self as first and foremost belonging to the human tribe.

The record of the conquest of the Aztecs by sixteenth-century Spanish conquistadors dramatically demonstrates the collision of the magical/mythical culture of the Aztecs with the modern technological culture of the Spanish. Based on reports of surviving Aztecs and written eight years after the event, Frey Bernardino de Sahagún described how the Mexican king Montezuma responded to the conquistadors in what was to result in the conquest of Mexico City. First, he sent out sorcerers to cast a spell on the Spanish. But this was to no avail: all were slaughtered. Then he sent a group of soothsayers, magicians, and high priests. To his amazement, they also seemed powerless to stop the advance: they could not bewitch the Spanish.[10]

The Mexicans could not prevail against the Spaniards, not simply because of Spanish technological superiority, but primarily because their worldview simply did not prepare them for the encounter. Their worldview left them defenseless against people who seemed strangely immune from the spells and magical incantations that both worked well and made so much sense within the Mexican world. It should be no surprise that the Aztecs were compelled to surrender almost immediately.

The surrender of one worldview to another does not, however, happen so quickly. Worldviews overlap and coexist, competing for the allegiance of the population in any society in any given age. Only slowly and over long periods does one gradually emerge as dominant. Strikingly, something like this sort of evolution of worldviews seems to happen in each and every individual in every age. We begin life in an undifferentiated cocoon dominated by egocentric thinking and move to the appreciation of larger and larger horizons that provide self-definition and suggest possibilities for action. But this development, while natural, is not automatic. When it does happen, it is dependent on environmental supports. It seems reasonable to assume that if you or I were raised in the tropical rain forests of Papua, New Guinea within one of the more than 850 indigenous groups that continue to live in that country, we would share much of their worldview—a worldview that remains best described as magical. Unquestionably, individuals can have a personal worldview that differs from that of the dominant culture. But as we shall see, there is a crucial communal and cultural context that always either supports or impedes the unfolding of any individual's worldview and consciousness.

These shifts in worldviews reveal possibilities for individual humans and our unfolding. What they show us is that it is possible for humans to move from one way of being in the world to another. Change is possible in our understanding of the relationship between our self and that which is beyond our self. It is possible for the deep framework that organizes our consciousness to change, and with it, for our way of living and experiencing life to change. Every one of us can make the journey from magical ways of relating to the world to more realistic ones. Each of us must make this journey on our own. But every one of us can move from egocentric to mythocentric (or ethnocentric) and then to world-centric frames of reference for relating to that which is beyond us. Every one of us can experience a broadening of our perspectives on life that offer our spirits more freedom to soar.

It is possible for fundamentalists like Saul to become free and allow love and life to flow through them as with the apostle Paul. Regardless of how we express our fundamentalist tendencies, whether this is in religious, political, economic, or other terms, it is possible to release our commitment to fortifying borders and soften the arbitrary boundaries we place around elements of existence that we most prize. It is possible to soften the defensive attachment we have to the small safe places we have created for our selves. And when we do, we expand our own personal borders of consciousness and align ourselves more fully with the flow of life as it moves us toward God. In short, we become more than we were.

The Value of Big Pictures

Big-picture maps such as we have considered in this chapter make us aware of developmental possibilities that are virtually impossible to see from the small, cramped places out of which we typically live our lives. If we listen with our heart and spirit, not simply with our mind, we might sense a longing to live in these larger places that lie beyond our present horizons. If indeed all of life is flowing in a direction that returns us to our Source, something within us calls us beyond our small self and the limited perspectives it offers us of life and the cosmos. That something is Spirit calling to spirit.

We easily settle for where we are in the human developmental journey because we fail to notice the ways in which our deepest longings point us beyond our self. We lose touch with the call of our own spirit to find our place in Spirit. This is the immense value of a big-picture map such as offered us in the Great Nest of Existence. It reminds us that everything in life flows out from God and back into God. It assures us that our Origin is our Destiny: we have a place in the great scheme of life, and this place is dynamic. Our place is moving along a transformational journey in which we are becoming who we most deeply and truly are in God.

These maps also alert us to the fact that human development is not simply small, incremental steps based on more of the same but might well involve much more major shifts and realignments of the self. In this regard, it suggests that transformation may be more than growth, may be of a different order. We will explore this much more carefully in upcoming chapters, but these big-picture possibilities suggest changes that may well be beyond our ability to simply engineer or achieve on the basis of effort. Particularly in the case of evolving worldviews, we get a glimpse of the social context in which these changes may happen, also something that we will examine more closely later. But however these changes happen, it is clear that they involve reorganizations of the self that are much more profound than the sort of changes that come from the self-improvement projects with which we are more familiar.

Yet such maps are not simply of value for us on our personal journey. Properly understood, they also have enormous implications for us as we seek to support the journey of others. Most efforts to nurture formation, re-formation, or transformation of persons lack a big-picture developmental framework. I am alarmed by how often therapists see only symptoms and problems and miss the developmental implications and possibilities of the moment. I routinely see parents getting caught up in managing behavior and solving problems without reference to the big picture of human unfolding that should guide everything they do. Those working in Christian ministry or spiritual formation also need better maps of the journey if they are to rise above simply assuming that the journey of others should roughly follow the contours of their own.

Although there is an inherent developmental framework in most approaches to spirituality, it is in the mystical expressions of the spiritual traditions that the vision of the self and its unfolding are best developed. Unfortunately, however, these mystical traditions are typically viewed with suspicion and therefore marginalized. Consequently, spiritual guides and practitioners usually operate with a limited vision of developmental possibilities and a modest or nonexistent understanding of the transformational potential of the encounters with the Transcendent that are a part of life experiences. The default focus in these situations is helping the other be a good Christian (or good adherent to their tradition). But for Christians, this confuses growth in holiness (or a deepening personal relationship with God) with spiritual growth—the two being related but not identical. Authentic spiritual growth will always make us more deeply human, more fully alive, more authentic, and much more. It will not simply be reflected in more conformity to religious standards or ideals.

Far too easily we settle for holiness rather than wholeness, conformity rather than authenticity, becoming spiritual rather than deeply human, fulfillment rather than transformation, and a journey toward perfection rather than union with God. Far too often we confuse our own spiritual self-improvement tinkerings with the much more radical agenda of the Spirit of God. The call of the Spirit—which is always gentle and therefore easily missed—is an invitation to abandon our self-improvement projects that are, in reality, little more than polishing our false self and become the unique hidden self in Christ that we have been from all eternity. The call of the Spirit is always a call to return home, to settle for no other habitation or identity than that of being in Christ and knowing the reality of Christ in us.

What if those of us who are in positions of influence in the lives of others were always watching for transformational possibilities and were better equipped to support others in their response to these moments? What if we were always attentive to where the Spirit of God is already active in the lives of those with whom we are involved and then made our first priority to align ourselves with God's big dream for them? To some extent this is exactly what the best parents, spouses, friends, spiritual directors, teachers, and psychotherapists do. They are not limited by the horizons of their own lives or even understandings but see and are able to support the larger developmental possibilities for others as reflected in the best maps of the journey.

But, having now set out the broad contours of the developmental framework offered by these big pictures, it is now time to increase the resolution of our map. We will do this over the course of the next two chapters. In chapter 3 we turn first to what are usually described as lines of development, which allows us to examine in more detail some of the most important things that change as we grow in the dimensions of development most central to the unfolding self. Then in chapter 4 we will turn our attention to the levels of development and think more carefully about what is actually changing as we progress up through various levels on those various lines of development.

Dialogue and Reflection

1. **How does the evolution of dominant worldviews relate to the awakening of the individual self?**

   Individual unfolding goes through stages that resemble this social evolution of consciousness. Consequently, we see in the social macrocosm hints of the changes that can also be discerned in the personal microcosm. If we continue to grow, we all move from egocentric thinking to the appreciation of larger and larger perspectives on the world and our selves. Later we will examine how our personal unfolding is influenced by communal and cultural contexts, and at that point we will return to the question of how we relate to dominant worldviews in our family and community and how they either facilitate or impede our journey of personal unfolding.

2. **Why do the possibilities of human becoming one with God frighten us so much?**

   This possibility is a threat to our small ego-self even while it is the great and indistinguishable hope of our much larger spirit self. Ego wants control and resists surrender. But surrender of control lies right at the heart of this journey into God. The kingdom of God turns the kingdom of the ego-self upside down, and ego will always resist that sort of radical transformation. Our spirits, however, will always respond to this invitation to surrender and journey into God with a sense of welcomed homecoming. Hints of this response can usually be discovered in our deepest longings—longings that, when properly understood, will always be seen to point us beyond our small self to our ultimate source and destiny: to our place in God.

3. Becoming one with God sounds like becoming God. What, if anything, is the difference between these two things?

To say that the source and fulfillment of all existence is God is not to say that humans or anything else in existence become God. But because everything that exists is held in existence in Christ, all of existence already participates in the life of God. This is why it is possible for humans—who, Christians believe, are created in the image of God—to participate more fully in the likeness of God by moving up the hierarchy of existence to spirit itself. This is the assertion of Christian mystical theology—that oneness with Christ can be our experience, not merely a theological proposition. However, participating in the life of God does not involve becoming the substance of God. This distinction was most clearly expressed by the sixth-century mystic Pseudo-Dionysius, who taught that although we can be united with God, we still remain in the image and likeness of God, never becoming God. It is difficult to specify the boundaries between us and God since God is in us and we are in God. Although God is in us, God is not reducible to us. God is both immanent and transcendent. So becoming one with God does not mean becoming God.

3

Growth and the Lines of Development

The question of human growth is a question of what changes as we develop. When we speak of children as growing, we are usually referring to their physical stature. Yet once that dimension of development reaches its pinnacle sometime in adolescence or early adulthood, when we describe someone as growing what we are typically referring to is maturation of the psychological and relational dimensions of their self. Unlike either physical growth or the early stages of the inner self's maturation that we see in childhood and adolescence, adult maturation does not come easily or automatically. It is quite possible to pass from adolescence to the grave without further significant development of the major dimensions of the inner self. Growth is possible, but it is far from the default option.

Freud was notably pessimistic about human nature. However, one of the places where that pessimism seems to have been most well founded was his observation that people coming to psychotherapy seldom want a cure for their neuroses. What they want is relief from the pain caused by their neuroses. I think he was quite right in this judgment. The default option for most people experiencing distress is to want to be rid of their problems but without doing the hard work of actually resolving them. Rather than resolving the developmental blocks at the root of our psychological distress and then getting on with the journey toward health and maturity, we often simply want to eliminate the symptom and reduce the distress. I don't pass judgment on this posture because I know it so well myself. But I do want to be clear about how profoundly this limits the possibilities for growth and development. Let me briefly tell two stories, the first to illustrate this default position and the second to illustrate openness to growth.

Crisis or Invitation

Keith was in his midforties when his life began to implode. He was a vice president of a seminary when he was arrested on charges of pedophilia. Though the seminary didn't dismiss him immediately, he knew immediately that his career in theological education was over—at least in his own denomination and at least for a while. As part of his pretrial evaluation, I was asked by the court to conduct his psychological assessment. This involved a number of interviews and a battery of psychological tests. These two sources of data told much the same story. Although he was devastated that he was caught and worried about the implications of his arrest for his marriage, his relationship with his children, and his reputation, he was far from open or honest with himself or me. He made excuses for what he had been doing, denied the significant problems that were obviously present, and showed no real interest in genuinely facing up to the truth. He lashed out in anger at the hypocrisy of the church and community; by the time I was finished with him, he had fired two lawyers who, he decided, were not up to the challenge of adequately defending him. He would have fired me if he had hired me, but I was a part of his experience that was beyond his control.

Although Keith's story involved a very public and dramatic collapse of a life, his response to the crisis he faced is not uncommon. For many people, their initial and sometimes continuing response to a major financial reversal, a medical crisis, or the death of a significant other is much the same: some combination of anger and despair, along with a longing to get back to some point in time before the crisis hit. But using a crisis for growth never involves going back: it always involves moving forward.

John was a few years younger than Keith when his life began to show signs of falling apart. He was a successful foreign affairs correspondent for a major chain of newspapers. Although he had long been aware that he was living on the edge, he felt that he had learned how to stay one step ahead of the potential disasters that he somehow managed to keep dodging. But, though he had avoided the physical dangers that had often been part of his life while reporting from the war zones of the world, he had not been able to escape his inner crisis. The first thing he noticed that told him something was seriously wrong was feelings of panic that had no basis in reality. Anxiety had always been on the edge of consciousness, but he thought it was simply the source of his creative energy. Suddenly, however, he felt overwhelmed with fears and a pervasive sense of dis-ease. He described it as a struggle for the very core of his being. He then went on to say: "Actually, I am not sure what that means because at the same time I have a very frightening sense that I have no inner core. It feels like experiences just flow through me without touching me. Maybe I am already dead at the center of my being. That's what most frightens me."

John spoke of burnout and exhaustion when he requested and received a two-month leave of absence. He had been working un-usually hard for the past several years, and he was seriously sleep deprived from his heavy travel schedule. However, he was also aware that something similar but less severe had happened nearly ten years earlier, and that the holiday he took at the time did little more than provide a short-term distraction from his distress. He was back at work within a few weeks; caught up once again in work, he soon felt he was past whatever he had been experiencing. Now he wondered if the problem wasn't more than work pressures. He didn't know what exactly that something more might be, but he said that it felt important to find out. Figuring out what was going on within him and recovering from the inner death he felt he was experiencing in his depths were, he said, why he sought help from me.

Notice the differences between Keith and John. Keith wanted to get back to how things had been while John felt that, as strange as it sounded, his present calamity might just be a disguised invitation to get his life back on track. Keith's posture is where we usually start. That is why I called it a default response. We will all receive invitations to awaken throughout the course of our lives. Sometimes they will come in the form of crises that may appear to be externally generated but which actually are largely shaped by the way we are living life out of touch with our depths. Our first response when we face these crises will usually be to try to get through them as best we can, restoring as much of our past life as possible.

But John's response of openness to growth is not simply due to the uniqueness of his personality. Like Keith, his natural orientation was to ignore problems and use the anger that he felt in response to their presence to plow through them. Keith and John were not as dissimilar as they appeared. But there were things that facilitated John's openness to growth. The first was the fact that he was already on an intentional spiritual journey and because of this was already at least minimally attentive to his inner world. He was a Christian, and his faith involved not simply beliefs and religious affiliation but also a sense of his life as being a journey of becoming something more than he was. Although he quickly told me how seldom he took time for personal prayer or any other spiritual practice, he was aware of a longing to grow more deeply as a Christian and as a human being; because of this, he had been reading some of my books. But there was also a second important factor that facilitated his openness. His wife had long been nudging him to take better care of himself, and particularly of his inner world. Deep down, even though he occasionally told her to stop nagging him, he knew that her gentle challenges expressed love and concern. John could not ignore the sense that God was in her, inviting him to find the same still center she possessed. He wondered if this might be his time to do so.

Neither of these facilitating supports—or any of the others that were present in his life—was enough to make John automatically open to growth at this moment. The possibility of growth still required his consent. However, the journey that John embarked on when he allowed himself to lean into his crisis and listen to the messages it was bringing to him left him forever changed. That change was slow in coming. How he wished it could have been as instantaneous as Saul's transformation into Paul seemed to have been. But slowly growth built upon growth, and eventually the very foundations of his life shifted.

Dimensions of Development

To understand John's growth, or that of any of the rest of us, we now need to increase the resolution of the big-picture maps we examined in the last chapter. They might suggest broad contours of the journey of awakening, but we now need to begin to fill in the details. The first step we will take in doing this is to look more closely at one of the two axes that I will use to describe growth and transformation. We can think of this first axis as dimensions of development. Psychologists have identified about two dozen of these dimensions and have mapped what development looks like on each. We have already encountered Piaget's work on cognitive development. Cognition is one of the central dimensions of the self's development because advances on each of the other dimensions is to some extent dependent on cognitive development. However, although cognitive development may be necessary, it isn't sufficient, and the major lines of development all show a striking degree of independence from each other. Ken Wilber suggests that each of the dimensions of the self that have been mapped in this way addresses one basic existential question faced by humans.[1] Adapting and extending his idea, table 3.1 presents twelve major dimensions of the self and the existential questions they address.

TABLE 3.1

Dimensions of Development and Existential Questions

Dimension of Development	Existential Question
Self	Who am I?
Values	What is important to me?
Moral	How should I chose?
Interpersonal	How should I relate to others?
Spiritual	What is of ultimate concern?
Needs	What do I need to be well?
Kinesthetic	How do I indwell my body?
Emotional	How do I feel?
Aesthetic	What do I find attractive?
Cognitive	What am I aware of?
Ego	How do I wish to appear?
Faith	Whom and how do I trust?

When we look at these dimensions in terms of the existential question they address, we immediately see how interrelated they are. Faith, for example, forms part of spiritual development, as do values and morality. Similarly, needs and aesthetics form part of values development; and ego, faith, kinesthetics, and aesthetics form part of self-development. In fact, calling one dimension "self" when all form parts of self further shows how interrelated they are. However, the reason for not simply lumping them all together is that development on these various lines is quite uneven. Recalling that cognitive development is necessary but not sufficient for development on all other lines, it should not be surprising to discover that many people are much more advanced in terms of cognitive functioning than, for example, emotional, moral, spiritual, or aesthetic functioning. This is the notion behind Howard Gardner's concept of multiple intelligences.[2] Some people are strong in logical thinking but weak in aesthetic appreciation, while others have highly advanced moral judgment but relatively weak emotional intelligence. In general, most people excel in several areas and are weak in most others. This isn't necessarily bad, but it does suggest that these dimensions of development are more independent than one might assume when you think about the relationship between the existential questions they each address.

One of the striking features of these lines is that in each case, development unfolds in a highly predictable manner—one stage at a time, in an invariable order. Almost never does someone seem to skip a stage or progress through the stages in an idiosyncratic order. The unfolding is sequential, and each of the hierarchical stages builds upon and incorporates the lower-level ones. We will examine the stages (or levels) of development more carefully in the next chapter; here we should notice that they function as something like a developmental platform. Stages can be thought of as relatively stable ways of organizing self and relating to the world. At any point in time, we are primarily settled within one or another of them on each of the lines of development. That does not mean that we always act in a manner consistent with that stage. Identifying a stage of development simply describes our default way of thinking and responding at that point in our journey. Let me make this clearer by looking at one specific developmental pathway and using it to illustrate these principles.

Faith Development

The most important mapping of faith development has been done by James Fowler.[3] He begins by making an important distinction between faith and belief. Belief, on the one hand, he argues, involves intellectual assent to concepts or propositions as set forth in religious doctrines and creeds. Faith, on the other hand, is the orientation of the total person that defines one's way of relating to that which is universal and considered to be ultimate. Faith, in Fowler's view, gives purpose and direction to life, shaping one's hopes, strivings, thoughts, and actions; as such, faith is a fundamental dimension of the human self. It is universal and is present in one form or another in all human beings, whether they claim to be religious or not.

Our faith involves our passions and intellect, our will and memory, our doing and being. Although we may try to put it into words, it is not something we can ever fully articulate. It will, however, be expressed in how we shape and live our lives. This is because our faith is not so much what we believe as how we believe. Because of this, the stages of faith identified by Fowler are strikingly consistent across religious traditions and cultures. Faith is more of a verb than a noun. It is our way of being in the world, our way of relating to life. If we are open to life, this way of being will evolve and change. Apart from this we cannot maintain integrity because being at one within one's self requires adjusting how we believe and how we live in ways that correspond to the changes in who we become as we grow and mature.

Yet we need to recognize that stages of faith development are not stages of salvation. They do not reflect one's relationship with God. Nor does progress through these stages reflect how good a Christian, Jew, Muslim, or anything else one is. The stages are simply markers on the human journey that reflect the growth and maturation of how we believe and how we orient ourselves to that which is beyond and transcendent to us.

Fowler outlines seven stages in the development of this foundational dimension of self.

TABLE 3.2

Stages of Faith Development

0	Primal-undifferentiated faith
1	Intuitive-projective faith
2	Mythic-literal faith
3	Synthetic-conventional faith
4	Individuative-reflective faith
5	Conjunctive faith
6	Universalizing faith

Stage 0: Primal-Undifferentiated Faith

Fowler's stage 0 is a prestage of faith. Normally lasting from birth to approximately two years of age, this is a stage of sensory, prelinguistic learning and adaptation to an environment over which the infant has little control. Given sufficient warmth and safety and a reasonable balance of satisfaction versus frustration, the infant will generally develop a capacity for basic trust. But given neglect or abuse or consistent frustration of basic needs, the infant's undifferentiated but all-pervasive faith response will be nonfaith. Faith at this primal and undifferentiated stage is hope and trust in continued safety.

Stage 1: Intuitive-Projective Faith

In the years between approximately ages three and seven, the young child's psychic experience is characterized by unprotected exposure to the unconscious. Imagination runs wild, unconstrained by logic and the ability to get perspective on experience. Life at this stage is a collage of disorganized images, fantasies, and impressions. There are no inner structures to help children sort these experiences. For that they are totally dependent on adults. This is why they are so influenced by the actions and moods of caretakers and so prone to absorb the strong taboos of family and culture.

Faith at this stage is fantasy-filled and imitative. Because this period of life is dominated by imagination, the importance of stories cannot be overestimated. Good parents have always known this and have told or read their children stories drawn from the storehouse of the world's best mythic tales. These help their children deal with their imagination. Timid parents sometimes are afraid to read these stories to their children, fearing that they may introduce things that might be frightening. Such parents have forgotten the boundlessness and vividness of children's imagination. There is nothing in these stories that their children haven't already imagined. What those children need is a symbolic container to help them cope with the fantasies that already fill their inner world.

The dangers of this stage lie in the potential for the child to be overwhelmed by images of terror and destructiveness. Its ideal outcome is when the child develops the ability to contain experience. Given the child's state of cognitive development, the best way to do this is by means of symbols and images as these are presented in stories that register the child's intuitive understandings and experience of life. Faith at this intuitive-projective stage is trust in superheroes who know the reality of inner-world and outer-world dangers but can be counted upon to deliver the vulnerable child from them.

Stage 2: Mythic-Literal Faith

The inner life of school-age children is also dominated by super-heroes, but faith is now based on the justice that children hope these heroes will deliver. Myths are interpreted literally, and through this process, the imagination is tamed of its worst ravages. This is made possible by the child's newly developed ability to think logically and adopt an external perspective, thus giving rise to the sense of fairness that now forms the basis of their faith. This sense of fairness continues to come from the stories of family, teachers, and community. The child accepts these stories and through them learns to make distinctions between "people like us" who are within the community of these stories and "those who are different." In this way the child takes the stories and beliefs that are central to the community as the child's own.

However, while this is normative for school-age children, it is quite possible and not uncommon for a person to maintain this faith posture for life. When this happens, symbols and moral rules continue to be interpreted literally. Stage-2 individuals have a strong belief in the justice and reciprocity of the universe. Their belief that the good will be rewarded and the bad punished provides comfort when they feel that they are within the bounds of goodness and leads to bargaining with God when they feel that they are outside this boundary. They define others by their roles and actions, with little reflection on what influences either the other's behavior or their own. The ideal outcome of this stage is the development of the ability to allow stories and myths to provide coherence and meaning for one's experience. The dangers are twofold: (1) either the treadmill of perfectionism and works righteousness or (2) the internalization of the judgments of others, leading to all-pervasive feelings of badness. Faith at this mythic-literal stage takes the form of reliance on the stories, rules, and implicit values of the family's community of meaning.[4]

Fundamentalists of all stripes are the best examples of the mythic-literal stage of faith development. They also illustrate how much faith can be defined more by *how* we believe than by *what* we believe.[5] We see this in the fact that fundamentalist Jews, Christians, and Muslims are more like each other than their more relaxed and progressive fellow religionists. Yet fundamentalist religionists are also more like secular fundamentalists than we usually assume when we think of fundamentalism as a religious phenomenon. Consider, for example, liberal fundamentalists or conservative fundamentalists who literally interpret the doctrines of classic liberalism or conservatism in a rigid exclusionary way and dismiss the validity of those who do not organize their life in the same way. Fundamentalism is built on rigid literalism, and regardless of whether it manifests itself in religious or secular terms, it reflects the mythic-literal stage of faith development.

Stage 3: Synthetic-Conventional Faith

The synthetic-conventional stage of faith development is first seen in adolescence, although it once again is far from limited to this stage of life. By "synthetic," Fowler means that the individual now begins to draw together the disparate elements of one's life into an integrated identity. By "conventional," he means that the values and beliefs that are held are derived from one's cultural or religious context and for the most part are accepted without critical examination. Because of this, faith at this stage is characterized by conformity: various contents of faith are drawn from one's group and pulled together in a way that involves conformity to the majority positions held by the group.

Beliefs at this stage are defined by authority (one's religious leaders, traditions, or sacred texts) or common adoption (the mainstream views held by the majority within a community or cultural group). Identity is based on alignment of one's self with a community and its beliefs, values, and perspectives; by means of this alignment, one discovers order, meaning, and direction in life. Critical reflection on the resulting faith posture is discouraged by the community. To challenge or no longer be able to support the perspective or core beliefs is a disloyalty that results in one's being identified as a nonbeliever, or no longer in the mainstream of the group. This describes the faith of the majority of the population of most Western societies.

Stage-3 faith is acutely tuned to the opinions and expectations of others. People at this stage of faith development lack sufficient confidence in their own judgments to develop an independent perspective. This does not mean that they do not have deep convictions, only that these convictions have typically not been critically examined. Because the opinions and expectations of others are so important, those who live out their faith life within a church tend to relate to God in the same way: seeking a relationship with God and hoping to live up to God's expectations. Such people tend to have a strong sense of the church as an extended family. Sometimes this is a rather romanticized family that gives more emphasis to the provision of support and experience of emotional closeness than to the opportunities for growth that might come from challenge, accountability, or higher levels of authenticity.

The dangers of this stage of faith development are twofold: (1) the expectations and beliefs of others can be so deeply internalized that later autonomy of judgment and action can be compromised; (2) people believe the message that their churches and communities of reference tend to give—that they have arrived. The ideal outcome is that personal perspectives, values, and beliefs are organized in a personally meaningful way. In general, however, one's faith at this synthetic-conventional stage is shaped by the beliefs, values, and perspectives of one's community or cultural group.

Stage 4: Individuative-Reflective Faith

Though we are often preoccupied during our twenties with education and entry into our careers, during our thirties we often find our attention, at least periodically, being drawn from the outer to the inner world. Now we are not merely entering into jobs but also entering into significant personal relationships. We may also be faced with the first questions about our fit with our chosen work, and we may well also have experienced the first failures and frustrations of intimate relationships. These experiences offer an invitation to confront questions regarding identity and belief that have often been lingering on the edges of consciousness since adolescence. Attention to this invitation is far from automatic. But if we offer attention, we approach a portal to a new and deeper faith experience that is first accessible at this stage of life.

By the mid to late thirties we may also discover that our personal journey has drawn us beyond the defining group from which we formerly drew our identity. We may begin to feel the need to take personal responsibility for our values, beliefs, and orienting faith framework. This is a stage of demythologizing, where what was once unquestioned is now subjected to critical scrutiny. Consequently we may feel overwhelmed with questions that we haven't faced for many years and were left unanswered when we thought we had left them behind—questions such as the meaning of life, who we are, and what we most deeply desire. This is often an uncomfortable place to be. Disillusionment and cynicism lurk at the edges of the path. We begin to see that the world is more complex than our synthetic-conventional faith allowed us to experience.

If and when movement into stage-4 faith happens, it almost always happens slowly. The journey through this portal is often quite destabilizing for the individual. It can also be unsettling for spouses, partners, and family members. Because it involves a relocation of authority within the self, it requires a corresponding reexamination of one's beliefs. The result will often involve a shift in identity. No longer defining one's self in terms of the beliefs of a community, the individual now needs a new, larger identity, and in this process of reflection and realignment, one's faith becomes uniquely one's own.

Although individuals at stage 4 strongly value personal autonomy and responsibility, they continue to identify with reference groups of others. Thus, while they no longer follow a crowd, they may identify with and feel themselves part of a reference group that will likely be larger and more inclusive than the more narrow ones with which they identified in stage 3. They now recognize the obligation to take the claims of other classes, ethnic groups, sexual orientations, and religions seriously, paying particular attention to the wisdom and perspectives on important matters of faith and life that they offer.

The danger associated with this stage is an overemphasis on self-sufficiency that leads to ego inflation and elitist, judgmental attitudes toward those who do not share this lofty perch of faith development. Let me briefly illustrate this danger with the story of Laura. Raised in a conservative Christian family, Laura seemed to be following her family's faith path through her college years. After graduation she told her family that she wanted to move to India to study and immerse herself in Hindu culture. Leaving soon thereafter, they did not see her for the next six years. During this time Laura kept in periodic contact but spoke more of the conditions of her outer life than of her inner journey. Her family knew she had been living on an ashram and gathered that she was enjoying her studies, but they did not know much more than this. When she came home for a visit, they quickly discovered how much had changed. She introduced a young woman who had traveled with her as her partner and told her parents that she had come to realize she was a lesbian. Even more shocking for her parents, however, was to hear her assert that she no longer considered herself a Christian and had even come to see that religion was the enemy of individuals and societies since religion made it harder for them to take responsibility for themselves and the world. She proudly declared herself to be an atheist and, as it quickly became obvious, was a rather militant one at that.

It was this militancy and the anger that underlay her commitments and value expressions that most clearly revealed the fact that this had not been an entirely healthy transition. It appeared to have been more of an escape than a true movement of self-transcendence. Rather than take the best of her earlier life forward with her on her journey, she was trying to leave behind as much of it as possible and become a new person. But her earlier life was far from behind her. Her anger at the church, and religionists in general, clearly showed that she had not dealt in any satisfactory way with the issues she needed to face. Her identity was now based much more in what she was against than what she was for. Her faith and life were full of reactivity and lacked the inner freedom that would have accompanied a more healthy movement of transcendence. Her faith was no longer stage 3, but she had not fully moved through the threshold into a healthy stage 4. I tell her story to point out that not all movement beyond a stage necessarily reflects growth. However, this transition can be negotiated successfully, and it can lead to significant growth in faith. A successful passage into stage 4 involves critical reflection on previously tacit and unexamined convictions and beliefs, which then become matters of explicit commitment. Faith is now personal, integrated, and internalized; because of this, faith is well on its way to enhancing life for the individual and others.

Stage 5: Conjunctive Faith

If a person has a midlife crisis, it is likely to be in the late forties or early fifties. If nothing of crisis proportions appears during this time, this is still the period when most people are ready for a midlife realignment. Neither crisis nor realignment automatically ushers in conjunctive faith, but if individuals have successfully managed the challenges of personalizing their faith and not simply borrowing the faith of their primary reference group, they might be ready to respond to their midlife crisis or realignment in a way that serves as a passage into stage-5 faith.

Midlife offers us invitations to broaden and deepen our faith because it reminds us of the inevitability of death and the fact that there are aspects of our life and identity that we cannot change.[6] It invites us to hold, rather than try to solve, the paradoxes of life and polar tensions of our existence. It invites us to relinquish reductionistic attempts to possess and control truth and be willing to approach it with a second naïveté that is expressed in a willingness to participate in the truth as it is expressed in both symbol and myth, thus allowing symbolic power to be reunited with conceptual meanings. It invites us to live the questions we cannot answer in a dynamic, trusting relationship with God. It is an invitation to move beyond rationalism so that we might grasp the greater reality that resides in the symbols of our chosen faith tradition, as well as the traditions of others. The larger-than-literal truth of mythos can now be held comfortably in balance with the more propositional truths of logos.

Stage 4 involved the demythologization of the world; now stage 5 involves its resacralization. Conjunctive faith involves seeing the bigger picture that had been obscured by our small perspectives; the spaciousness of this larger place fills us with wonder, humility, and gratitude. Such are the gifts of stage-5 faith.

As with previous stages, stage 5 also has its dangers. People can be drawn into a private world of their own spirituality and can be vulnerable to forgetting how much they still need and can learn from those at lower levels of faith development. They also run the risk of developing a sense of homelessness unless they learn to commit to a tradition and live within it. At its best, however, stage-5 individuals are alive to paradox and the presence of truth in places of apparent contradiction. Consequently they thrive in being able to unify opposites within themselves and in the world. They are available, therefore, to join the ranks of the wisdom figures of their generation, something that every generation desperately needs. Faith at this conjunctive stage is the ability to see and live one's tradition's most important visions and meanings while still recognizing that they are relative and imperfect apprehensions of transcendent truth.

Stage 6: Universalizing Faith

Sometimes described as enlightenment, stage-6 faith is characterized by a pervasive, even if not always present, sense of being at one with oneself and others in God. More visible to others is the fact that people at this stage invest their lives in social and religious causes without any concern for personal cost. Fowler observes that this decentering of self coupled with a continued widening of the circle of "those who count" challenge our usual criteria of normalcy and give their lives an extraordinary and often unpredictable quality. He goes on: "In their devotion to universalizing compassion they may offend our parochial perceptions of justice. . . . Their enlarged visions of universal community disclose the partialness of our tribes and pseudospecies. And their leadership initiatives, often involving strategies of nonviolent suffering and ultimate respect for being, constitute affronts to our usual notions of relevance."[7]

Fowler acknowledges that very few people reach this stage of faith development. The examples that he cites include Mother Teresa, Dietrich Bonhoeffer, Martin Luther King, Mahatma Gandhi, and Jesus. Each of these people was understood as subverting the religious and social structures of their world, and each gave up their self for the sake of not just their community but also humanity as a whole. Each illustrates the central feature of faith at this universalizing stage: eschewing utilitarian considerations or selfish concerns, expressing a sense of solidarity with all people, and living out compassion for them.

Patterns of Growth

Faith development follows the same sort of patterned unfolding that we see in all the other major dimensions of the self. The names of the stages seen in moral development, ego development, cognitive development, or spiritual development all differ, but the stages show a path that involves the same broadening of perspectives. Growth on any of the lines of development involves expansion of boundaries and what we could call a differentiation or emergence from embeddedness.[8] We begin to see ourselves and the world differently because we become aware of things that were previously beyond awareness. Robert Kegan observes that this differentiation from what was previously background always involves a reorganization of our sense of what is self and what is other.[9] It is also characterized by a shift in our identifications. This is the reason why growth on any of these developmental lines has such implications for our identity.

We will examine all of these patterns more fully later, but first we turn our attention to the other axis of development, the levels of development through which we pass as we grow on any of the developmental dimensions or lines. This should begin to open the door to our understanding of transformation.

Dialogue and Reflection

1. **You refer to faith and spiritual development as separate developmental paths. How do you distinguish them?**

   As I suggested when discussing the existential questions each of these dimensions of human existence address, faith deals with the question of whom and how I should trust while spirituality speaks to the broader question of what is of ultimate concern and how I should relate to this matter of ultimacy. Although it is clear that these are related, I think they are, at least to some degree, independent. I know many people who are more advanced in faith development (whom and how they trust) than they are in spiritual development (consideration of and response to matters of ultimate concern). They have a background implicit spirituality but have not advanced very far in this line of development because it has never emerged from the background as a life priority. I am less sure if I can think of examples of people who are more advanced in spiritual development than faith development and suspect that this might suggest that spirituality cannot progress far without faith, even though it is not reducible to faith.

2. **I have always thought of spiritual development as not simply one among many lines of development but as primary and foundational to all the others. How would you respond to this?**

   I think the temptation to classify spirituality as somehow separate from the other lines of development is dangerous and should be resisted. Trying to privilege one line of development like spirituality makes it less integral to human personality. I understand spirituality to be the orientation of the total self toward that which is beyond or transcendent to the self, not the response of some special part of self that is more spiritual than the other dimensions of self.

3. Because Christian faith is very much tied to an object of faith (God), some Christians might feel that Fowler's separation of faith and its object is a threat to Christianity. How do you respond to this concern?

> I count the fact that Fowler treats faith independent of the object of faith to be a strength of his approach. The fact that his description is as applicable to a Muslim as to a Hindu or Christian is what makes it most valuable, as is the fact that it is also equally applicable to fundamentalists, liberals, atheists, and agnostics. What he describes is *how* we trust, not whom we trust—*how* we believe, not what we believe. Christians who place their ultimate trust in God have the same potential to grow in their faith as those who place that trust elsewhere. Regardless of what we believe, we can all mature in how we place our trust in those beliefs. There is nothing to fear in faith that is broader, deeper, and more mature. Mature faith is reflected in how we orient ourselves to that which is beyond and transcendent to us and which should be prized by Christians as much as anyone else.

4. You describe faith development as involving a broadening of perspectives. But doesn't this help us understand at least part of the reason why we often resist growth?

> Very good point. I think it does. We feel safe and comfortable in small places and fear adopting broader perspectives that force us to renegotiate our relationship to our selves, others, and the world. This becomes even more of a concern in the next chapter, when we turn our attention to transformation and begin to see the even bigger implications of allowing our perspectives to broaden. But remember, the threat is just to our small ego-self. Our spirits want us to soar, not just stay safe. If we dare to begin to attend to our deepest longings, they will always pull us forward as we respond to the invitation of Spirit to become more than we presently are.

4

Transformation and the Levels of Development

In chapter 3 I briefly identified the major lines of development, and we examined one of them—faith development—in some detail. As we saw, faith can be understood to develop through a number of separate stages, each representing a stable way of relating to self and that which is beyond the self, and all hierarchically organized so that each higher one builds upon and incorporates all the lower ones. We also noticed that progress through these stages is linear and that each is encountered in an invariable order. The picture is the same for each of the other dimensions of self: the number and names of stages vary, but each introduces a larger perspective and a larger self.

This brings us to the second axis that needs to be part of any comprehensive map of development. The first axis consists of the various dimensions of the developing self; the second axis shows the levels of development experienced in each of those domains. Let me present a graph to illustrate how these two axes go together.

What we see in this graph is a display of five dimensions of the development of a hypothetical woman—someone whose cognitive development outstrips her faith, moral, and ego development, with interpersonal development showing an even more notable lag. At the

FIGURE **4.1**

Sample Lines and Levels of Human Development

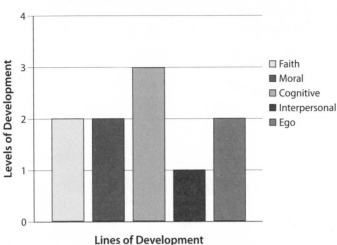

Lines of Development

moment the numbers on the vertical axis are not important. The question, however, is what movement up through these levels means, particularly when the overall level increases. How could we describe the overall change in this individual if at a later point in time her scores on all five of the self's dimensions mapped in figure 4.1 had, for example, increased by one level?

Centers of Gravity and Consciousness

Like all the rest of us, the hypothetical individual I have presented in figure 4.1 is not functioning at a single level. If more lines of development were measured and graphed, we would see even wider divergence among the developmental levels of the various dimensions of her self. Yet at any point in time our way of being in the world is usually organized around a single center of gravity. For each dimension of development, this center represents the average level of development. For the individual presented in figure 4.1, this would be level 2. Some aspects of her development are beyond this and some behind it, but this is where most cluster—just as they tend to cluster around a single center in the developmental psychograph that could be drawn for each of us.

Average levels of development can also be thought of as our developmental center of gravity. This represents a relatively stable platform on which we stand as we engage with life and the world. It includes our worldview but is much more basic than our beliefs. Largely unconscious, it organizes how we approach life and how we try to make meaning out of our experiences. Because it is the platform on which we stand, we don't tend to see it. But we will notice when it begins to shift beneath our feet.

Ken Wilber suggests that this platform is our overall level-of-consciousness development.[1] This determines our way of being in the world because it is built around our working understanding of the relationship between self and everything that we perceive to exist beyond our self. It therefore is the core of our identity.

Consciousness is not so much a thing as that which allows us to experience things. Ken Wilber describes it as simply the degree of openness or emptiness that we possess.[2] Openness and emptiness enable us to experience phenomena. An absence of openness and emptiness results in a constriction of consciousness, and the result is that self-preoccupation blocks meaningful experience of anything beyond those preoccupations.

Consciousness is not itself a phenomenon. It is the space within which phenomena and our awareness of them arise. It is the platform on which we stand as we engage with the phenomena of both the inner world and the outer world. While consciousness is not simply reducible to awareness, our consciousness grows and expands as our awareness increases. Consciousness also provides our framework for organizing experience in that it allows us to make sense of and respond to that which enters awareness. It includes our sensations and perceptions, thinking and willing, awareness, and our response to experience. All have a place in consciousness, and all can be brought more fully into awareness. It is this framework that changes during the process of transformation; the most central part of this change, as we shall see, is the boundary between what is considered self and what is considered to be beyond or not part of self.[3]

But how then does consciousness relate to the various lines of development? How does growth in the various dimensions of self affect this spaciousness? And how does that affect how we experience phenomena? Wilber offers a metaphor for how this works that I find very helpful. He suggests that each of the lines of development is like a path up a mountain, each offering its own unique view. What each allows us to see is related to the existential question that each addresses. Thus, for example, as the path of faith development rises, one sees more clearly how to trust; while climbing the path of moral development, one sees more clearly how best to make choices. Wilber points out, however, that the view on different paths is similar at similar elevations. Higher altitudes on any of these mountain trails represent broader and more inclusive perspectives. The stages or levels of development therefore represent the perspective from a particular elevation: increasing elevations represent increasing openness to apprehending reality on its own terms. This accounts for the fact that for various dimensions of self, descriptions of the higher levels of development all tend to converge. Just as mountain trails to the top of a mountain all converge as one nears the summit, so too do the higher states on all the various lines of development.

The elevation markers are the levels of consciousness development. They are without content. They are empty, just like consciousness is empty. But each of the paths can be measured in terms of its altitude, and this is what we were examining in the last chapter when we looked at the stages of faith development. All developmental lines move through the same altitude gradient. But recall my suggestion that the cognitive line is necessary but not sufficient for all other development. The reason for this is that a person needs to be aware of something if one is to act on it, feel it, identify with it, need it, or in any other way engage with it. Cognition is the capacity for awareness. This is why cognitive development appears to form a ceiling on consciousness development.

In summary, therefore, we can say that shifts in our center of gravity represent shifts in our consciousness. At a minimum this will always involve a change in two things: our sense of our self (identity) and our view of life and the world (perspective). Movements up the vertical axis correspond to bigger selves and larger perspectives. At the core of both of these is increased awareness. So we have introduced the levels of development; now it is time to turn to the question of how transformation relates to movement up this vertical axis of consciousness development.

Transformation and the Expansion of Consciousness

Transformation is a term that in common usage simply implies change. Sometimes the bar is set rather low, and the change might be quite small. Someone, for example, might speak of a spa treatment as having been transformational. They probably mean that it was refreshing. At a slightly more profound level, another person might speak of having lost a lot of weight as transformational. By this, they might mean that they feel like a new person. At what is likely a still more profound level, another person might describe a dramatic conversion experience or mystical encounter as transformational.

My use of the term is quite specific. By *transformation* I mean an enduring expansion of consciousness that expresses itself in four ways:

1. increased awareness
2. a broader, more inclusive identity
3. a larger framework for meaning making (how we understand and make sense of our self, others, God, and the world)
4. a reorganization of personality that results in a changed way of being in the world

Moments of awakening and consciousness expansion can be quite temporary. Altered states of consciousness do not automatically—or even easily—translate into changed stages of consciousness. Exogenous drug-induced states of consciousness expansion, for example, are generally temporary. Changed states of consciousness are not, therefore, enough to warrant being called transformational experiences. They may have transformational potential, but as I use the term, transformation involves an *enduring* expansion of consciousness: increasing awareness that expresses itself in terms of a more inclusive sense of self, a larger framework for meaning making, and a changed way of being in the world.

Unlike the small, incremental changes that may accompany becoming healthier or more mature, shifts in the platform of consciousness are more like the major leaps involved in quantum changes. Many small, unseen background changes may make them possible, but suddenly we notice that our center of gravity has shifted, and the ground from which we view others, the world, and ourselves has changed. Genuine transformation is not, therefore, simply the result of self-directed efforts at change. Nor is it simply the result of either maturation or life circumstances. We do, as we shall see, have a role in making it possible, but it is more a gift than an achievement.

Genuine transformation involves a reorganization and realignment of personality that results in a changed way of being in the world. The

Jungian analyst Murray Stein suggests that it involves a movement of psychic energy from one organized way of being to another in which "underlying latent structures come to the surface and assume leading positions, while other features that were prominent change radically or disappear."[4] The result of this movement is a larger and truer self, which will be reflected in more authenticity and vitality, increased wholeness and integration, larger horizons, an expanded sense of identity, and a greater sense of meaning and purpose in life. In short, transformation is movement from a lower order of life to a higher order.

Despite the rhetoric, transformation is seldom truly desired by most Christians or welcomed by most churches. Most of us prefer to keep the change process under our control and limited to the small tinkerings associated with our self-improvement projects. If we are genuinely open to the unfolding of self that is involved in transformation, we will generally encounter resistance in most of the places that we normally expect support. Families, community, and culture often conspire to keep us safely in a place of conformity. As noted by Richard Rohr, most religion—and this certainly includes Christianity—is more tribal than transformational.[5]

Genuine transformation is a change process that is not under our control. Unlike growth, transformation is impeded by effort, but it is facilitated by consent. If change is to come in the deep places of our self, it must come from some point beyond our self. Attempts to make transformation into a self-improvement project simply strengthen the false self. When this happens, the truth of our being becomes even more distant from us.

Transformation and Identity

Transformation involves a shift in the self that occurs at the boundary of what is understood to be self and non-self. Robert Kegan describes each level of consciousness as a temporary truce between self and non-self, a truce that lasts until the transition into the next level of consciousness, when the self once again broadens and the division between self and non-self once again changes.[6] Transformation affects our identity by changing our identifications and attachments. Identity is grounded in our attachments. We are what we most identify with. If my body is what I most deeply identify with, then I am my body.

If, however, my thoughts, history, religion, symptoms, accomplishments, reputation, competencies, or longings are what I most identify with, then this becomes my identity. I am what I am most strongly attached to.

Notice, for example, how this happens with those who have defined themselves by a history of trauma or abuse. We speak of them as having a victim identity. Being the consequences of abuse is much more serious than simply having symptoms that result from abuse. Similarly, it is easy to identify with your life circumstances and base your identity on this. Thus, instead of living with health challenges, you can slip into defining yourself as weak or sick. Or, instead of simply living in poverty, you can define yourself by your economic standing or social class.[7] Similarly, *being* my thoughts, beliefs, or opinions results in a much smaller self than simply *having* thoughts, beliefs, or opinions. If you doubt that there is a difference between the two (being and having), simply think of someone who is overly attached to their opinions or beliefs and observe how that investment makes their self smaller and more constricted. Notice also how it makes them less available for genuine intimacy and presence. Their intimate space is already filled by their opinions and beliefs. It is hard to be present to both one's own ego attachments and to others. In the same way, a primary attachment to one's accomplishments, reputation, possessions, or any other finite thing will all serve to define our identity and limit our self's unfolding.

These sorts of attachments are what we are usually talking about when we speak of a false self. The problem with this language is that it suggests a binary state: it implies that our self is either true or false. This is overly simplistic. The falsity in our self is a result of our inordinate or disproportionate attachments (in Christian terms, loving anything more than God) that keep us from knowing the truth of our larger self. Knowing that truth always requires adjustments to our identity because the truth of our self is much greater than most of us ever imagine. This truth and this way of being are at the root of a genuinely unfolding consciousness and self.

Robert Kegan provides us with a very helpful framework for understanding how shifts in identifications lead to shifts in consciousness. He observes that during psychological development the "I" of one stage becomes the "Me" of the next.[8] What this means is that what we are identified with—what we experience as "I"—at any stage of development tends to be transcended and no longer identified with as we move to the next higher stage. This means that we can now see more objectively what we were previously identified with. We could also say that the subject of one stage becomes an object in the next. Described in terms of consciousness, this means that the "I" doing the seeing is more objective about things that were previously embedded in the background of awareness and simply taken as a part of self.

Think, for example, of the way in which the young infant is identified almost solely with its body. However, with the development of conceptual thinking, the mind becomes the self, and the infant can then begin to see its body more objectively. Now, instead of *being* its feelings or hunger or pain, it *has* feelings of hunger or pain. This is the core pattern of human development. It's a process of being embedded and identifying with our experience of that embeddedness, slowly disembedding ourselves or transcending those experiences and beginning to see them more objectively, and then reestablishing a new embeddedness with a new set of identifications and a new and larger identity.

For an adult example, let us return to the story of John from chapter 2, the journalist facing a sense of inner emptiness and wanting to use this experience as an opportunity for growth. John's strongest identification was with his writing, with what he described as his ability to see a story. He often felt that if he couldn't write, he didn't know who he would be. Consequently, he measured his worth and success in terms of writing. He was far from immune to what his editors and the general public thought about his columns and books, but he was also quite able to judge when he had noticed something that could be turned into a story and always felt deeply satisfied when it was written. You might wonder where the problem is in this. It sounds rather ordinary to be identified with your work, your abilities, and your accomplishments.

However, John's crisis did not have to do simply with his identifications and identity but with an inner conflict. For many years he had felt himself being pulled to a larger, freer, and truer self—to a way of being in himself and in the world that would not be as bound by his ego and its attachments. But up to the point where I met him, he had resisted this pull. He recognized the truth of Jesus's words that if you want to find your self, you must first lose it. He didn't understand the words, but they spoke to deep places in his spirit that he had been ignoring but that he knew were inviting him on a journey. He kept telling himself that his life was good and that he was almost as good a Christian as could be reasonably expected for someone in his life circumstances. But he was in conflict.

I began by asking John what he most deeply desired. His answer came quickly: inner stillness and peace. His restless spirit had, he said, served him well, and he didn't want to lose it. But, he said, he also wanted to be still, something that he said he could not now do. He had done some reading on meditation, but previous attempts to make this work for him had been unsuccessful. More recently he had read about centering prayer and wondered if it might be what he needed. I gave him a framework for beginning this practice and agreed to accompany him as a spiritual guide on his journey.

As is usually the case, John's early experience of centering prayer was quite frustrating. But, as he over and over again released the thoughts that came into his head during his times of centering, he began to experience freedom and detachment from things that had been so close to him that he thought of them as himself. He began to see that he was not simply his thoughts or his abilities. He had both, but they did not define him. Increasingly he began to feel that what defined him was more his heart and spirit than his mind. More and more he felt that his life might still take the same outer form but that the furniture in his inner self was being radically rearranged.

This is what I mean when I describe the transformation of consciousness in terms of embeddedness and identifications being replaced by a process of dis-identification, fresh identifications, and new embeddedness. John had been embedded in the life of the mind and was shifting toward a self that was embedded in spirit. This is the sort of transition that is going on when the platform on which we stand shifts so that we feel ourselves looking at our self, others, God, and the world through new eyes. John was looking onto the world from a new perspective and through the eyes of a new consciousness. But he was also looking with those same new eyes at himself, and consequently his sense of identity also shifted. These shifts in consciousness are the central dynamic of the transformational journey into God.

If transformation is not an accomplishment but is something that must come from beyond the small self that we presently are, where does it come from? I have no better answer than that it comes from God. This God, who is both within and beyond us, constantly calls us to be more than we are. All growth, healing, and transformation are mediated by this outpouring of the divine Self. They come to us as gifts, but there is something we must do to accept them.

Transformation and Faith

That something is responding to life with a *yes* of openness, acceptance, and gratitude and then living with the inner stillness and presence that is part of being a good host to the Spirit of God, who dwells
within. In a word, it is "faith."[9]

Yet recall from our discussion of faith development in chapter 2
that faith is much more than beliefs. Faith as belief—this being how
it has commonly been understood in Christianity since the Enlightenment—is far too weak to transform anything. However, faith involves
much more than giving cognitive assent to propositions. It is a whole-
person orientation of trusting openness. Faith in God is leaning into
God with trust. It therefore is inseparable from openness. This is why
genuine openness to life is openness to God, and openness to God is
openness to life.

Faith as Openness

God comes to us disguised as our life, and if we fail to be open to
the flow of our life and the gifts it brings us, we cannot be genuinely
open to God. If we are open to our life, God will introduce into it the
grace that we need to grow up into the fullness of our true self-in-
Christ. Often this grace will come in the form of experiences that we
might not have ever chosen but which hold the possibility of helping
us awaken. But grace comes most regularly in the form of the people in
our life whom we normally do not notice but who bring to us this most
precious gift of God—the gift of our becoming. This includes people
with whom we come in contact who are living with more openness
and with a larger consciousness than us, and who can, by their ways
of being in the world, point us to possibilities for our own becoming.
It will also include people who are living with more openness and
hospitality to the Spirit of God than we are. And it will include people
who can hold the tensions of longings and unfulfillment and who can
continue to trust and hope in openness and faith. Unfortunately, our
knee-jerk reaction to these people is often to dismiss or ignore them.
We immediately notice that they are different from us but, rather than
noticing the traces of the Transcendent Other in their otherness, we see
only threat to our way of being in the world and consequently distance
ourselves from them. Receiving the gifts they have to give us simply by
their way of being starts with hospitable openness to their otherness.

This posture of openness in faith reflects the essence of prayer. Prayer is openness to God in faith.[10] It is allowing the life of God to flow into and through us. This is the faith that we receive as a gift when we turn in openness and trust to God. Once we begin to trust that our life comes to us as a gift from God, we are able to respond to it with a yes of basic acceptance and openness. Richard Rohr correctly points out that the ego is always strengthened by constriction, opposition, and reaction, and that when religion starts with no rather than yes, it always ends up obsessed with purity codes and does not lead to compassion, justice, and a truly transformed heart and mind.[11]

Dag Hammarskjöld describes the way in which saying yes can transform the spirit: "I don't know Who—Who–or what—put the question, I don't know when it was put. I don't even remember answering. But at some moment I did answer 'Yes' to someone or something. And from that hour I was certain that existence is meaningful and that, therefore, my life, in self-surrender, had a goal."[12] Saying yes to life does not mean that you must pretend to like everything that life brings you. It simply means that you receive it with openness of heart and mind, an openness that allows you to see yourself, your life, and the world with new eyes and to respond to it out of a bigger heart. This is faith, and such faith opens us in hospitality to the Spirit of God, who is already present within us and who is the source of all becoming.

That same faith prepares us for the free fall that is also always a part of transformation. The human journey of becoming is not one slow steady climb up a hill. Rather, it is much more as described in a poem widely attributed to Guillaume Apollinaire but actually written by Christopher Logue, to celebrate Apollinaire's daring spirit:

> "Come to the edge," he said. They said, "We're afraid."
> "Come to the edge," he said. They came.
> He pushed them . . . and they flew.[13]

My daughter-in-law ends all her emails and messages with the sign-off "Feel the fear and do it anyway." She embraces life on the edge because she knows it is a place of becoming. She knows that only when we dare to leave the safe places of life are we truly able to enter the fertile places that are pregnant with transformational possibilities. It's natural to want to have our leading foot on something solid before we lift the other one, but genuine becoming does not allow this safety net. Recall the words of Jesus: we must lose our life before we can truly find it. We must let go of our life and feel the fear of free fall before we can know our self to be truly held. We have to let go of the old and go through a stage of unknowing or confusion before we can enter the promised land. This is what it means to live by faith: we trust that we are being led to a place that we do not know, on a journey that we do not control.

Transformation is not for the fainthearted. But it is for those whose hearts and spirits and minds are open and ready to become even larger. It is for those who long, those who dream, those who seek. It isn't for the contented. Rather, it is for the seeker that is in all of us—seeking the larger places for which we were born, seeking the larger self we dare to hope we really are, seeking the truer self we trust must lie hidden in the clutter of the various selves of our own construction. It is for those who hunger and thirst after being all they can be and are not prepared to settle for anything less.

Faith as the Courage of Inner Stillness

Faith has another important expression in making ourselves available to God for the divine work of becoming all we can be: inner stillness. One of the ways in which we most securely insulate ourselves from transformation is by having lives that are too full for stillness and solitude. We tell others that we wish we were less busy, and we may even believe this lie ourselves. Our busyness is a distraction that keeps us from facing our inner self. Stillness may feel superficially attractive, but what we really want is diversion and relaxation, not space for presence to self and to God. Our avoidance of those things is the root of our addictions and keeps even our religious life wound up in a frenetic treadmill of obligations and activities.

For the last two decades my wife and I have spent about half of each year in leading contemplative retreats around the world. Doing so has convinced me that real transformation seldom comes simply from reading a book or listening to a lecture. It requires the fertile place of solitude and stillness. It demands the openness of heart and mind that can only be given when space is created for whatever measure of stillness we can receive from God and are then prepared to offer back to God as our gift. Seeking silence, solitude, and stillness is always, therefore, a response to the Spirit, who calls us within our spirit to deeper places. It's a response to a longing that we may not even know is present. Acknowledging and responding to this longing is itself a way of expressing faith and saying yes to God.

There is also an important place for an encounter with Presence in moments when we are doing something we seem profoundly meant to do. A friend of mine calls this transcendence in action.[14] But we will never be able to discern these encounters if we have not first learned to discern Presence in stillness. Then we are able to experience an inner stillness that is deeper than inactivity, a stillness that can even be experienced in action.

It begins with the intentional practice of stillness to self and God. This contemplative presence needs to last just long enough for a single taste of the mystery that is God. As soon as you taste this transcendent mystery for yourself, you will long for an even deeper encounter. In this place of stillness, faith is simply your intention of offering presence to One who is present to you. Your presence is simply a response to Presence, just as your own being is a response to the One in whom you have your being. Your depth of knowing both God and yourself and your depth of transformation will be as great as your readiness to offer presence to your self and God. Presence requires stillness because there is no real meeting, no genuine encounter, without presence. And without encounter, there is no transformation.

It is striking that for all the emphasis Jesus placed on love, he praised faith even more than love. "Your faith has saved you," he tells us in Luke 8:48. Faith transforms us because faith is a readiness to let go and take the next step—even when it isn't clear where you will be putting your foot down. It is daring to allow yourself to be still and face your inner demons, or step over the edge when nothing but the abyss seems to be below. You no longer need to hold on because you know that Someone is holding on to you!

Transformation and the Awakening Self

I will have much more to say about transformational dynamics as we proceed. Yet before ending this chapter, let us step back for a moment and connect transformation and awakening. As I am using the terms, *transformation* and *awakening* represent two perspectives on the same phenomenon. Both describe a change of consciousness: awakening emphasizes the emergence from a state of oblivion to one of awareness, and transformation points to the implications of this emergence.

With each expansion of consciousness, we do not simply become aware of new things; we also experience a change in how we organize these new contents of consciousness. This movement of increasing the contents of consciousness (awakening) and reorganization of those contents (transformation) is what we will be examining as we consider the journey of the awakening or unfolding self. In psychological terms, what I am proposing is that human development is primarily organized around this expansion of consciousness and the reorganizations of the ways of understanding the relationship of self and non-self that are involved in it. Each shift to a new platform on which we stand and from which we view our selves and the world is associated with changes in how we organize our experience and consequently with changes in our identity.

This transformational journey of successive awakenings and the associated expansions of consciousness is the journey of the unfolding self. But this journey is not simply one of ascent. Rather than mapping the journey on the two axes we have considered to this point, if we were to add a third dimension of progress or regress, we would see a looping series of spirals that go up and down in ever-widening and more-encompassing circles. Unlike growth—which (as we have recognized) progresses in a rather linear manner through ordered stages, none of which appears to be able to be skipped—transformation moves backward and forward, up and down, as we prepare for a shift to a larger self and expanded consciousness. Transformation is at least as much about descent as ascent, death as new life, loss as new discovery. This is because the process of becoming more than we now are often requires re-formation that must precede transformation, and healing that must come before increasing wholeness.

The journey therefore is far from linear. Do not trust any map of the journey that reduces it to a formula or leads you to expect a simple straightforward path. The walk is the same from beginning to end: openness and faith that expresses itself in sufficient stillness and solitude to allow you to be a good host to the Spirit, who is the inner engine of transformation. But the path is far from straight and far from simply one long gentle incline of ascent. It is a path that must take you right through the middle of life as it comes to all of us—with its great losses, loves, suffering, hopes, disappointments, disillusionments, and fulfillments. In the midst of these we must learn to open ourselves in faith—and stay open—to the Spirit, who meets us through the circumstances of our lives and in the depths of our being.

It is there that we learn to open both heart and mind so that both might be transformed: both have a crucial role to play in a Christian understanding of the expansion of consciousness that is ours as we participate in the life of the Spirit.

In overall terms we could describe this participation in the life of the Spirit as returning to our home in God. It is a progressive knowing of the truth of our being: we are already in God. Our separateness from God is an illusion, an illusion based on what theologians call sin. But it is an illusion that has tremendous existential, psychological, and spiritual consequences. Awareness of the truth of our being is at the core of our expanding consciousness. And this growing awareness allows us to move more fully into our life in God and God's life in us.

Teresa of Avila spoke of this journey of finding your self in God and God in your self.[15] Thomas Keating describes it as a journey through four "yous": (1) the you of ordinary everyday awareness, (2) the you of your personality and character, (3) the you that is in relationship with those who love you for exactly who you are, and (4) the you that at the deepest level is not separate from God—distinct, but not separate. It is God sharing the divine life with us.[16]

Although some contemporary writers speak of this as a journey toward Christlikeness, I prefer to describe it as an increase of Christ-consciousness. Too easily becoming like Christ gets reduced to changed behavior. Genuine transformation involves something much deeper: changed being. It is taking on the mind and heart of Christ and consequently living with the awareness that we participate in the life of God without any loss of our uniqueness. This is the destiny of all humans. It is the Word of God made flesh and enlightening everyone who comes into the world (John 1:9).

But even those of us who find something in this language of a journey into God that corresponds to our deepest spiritual longings live most of our time in a place where it is far from our consciousness. We may have moments when we suddenly have a sense of the reality to which the words point, but most of the time it is not part of our experience. Consequently our consciousness and identity exclude what we in our beliefs may profess as central. This is the gap between our theology and our spirituality.

No one has more to teach us about the remedy for this gap than the Christian mystics. Their theology is spiritual theology. It is grounded in their experience. As we shall see, what defines them is not so much their experience as their desire to move their knowing God from their heads to their hearts and to the centers of their being. They are not prepared to settle for anything less than to drink deeply from the living waters promised by Jesus—waters that will not only quench our deepest thirst but that will also spring up from within us as a well of everlasting life (John 4:14). This and nothing else is the one taste that we need if we are to be healed of the gap between our beliefs and the realities of our inner life.

Dialogue and Reflection

1. **You described consciousness as the openness and emptiness that enable us to experience phenomena. But what is this emptiness, and how do we create it or contribute to its development?**

   I appreciate the way you worded your question because it suggests some sensitivity to the possibility that we may not be responsible to create this space. We are not responsible to create it because there is nothing we could or need to do to accomplish this. The space is already there. We simply need to be aware of it and stop filling it up. So much spiritual practice constitutes efforts to fill the self rather than empty it. Along with all the great spiritual teachers of the world, Jesus emphasized the importance of emptiness. He actually epitomized it: the whole trajectory of his life was one long journey of self-emptying. This is the spiritual journey of discovering the God who is within, and this is the source of the inner space. It is the journey of surrendering one's ego-self to the Spirit and allowing that small ego-self to be displaced by one's true self-in-Christ. It is discovering that the space I seek for awareness is not something I need to create but something that has been mine all along—something that I can receive as I let go and allow my frantic inner grasping to lessen as I open my self in trust to the One in whom I am held and have my being. This is a spiritual response and is part of the reason spiritual practices have the potential to play a crucial role in this process. But we will have to wait for a later chapter for me to take that topic up more fully.

2. **How do changes in consciousness lead to the other broader changes you say are part of transformation?**

Changes in consciousness are moments of awakening, and awakening operates as Fritz Perls describes it in chapter 1: recognizing every moment of seeing more clearly what truly is as being pregnant with possibilities of change. As I have said, genuine transformation does not happen automatically. Saul did not become Paul just because of what happened to him in his encounter with Jesus on the Damascus Road. He had to consent to the changes that began in that moment of disorientation and that were grounded in his vulnerability and openness. But it all begins with a moment of awakening and the choice of staying sufficiently open to allow light and life to flow into one's soul.

3. What is the relationship between transformation and growth?

Growth is hard, plodding work. There are no shortcuts: what we avoid dealing with will always hold us back. Small steps of growth usually occur within a single line of development. But recall that the lines converge as we move up them, so eventually growth in our emotional functioning, moral development, or self-regulation will begin to spill over into other closely related lines of development. When they do, this enhances our readiness for transformational shifts of consciousness by raising the platform on which we stand and from which we view the world. Transformation is a movement between the major platforms. It isn't just a slightly larger perspective but a whole new view, a whole new platform on which we stand and engage the world. Growth is incremental, but transformation is more like a quantum leap forward or a major paradigm shift. The big shifts of transformation are best recognized after the fact. The new and larger platform we suddenly find ourselves standing on isn't something we have built ourselves or achieved through our efforts. It is a gift that we were able to receive by being ready to take the risk of letting go of old ways of seeing and living. Our growth prepares us for it but can never produce it. It is what Christians call a grace.

However, this distinguishes growth and transformation but doesn't answer your question about the relationship between them. Although I don't think that growth leads to transformation, it can prepare us for it. And apart from openness to growth, I don't think there is any meaningful openness to transformation. Growth is also usually a by-product of transformation. Transformation usually involves a burst of growth involving enough momentum that it can facilitate a significant period of growth. We will see how this works more clearly in a later chapter when we consider the spiraling nature of growth and transformation and the way in which transformation requires and invites gathering up all the parts of self that have been left behind and are lagging in developmental maturity.

4. **The picture you paint of transformation as an expansion of consciousness is so much bigger than what is usually presented in Christian spirituality that it makes me wonder if it really is Christian spirituality. If it is, why haven't I heard more people talk about it in these terms?**

The Christians who have spoken this language are the mystics, and their marginalization within our tradition has resulted in the loss of this big picture that I have presented. They talk about a journey toward union with God, but the church has often reduced this to a journey of sin avoidance, faithfulness in religious practices, and personal piety. Christian mystics talk about taking on the mind and heart of Christ, but the church talks about adopting certain beliefs and practices. Mystics understand that the heart of transformation is the heart, but the church has too often been content to focus on behavior. So, if we are to recover this much broader understanding of transformation, then we must look to the Christian mystics.

5

Learning from
the Christian Mystics

With the exception of Hinduism, which is so thoroughly mystical that it is redundant to speak of mystical Hinduism, mystics tend to make their fellow religionists nervous. Consequently they are usually marginalized—sometimes revered but usually invested with enough suspicion to hopefully minimize their contamination of ordinary Christians, Jews, Muslims, or other religious practitioners. Mystics are treated with suspicion because they seek direct personal knowing of and union with the Divine, threatening those who try to mediate this access as a way to control the faithful and shape their beliefs, expectations, and practices.

Yet every religion has its mystics. In Christianity that began with Jesus. Reading his assertions of being one with God (whom he called his Father) as theology misses the fact that these were not statements of belief but of experience. Jesus was describing his spirituality when he tells us that he was sent by his Father (John 8:42), would return to him (14:12), and did or taught nothing that did not come from his Father (7:16). He was describing his spirituality when he said that he and his Father were one (10:30). His prayer for the world was that we too might know the union with the Father that he knew, and in so knowing, we might share his same spirituality and the same life of God (17:21). Unquestionably this was a mystical spirituality. The marginalization of our mystics shows how much Christianity has distanced itself from this cardinal feature of the spirituality of Jesus and become a religion of beliefs rather than a spirituality of transformation.

Like mystics of all spiritual traditions, when Christian mystics speak of God, they emphasize love. They do not do this simply because of theological assumptions about the nature of God but because their encounter with God demands that their story of God—which is what theology is—be centered and grounded in love. Love, they tell us, is at the core of existence. It is our origin and our fulfillment. Born out of the love of God, our very being is being-in-Love, for our being is in the God who is love. Love, they argue, is not merely one characteristic of God but is God. Echoing 1 John 4:7–8, they assert that where love is, there is God; and where God is, there is love. Consequently nothing is more important than knowing God in love, for it is in this knowing that we reach our ultimate end: loving union with Perfect Love.

But this is not just the teaching of Jesus or more-modern Christian mystics. It is also the teaching of Scripture. With shockingly bold language, Peter describes the mystical possibility of union with God as participating in the divine nature (2 Pet. 1:4). Paul speaks of having been crucified with Christ and no longer living his own life, but the life of "Christ who lives in me" (Gal. 2:20 NRSV), and John states that although we already are the children of God, in the future we shall be like God and shall see God as God really is (1 John 3:2). These possibilities—of experiencing a union of the human spirit and the Spirit of God and of a full knowing of God in which we can experience God as God rather than "through a glass, darkly" (1 Cor. 13:12)—are biblical teachings that became central themes in the writings of later Christian mystics.

Christian mysticism is participation in this transformational journey toward union with God in love. But it is not just mystics who are invited on this journey. This journey is the calling of all of us. All humans are called to live the mystery of our life in Christ by allowing grace to transform us into our true selves and thus letting us begin to know the reality of our mystical union with God. This journey into union with God does not come from leaving the world and seeking mystical experience but by living out our life in the world. But this raises the question of where mysticism fits within this journey and, an even more basic question, what it means to be a mystic.

Demystifying Mysticism

One of the reasons why mysticism is so often mistrusted is that the mystics are seldom allowed to speak for themselves. Instead, too often people let others tell them what the mystics are supposed to say and believe. Recently I gave a talk on learning from the mystics to a group of seemingly intelligent, well-educated Christians. After hearing an appreciative reference to Thomas Merton, someone asked me how I could take the Christian mystics seriously since they were obviously such fringe characters, pursuing ecstatic visions and encounters and dabbling in extraordinary supernatural phenomena. I asked this man which mystic he was referring to. He replied, "No one in particular: really, all of them." I then asked which of the Christian mystics he had read. He said that while he had not read any of them, he had been taught by his church that they were not to be trusted. This uninformed dismissal of an important Christian tradition is tragically common.

The mystics themselves repeatedly warn about the dangers of seeking ecstatic or mystical experience. Although occasionally some of them become distracted by visions or personal revelations, they frequently remind us that if we are to love God with all our heart, soul, and mind, we must desire nothing more than God (Matt. 22:36–40). Thomas Merton states that "in order to possess Him Who is all, we must renounce possession of anything that is less than God,"[1] everything else that can be seen, known, enjoyed, or possessed. Gifts that we receive from God (including mystical gifts) must never be confused with or valued more than the giver of all good gifts: God.

Christian mysticism should therefore not be confused with experience. Instead, it should be understood as participation in the mystery of the transformational journey toward union with God in love.[2] The pursuit of visions, raptures, or other high-octane experiences can be a dangerous distraction from this journey. The goal of the journey is to know God in love. John of the Cross said that because God is love, God can only be known by love, not by thought. But to know this love is to know God. Recall Paul's prayer in which he asks that out of God's infinite glory, you may receive the "power through God's Spirit for your hidden self to grow strong, so that Christ may live in your hearts through faith, and that, planted in love and built on love, you, with all the saints, will be able to grasp the breadth and the length, the height and the depth of God's love; until, knowing fully the love of Christ which is beyond all knowledge, you are filled with the utter fullness of God" (Eph. 3:17–19). A mystic is simply a person who seeks, above all else, to know God in love. Mystics are, therefore, much more defined by their longing than by their experience. They long to know God's love and thereby to be filled with the very fullness of God.

This sort of knowing is beyond reason, but it is not irrational. It is transrational. It is knowing of a different order. It is a form of knowing often described as contemplative. And this is its connection to mysticism. Contemplation is apprehension uncluttered by thought—particularly preconception and analysis. It is based on direct and personal encounter. When you know something by means of such encounter, you may not be able to express it verbally—at least not in a compelling, coherent, or exhaustive manner. But you do know that you know because your knowing has a depth and immediacy to it that is never present in simply knowing *about* things—even merely knowing *about* God.

A Modern Mystic

Let me make this more concrete. I will introduce you to a woman who lived an ordinary married life in the modern world but who, since her death, has been widely recognized as one of the great mystics of the twentieth century, someone who has done more than anyone else to make mysticism of practical relevance to ordinary Christians.

Evelyn Underhill was born in 1875 into an English home that she would later describe as tolerantly agnostic. Raised apart from any religious influence, her teenage curiosity about religion led her to visit a church and, to the surprise of her friends and family, shortly after that to be confirmed into the Church of England at age sixteen. On the day of her confirmation, she made the following entry in her journal: "As to religion, I don't quite know, except that I believe in a God, and think it is better to love and help the poor people around me than to go on saying that I love an abstract Spirit whom I have never seen. If I can do both, all the better, but it is best to begin with the nearest."[3] Although her subsequent church involvement and spiritual development would be quite minimal for many years, this journal entry hints at what would become hallmarks of her mature spirituality. The most important of these was her conviction that talk of loving an invisible God that does not translate into actions of loving the very visible humans who populate our life is worthless and dangerous. As it subsequently emerged, her spirituality and approach to mysticism were far from otherworldly, both being firmly grounded in life in the world.

Her spiritual unfolding was, however, slow in coming. Eventually it did arrive through travels in Italy that finally led to her spiritual awakening. Caught up in rapturous attention as she sat and looked at the great art she encountered in the Florentine galleries and churches, she wrote that "this place has taught me more than I can tell you: a sort of gradual unconscious growing into an understanding of things."[4] The understanding that she came to was of our fundamental orientation toward the divine, and the capacity of all humans—not just religious or spiritual elites—to personally experience the love of God that touched her as she sat and looked at the religious paintings she encountered in Florence.

Evelyn Underhill thought of mysticism as simply knowing God in love. Although she studied the lives of the great Christian monastic mystics and came to a deep appreciation for their calling, she saw no need to leave the world to come to this knowing. She was convinced that such knowing was possible for all human beings. Made in God's image, the spirit of humans was, she argued, capable of immediate communion with God, a communion that expands consciousness, allows us to see things as they truly are, and attunes us to the realities of the world.[5] The cultivation of this communion with what she called the One Reality is a lifelong process that is practical and active. It develops within the context of the regular practice of adoration and charity. "Adoration is caring for God above all else. Charity is the outward swing of prayer toward all the world, . . . embracing and caring for all worldly interests in God's name."[6] Mysticism, as she argued and demonstrated by her life, involves a development of the whole self under the impetus of its search for the transcendent; mysticism ultimately expresses itself in our participation in God's redeeming work in the world.[7]

The mystics have many gifts to offer us. Let me briefly comment on four that I think are most important: trust in the darkness, the alignment of head and heart, healing the wounded self, and unifying a divided consciousness. Taken together, and when combined with a passionate desire to know God, these form the foundation of the spiritual consciousness that allows us to taste the One Reality to which Evelyn Underhill bore witness.

Trust in the Darkness

Moments of spiritual awakening are usually accompanied by a sense of peace, joy, and expansive lightness of being. However, if you manage to stay awake and allow yourself to be carried along by the Spirit, eventually you will enter into a very different season of the journey. Suddenly it seems as if the lights have been turned off. Struggles, discouragement, and suffering replace peace and joy. Worse, it seems as if God has now left you in the darkness and is nowhere to be found. But this too is a stage of the spiritual journey, a stage that the sixteenth-century Spanish mystic John of the Cross calls the dark night.[8]

Contrary to our frequent assumption that mystics live in states of continuous (or at least frequent) bliss, the reality is that like us, darkness characterizes more of their lives than bliss does.[9] Consequently they have much to teach us about learning to live in these places where our senses are darkened and our souls clouded. And what they tell us is that if, rather than expect the darkness to be eliminated, we continue to consent to the inflow of grace, we will learn to see in the darkness and to know God's presence with us even when we are in the cloud of unknowing. They actually assure us that we can learn not only to trust God's presence in the darkness but also to prefer darkness to light as we learn to float on the dark river of God's love. As we do so, we receive the gift of a deeper knowing than that which is ever possible by means of our senses. We receive the gift of knowing in faith and love.

One of my favorite medieval mystics is Julian of Norwich. Although she is primarily associated with the mystical revelations of Love that she received late in her life, I believe that her most valuable gift to us comes from the many years of darkness that preceded these revelations. This was a protracted period of suffering, unfulfilled longing, and waiting in trust; what she learned from this was at least as important as what she learned in her later experiences of Divine love. She summarizes the gifts she received from this period of waiting in darkness:

> By this I was taught to understand that our soul's continual seeking
> pleases God greatly; for we can do no more than seek, suffer, and trust,
> and it is worked in the soul by the Holy Spirit; and when we find him
> clearly this is by special grace at a time he chooses. Seeking with faith,
> hope, and charity pleases our Lord; and finding pleases the soul and
> fills it full of joy. And so I was taught to understand that seeking is as
> good as beholding all the while he allows the soul to labor. It is God's
> will that we continue to seek him and strive to behold him, waiting
> for the moment when he chooses by special grace to show us himself.
> This does him the most honor and profits you; it happens gently and
> effectively with the guiding grace of the Holy Spirit. For when a soul
> fastens itself to God truly trusting, whether in seeking or beholding,
> this is the best service it may render him.[10]

Julian's life and writings illustrate trust in the God who comes
to us in a cloud of darkness, desolation, and unknowing and meets
us with grace that can never be received in the light, in states of
consolation, or with the knowing that comes through reason or the
senses. This is the grace that allowed her to wait on God with such
hope and trust during long years of suffering and unfulfilled seeking
with such hope and trust. It is also the grace that allowed Thomas
Merton to turn with such confidence to God amid his time of darkness and unknowing. Listen to his poignant journal entry expressing
trust that is only possible in darkness: "My Lord God, I have no idea
where I am going. I cannot see the road ahead of me. I cannot know
for certain where it will end. Nor do I really know myself, and the
fact that I think I am following your will does not mean that I am
actually doing so. But, I believe that . . . you will lead me by the right
road, though I may know nothing about it. Therefore I will trust you
always though I may seem to be lost and in the shadow of death. I
will not fear, for you are ever with me and you will never leave me
to face my perils alone."[11]

This is living by faith, not by sight or the certainty of reason or the
senses. When faith is exercised in this way, such trust in God's loving
presence increasingly becomes the light that illumines our existence
even when we are engulfed in the darkness of pure faith.

As promised by Jesus in John 14:27, peace now becomes dominant
over anxiety, and hope over despair. We don't simply believe that
we are in God's hands; we also know this—a knowing in faith that
comes from turning in trust to God in the darkness and, as we do so,
receiving the faith to know that we are not alone.

Trusting God in the darkness is learning to know God beyond images and concepts. It is a spiritual knowing, not merely a mental (sensory or intellectual) knowing. It is coming to know Christ as the light that burns darkly but with fierce intensity—a light that is best seen in the darkness. Pseudo-Dionysius imagined this place of receptivity to the fierce love of God that burns so hot as to consume light and described it as the "divine darkness." This darkness has a place of special importance in the mystical theology of the Christian church, and the mystics' encouragement to trust God in the darkness is one of their special gifts to the rest of us.

The Alignment of Head and Heart

In the last chapter I defined transformation as an enduring expansion of consciousness and noted that how adequate this definition is depends on how we understand consciousness. If by consciousness we mean simply the contents of awareness (as is common in many psychological understandings) or mental processes (as when the transformation of consciousness is understood in more spiritual terms as enlightenment), then the mystics agree that this is far too narrow an understanding. The journey into God, they argue, must change both heart and mind. Both are foundational to how we organize experience, and therefore both are important parts of consciousness. But for the self to optimally unfold, the heart and the mind must be aligned with the other and formed by the heart and mind of Christ.

In general, the mystics understand hearts and minds as perceptual organs: as means by which we acquire knowledge about the world and God. The heart is the center of our being. This is what Jesus meant when he spoke of thoughts and actions emerging from and expressing the realities of our hearts (Matt. 15:19). In itself the mind is incapable of knowing the ultimate mystery of God, nor even, through its own power, of consistently doing the good that is desired by the heart. To live in truth, the mind must surrender to the wisdom of the heart that is received through faith for, as Pascal argues, "it is the heart that experiences God, and not the reason."[12] But for this to happen, both head and heart need realignment with each other.

It is in contemplative stillness before God and self that we experience the most potential for this healing of the split of head and heart. This is where we encounter divine mysteries that cannot be captured by either but which can be received by both when they are aligned. This is not something we can accomplish but is something we can experience as we cultivate a contemplative knowing of God in love. Through this we acquire the heart and mind of Christ; in so doing, our heart and mind are aligned with, and unified with, Truth. While it is profound arrogance to think that we could ever possess truth, the mystical hope is that we can know ourselves to be possessed by the Truth. To be possessed by the Truth is to be in Truth, and this is infinitely more valuable than to have opinions about truth, no matter how accurate those opinions may be.

To be possessed by the Truth is to be made over into the heart and mind of Christ. But we cannot take on the mind of Christ unless we are also willing to take on the heart of Christ. And neither is something we can simply accomplish by an effort to re-form our minds or hearts. Both are the result of being healed by God's love. Changing our thoughts, embracing certain propositional truths, or willing our self to change—all these are woefully poor alternatives to being made new in and through love. The role of heart and mind is to cooperate with truth by opening to love. We need the mind to know the truth of the heart, and we need the heart to know the truth of the mind. Both must participate in the transformational process if we are to access grace. This and this alone allows us to receive divine love and then let it flow through us to others and to the world.

As long as we are open for even the smallest measure of this divine love, we will begin to be healed by it, and part of this healing is the readiness for even greater openness. This is the way in which heart and mind are transformed as we journey into God. That readiness may begin in either head or heart. Each act of openness provides the doorway to the next. Our part is to consent to the inflow of the life and love of God. This consent will be, in part, expressed by our desire for union with God and by our cooperation with grace by making our selves available to the means of grace, such as prayer, the sacraments, the Word, stillness before God and self.

Healing the Wounded Self

One of the misunderstandings of the mystical journey into God is that it is a journey of encounter with God that leaves self progressively behind. This is absolutely incorrect. The journey into God involves the maturation and completion of our self; because of this, it is a continuing and ever-deepening encounter with both God and self.

Central to the journey into God is healing our self's wounded parts by God's love. Perfect Love alone can heal both these wounds and the life-destroying ways we have developed to avoid their pain. The journey into Love cannot help but engage these broken parts of us and bring healing to the fragmentation and inauthenticity that has resulted. Movement toward our true self in Christ would be impossible if healing were not a central part of this journey. But a developing relationship with Christ that includes prayer, the means of grace, and participation in God's kingdom work of making all things new in Christ will always involve the healing and restoration of our true self.

This does not mean that healing of these wounds cannot happen apart from a developing conscious relationship with Christ: here the key word is *conscious*. Any growth or healing that we experience demonstrates that we already are in relationship with God because apart from this relationship, not only would there be no growth or healing, but there would also be no existence. While it is quite clear that we can be in relationship to God without awareness, awakening (which includes increased awareness) will always bring increased opportunities for participation in this healing as ever-deepening knowing of God leads to ever-deepening knowing of self.

Each awakening involves a brush with the Divine. And each encounter with the Divine increases our appetite for more. Rather than satiation, we experience increased longing for a deeper taste and a fuller knowing of God. But as I have argued elsewhere[13] and as the mystics themselves have repeatedly affirmed, deep knowing of God and deep knowing of self are so inextricably interdependent that neither can happen apart from the other. Consequently each awakening involves a progressively deeper awareness of our longing to fully become our true hidden self in Christ. Echoing a central tenet of the mystical theology of Teresa of Avila, John of the Cross, Bonaventure, and many others, Thomas Merton puts it this way: "There is only one problem on which all my existence, my peace, and my happiness depend: to discover myself in discovering God. If I find Him I will find myself and if I find my true self I will find Him."[14] Our participation in the journey into God takes the form of embracing this priority pursuit. And as we express faith by being open to our self and God, Christ restores our being in love.

Part of this restoration is the healing of our unconscious. The mystics understand this primarily to be the result of prayer, particularly contemplative prayer. This is the place where the stillness before self and God, earlier described as expressive of hospitality to the Spirit, come together. Consequently it is in this place of prayerful openness in stillness that the healing of our deepest wounds occurs. We understand the way in which this healing occurs much better as a result of developments in depth psychology over the last century. But the foundations of this psychological understanding were laid in the spiritual writing of such mystics as Richard of Saint Victor, Bonaventure, John of the Cross, Teresa of Avila, and Gregory Palamas. Some of the most helpful discussion of the dynamics of this deep healing through contemplative prayer is found in the writings of two contemporary Christian mystics, Thomas Keating and Cynthia Bourgeault.[15]

In John 8:32, Jesus said that the truth will make us free, and I am convinced that the principal way in which this happens is through this deep healing of our unconscious. Jesus is The Truth that leads us to freedom by means of the knowing of self, particularly through an encounter with the lost parts of our self that remain hidden in the dark recesses of the unconscious. The integration of these lost members of the family of self is an essential part of establishing our true self in Christ. Although this might sound like an insight of modern psychology, it once again comes to us from the rich tradition of Christian mysticism.[16] The journey into God is a journey of restoration of the unique self that we are—the self that was created in the image and likeness of God and which, from eternity, has had our name. It is a restoration of the whole person to a knowing of love of God and our self-in-God.

Unifying a Fragmented Consciousness

One final aspect of the self that is restored during the journey into God and that deserves discussion is consciousness. Because the mystics understand mind and heart as ways of knowing and because they understand the goal of life to be knowing God in love, they have always had a special interest in consciousness since it is our consciousness that shapes our knowing. It is a problem of consciousness if we are already in God and God in us, but we are not aware of this fact. And if nothing is more important than our deep knowing of God's abiding presence in us and love for us, then right at the heart of our restoration must be the transformation of our consciousness.

There are several ways in which the mystics have described this problem in our consciousness. One is in terms of our lack of awareness. We have already covered this lack when we discussed spiritual awakening, noting the emphasis that Jesus placed on awakening and the way in which it can be considered the core of conversion. But even after our eyes begin to open and ears begin to hear, we continue to process our experience through our still-fragmented consciousness. The name that mystics give to this fragmentation is duality. Its opposite is seeing through the eyes of truth and understanding that allows us to apprehend reality as it truly is, a way of seeing that the mystics call contemplation.

Contemplative seeing and knowing are not opposed to other ways of seeing and knowing. Instead, they complement them. Richard of Saint Victor, one of the most influential mystical theologians of the twelfth century, argued that humans possessed three sets of eyes. The first, the eye of the flesh (*oculus carnis*), is the means by which we see physical reality. The second, the eye of reason (*oculus rationis*), is how we discover order. The third, the eye of faith (*oculus fidei*), is how we see spiritually. Each eye raises the level of gaze to the next, thereby overcoming any sense of incompatibility between the physical world, reason, and the sacred. The mystics do not reject the first eye, of the senses. Nor do they reject the second eye, of reason. They know better, however, than to confuse knowing with the acquisition of sensory data or the fruits of reason. As explained by Evelyn Underhill, contemplation supplements reason and the senses. It unifies consciousness, pulling together the fragmented ways of knowing and experiencing. In emphasizing the relational nature of this unification, not simply its perceptual features, Christian mystics describe this state of unified consciousness as mystical union with God. Mystics therefore are those who have moved from knowing that is simply based on either the senses or the mind to a knowing that grows out of union with God. Richard Rohr describes this as "movement from mere belief systems or belonging systems to actual inner experience."[17] This movement could be called conversion, enlightenment, transformation, or sanctification. It is Paul's "third heaven," when he encountered things that cannot be put into human language (2 Cor. 12:2, 4).

A unified consciousness is an expanded consciousness. It comes from being at one within ourselves as we learn to live the truth of our being at one with God. It is seeing the world from this place of union with and in God. Genuine openness to God brings with it an openness of our whole being to the whole of reality. Contemplation is this posture of knowing in openness. Contemplation keeps things open: "It remains vulnerable before the moment, the event, the person—before it divides and tries to conquer or control it. Contemplatives refuse to create false dichotomies, dividing the field for the sake of the quick comfort of their ego. They do not rush to polarity thinking to take away their mental anxiety. . . . [It] is an exercise in keeping your heart and mind spaces open long enough for the mind to see other hidden material. It is content with the naked now and waits for futures given by God and grace."[18]

Treasures and the Heart

The mystics are our most helpful cartographers of the transformational journey of the awakening self. It is to this journey that we now turn in the next four chapters. Table 5.1 presents an overview of the framework that I will use to organize these chapters. It is built around four levels of consciousness that, as far as I can discern, are also the four major available frameworks for organizing identity. These options for self-organization are the body, mind, soul, and spirit.[19] Although the journey of the awakening self is far from sequential, it generally unfolds with a progression from body to mind, to soul, to spirit—each, at least potentially, becoming the new center of consciousness and identity.

Another way of thinking about these four levels of consciousness or frameworks for self-organization is to think of them as four major options for storing up treasures. In the Sermon on the Mount, Jesus taught that where our treasure is, there also will be our heart. He also said that rather than laying up treasures on earth, we should invest in the treasures of heaven (Matt. 6:19). Often this teaching is interpreted too literally as simply a warning against materialism. But the point he was making was much more profound than this. What Jesus was teaching was that our treasures (those things to which we are most attached and in which we are most invested) will determine the center and orientation of our life (our heart). Anticipating the best contemporary psychological and spiritual understandings of these matters by two thousand years, what he was teaching was that our attachments shape our identity and consciousness.

TABLE 5.1
Consciousness and the Awakening Self

Level	Experiential Focus	Self	Identity
BODY	Bodily impulses, sensations, and needs	Body self	I am my body.
		Public self	I am my image.
		Material self	I am my possessions.
		Role self	I am my role.
MIND	Thoughts, feelings, opinions, beliefs, morality, and meaning	Mental self	I am my thoughts.
		Ideological self	I am my beliefs.
		Communal self	I am my community.
		Individual self	I am myself.
SOUL	Experience, authenticity, actualization, and fulfillment	Reflective self	I am my experience.
		Shadow self	I am my shadow.
		Divided self	I am not always my true self.
SPIRIT	Ultimacy, mystery, being, and union	Essential self	I am.
		Divine self	I am one with God.
		Cosmic self	I am one with everything.

Obviously there is quite a range of things we can make our ultimate treasure, material possessions being far from the only option. The four frameworks for organizing consciousness are, at heart, four categories of attachments: things associated with the body and materiality; with our mind and its mental processes and contents; with our soul and the reflective space between events and meaning; and with our spirit and our engagement with the Transcendent. While there are many places between heaven and earth where we can store our treasures, as Jesus taught, wherever our treasure is, there will be the core of our identity and the ground of our consciousness.

Each of the following four chapters will focus on one of these four major levels of consciousness and identity and the way in which attachments are organized and treasures stored within it. For each level, I will also identify several different ways in which this self-organization can appear. Although some of these sometimes unfold in the sequence in which I present them, I do not mean to imply that they are substages through which we must proceed in that particular order, or even that all of them will always be present as we move through a level. Even organizing the four major levels in this way suggests more separateness and linearity between them than is usually seen in real life. In a later chapter we will return to this unfolding and examine more carefully the nonlinear, way in which it actually occurs.

Dialogue and Reflection

1. **You said that mystics are people who love God a lot. Is mysticism really just loving God and coming to know God's love?**

   Mystics are characterized more by their longings than their experience. This means that Christian mystics are not so much characterized by loving God a lot as *wanting* to know God's love. Their deepest and most persistent longing is to know God more fully, and personally and what they already know is that this knowing must be a knowing of the heart, not merely a knowing of the head. Nothing is more important to them than this knowing of God in love. Nothing will be accepted as a substitute for it.

2. **I don't understand what you mean when you speak of contemplative stillness or contemplative knowing. What is contemplation, and why is it so important to the mystics?**

   I define contemplation as an apprehension of reality that is relatively uncluttered by thought—particularly preconception and interpretation or analysis. As a way of knowing that complements reason and the senses, it allows us to encounter things as they really are, not as we think they should be. This is what it means to speak of contemplation as a way of knowing in openness, and this is why it is so prized by the mystics. It is also why contemplation is such an important part of any spiritual practice that is designed to help us open our self to God. Such spiritual practices start with stillness as we seek to step aside from words and thoughts and simply be with God in openness and trust. But I will have much more to say about these contemplative spiritual practices later when I will explain why they have such a singularly crucial role in the journey of the awakening self.

3. **Your discussion of the way in which the mystical journey into God involves a unifying of our fragmented consciousness reminds me of Richard Rohr's teaching on nondual consciousness. Are you talking about the same thing as he does at this point, and what do you think of his strategies for ways of healing our duality?**

Yes, I am talking about the same thing, and there is no book I more quickly recommend than his *The Naked Now*[20] to better understand duality (or a fragmented consciousness) and to place it within a Christian context. However, I think that the very practical nature of his writing can lend itself to misinterpretation when he offers what you describe as strategies to heal our duality. I do not understand him as in any way suggesting that we can heal ourselves by means of self-applied cognitive therapy. What I understand him to be offering are ways of opening our self—both heart and mind—to the Spirit, who effects the deep changes in consciousness that we need if we are to get past our confusion of thoughts and know direct, unmediated experience of God. Nothing like union with God is even remotely possible until we move into this primary realm of openness to what actually is as it exists beyond our thinking and understanding. This is why the most basic teaching of his book, that nondual presence prepares us for an encounter with Real Presence, is so valuable.

6

The Body-Centered Self

The human self is a vaporous and insubstantial thing. Unlike the body, the self lacks form, and its substance can be shaped in a great variety of ways. It is no wonder that it is so hard to define and so elusive when we search for it. This insubstantiality makes it easy to lose the true and authentic self by confusing it with imitations of our own creation. Thus false selves are simply proxies for our true self, poor imitations of the authentic original. In some deep part of our knowing, we sense that we are a unique reflection of our Source, but we are easily seduced by the urge to be our own source. It should not be a surprise that we then experience a profound sense of alienation from our deep center and from our true Source.

The lightness of being a human self leaves us vulnerable to these distortions. And so, seeking form and substance, it is not surprising that our first attachment is to our body. The body provides such a substantial framework for the self that many people never move beyond the body self that should be simply the first stage of human unfolding. But it is the first stage for all of us, and important residuals of this way of organizing self remain in all of us for the rest of our life.

To be human is to be embodied. Fashioned from the dust of the earth and animated by the breath of God, humans do not merely have bodies: we are our bodies—just as we are our minds, souls, and spirits. We are not, however, reducible to any of these expressions of self. But if the self is ever to soften its attachment to body and trust its more ethereal nature, it must first embrace its rootedness in the body. Any attempt to escape our bodies leads to distortions of mind, soul, and spirit and ultimately also damages the body. Even if and when we move to higher centers to organize our self, our body remains our connection to matter. In the words of Scripture repeated in funeral masses and graveside homilies in all branches of the Christian church, from dust we have come, and to dust we shall return (Gen. 3:19).

The infant's earliest consciousness does not afford any differentiation of self from non-self. Expressed in more positive terms, Freud has described this as an oceanic consciousness that involves an experience of being at one with everything.[1] Awareness of separateness and identification with "my" body therefore is an important developmental achievement. It provides the self with an identity that is more concrete than any other that will ever again be available to it. This is the power of this first crucial attachment of self to the body we relate to as "mine." The result we learn to call "I." And the first and primary contents of consciousness are now the sensations that arise in "my" body. "I am hungry" or "I am full" are statements of both awareness and identity as the infant begins to learn to identify with what arises within one's own body. These will remain the primary identifications for as long as the self is organized around the body.

But this developmental accomplishment, like many that follow it, involves both gain and loss. The loss is the sense of oneness with mother (or primary caretaker). This immediately introduces an existential crisis—a sense of detachment and separation that we unconsciously try to assuage by relating to our body as we previously related to the earlier undifferentiated self, which included mother and the rest of our world. The result is what I call the body self.

The Body Self: "I Am My Body"

The first option for an organization of consciousness and self is expressed in the sense of being my body. At this earliest level of organization of the self, this means that there is no room for any other competing identifications because at this stage "my self" is synonymous with "my body." As long as my body remains the framework for the organization of my self, any other identifications that may develop over time will be relatively minor.

Two quite different body experiences seem to be associated with this level of self-organization: the body as a source of pleasure, and the body as a source of pain. In both, that pleasure or pain is the person's primary identification and strongest attachment. It is the experience that is most characteristically "mine." It therefore becomes "me."

Sex addictions sometimes reflect this grounding of an identity in pleasure—or even more accurately, in excitement. The sex addict whose consciousness is organized around a body self hungers for arousal. Arousal is more important than even gratification because arousal is the ultimate pleasure, the ultimate assurance that one is alive. And because at this level no other form of arousal can compete with sexual arousal, this becomes the prized experience and primary identification. Recall the famous Cartesian formulation of identity: "I think, therefore I am." The identity of many sex addicts takes the form of "I am aroused, therefore I am." Sexual excitement is for them the ultimate pleasure. No other experience carries the same jolt of vitality. And consequently, no other experience better defines the self.

A body self based in pain is an even more common manifestation of this level of consciousness and self-organization. Elise, a mother of two teens and the manager of a surgical ward of a hospital, illustrates this level of self-development and organization. Elise's experience of her body was one of pain. Unlike some who have suffered from pain as the result of disease or physical injury, her pain was not continuous, nor was it always in the same parts of her body. The root of her pain was early childhood abuse and neglect. This involved a toxic cocktail of psychological and physical suffering that she stored in her body. She began her existence as an unwanted pregnancy, this leading, we later discovered, to an unsuccessful attempted abortion. Her suffering then continued for the first six years of her life until she was removed from her mother's care and placed in a foster home. However, once again she was sexually and physically abused by these foster parents—this again leading to her removal and eventual placement with a caring and wonderful family. Remarkably, unlike many who experience similar levels of abuse, Elise somehow managed to avoid adopting a victim identity. She had learned to keep her suffering private: consequently only her closest friends knew of it. But her body knew the truth. Her body served as her memory and as a container for what in others would normally be experienced as feelings.

Elise had great trouble describing her feelings. When I asked her about them, the best she could do was say that she felt numb. But this wasn't so much a description of a feeling as a way of telling me that instead of feeling the range of emotions that most people feel, she felt nothing—with the exception of pain. Sometimes this took the form of a burning sensation experienced most often in her abdomen. At other times she suffered severe headaches, skin sensitivity, and pain in her internal organs. Over the years the pain manifested itself in different ways, but it was usually present somewhere in her body. Medical investigations had consistently failed to identify any physical explanation for it. Several times she had been told that it was all in her head. A more sophisticated but still inaccurate diagnosis that she received from several doctors was that she was a hypochondriac. Actually, she suffered from a somatization disorder. But this is simply a technical way of saying what we have already noticed: instead of having feelings, Elise developed physical symptoms.

I said that Elise had not adopted a victim identity. That was because consciously she did not focus on her history or its effects. Her conscious focus was on her body. Her body carried what her feelings and memory were incapable of holding. Her body held not just her pain but also her story. And this was why she was so attached to it, so oriented toward it—not in a simple hypochondriacal way that expressed anxiety but in a way that expressed identity. Her body retained every drop of the pain she had suffered in the womb and for the first nine years of childhood. She had almost no conscious memory of these experiences—although they did leach into consciousness by means of very dark and sometimes graphic dreams that had tormented her all her life. However, apart from this little bit of leakage, her body had sealed her off relatively well from the consequences of years of horrific experience. But it did carry her story, and at a deep level she recognized the truth that she was her body. Her body was the center of her identity and consciousness.

Whether one's primary body experience is pain or pleasurable arousal, in both cases the fact that consciousness is organized at the level of the body means that emotional development is compromised. Just as Elise had very limited emotional differentiation or experience, the same is true of all those at this level of consciousness and self-development. For example, when asked how she felt, one woman who was compulsively promiscuous told me that she knew only two emotional states: boredom and sexual excitement. In spite of a very successful international career as a management consultant and an active social life, she told me that her work, friends, and life all bored her. It was only during sex that she felt alive, and so she lived for those moments and did everything she could to arrange them as often as possible.

However, despite the limited emotional development that is associated with the body self, the arrival at this platform of consciousness development involves both awakening and transformation. Awakening is seen in the expansion of the contents of consciousness. The awareness of one's body and the clear and strong identification with it means that awareness is quite different from what is seen in the undifferentiated stage of self-development that precedes it. The background of existence is now my body and the feelings associated with it. But this also represents a transformational step because the consolidation of the body self involves a reorganization of the sense of self. Consciousness is no longer undifferentiated. My body and my self form a sphere of experience separate from everything else. This reorganization represents the first stage of self-development; although the self that is involved is limited, at least it is my self.

Trauma that is transferred to and stored in the body is the most common reason people get stuck in this developmental stage. Everyone, however, seems to start here. But recall that when I speak of a level of development and organization of the self, I am talking about a center of gravity or a developmental platform. Most people are pulled forward by the Spirit to higher platforms. For this to happen, they cannot simply reject their body self. Transcending a developmental position requires that we first embrace it. Recall the pattern I identified: embeddedness and identification lead to dis-identification, eventual transcendence, and then an embeddedness and identification with a larger self situated on a larger horizon. Healthy transcendence always requires that we do not simply abandon a previous platform but move to a higher one that incorporates it. And this is what happens for the majority of people at this stage. Slowly they find themselves adopting a different perspective on their bodies; as they do so, something new becomes their primary identification and the center of consciousness.

The Public Self: "I Am My Image"

The way of relating to our body that usually emerges next involves the adoption of an external perspective on our self. No longer is it simply a matter of me identifying with my body but, while my body remains the primary focus, I now view it from the perspective of others. Now my primary identification becomes my image: how I am seen from that external perspective.

Once again, this is a very significant developmental advance. This capacity to take alternate perspectives lies right at the heart of the expansion of consciousness, and learning to adopt a secondary perspective represents a major developmental step. The world suddenly becomes much bigger. The self may not immediately feel bigger, but it is. Now, rather than simply looking at my body as my self, I am looking at my body as others see it. The new arena we have entered is the arena of the public self. Here what I primarily identify with is the way I think I am seen by others, or the way I want to be seen by others. And the new identity that results means that I see and experience myself as my image, as what I think (or hope) others see.

The awakening that this represents is the new view of the world that comes from adopting an external perspective. When you think about it, being able to do this is really quite remarkable. To be able to look at the world from the perspective of my body self was already quite an accomplishment, but now to be able to look at the world from an external vantage point is a great leap forward. It is like an out-of-body experience! But once again, this leap involves not just new contents of consciousness but also a change in how those contents are organized. What I experience as my self is now not simply my body but my body as seen by others as well. And this public self is the center of my consciousness. Although there are some obvious downsides to this shift, it nonetheless is significant enough that it is appropriately described as a transformation of the self.

The shadow side of this advance is, however, that we now have not just consciousness but also self-consciousness. Now we encounter the tendency to perform for the audience that constantly observes us, or at least those we count to be the most important spectators. Self-consciousness also introduces the anxiety that is familiar to all of us to some extent or another—anxiety associated with performance and the question of how we are doing in projecting the image we desire to project. This also represents a serious risk to authenticity. Now the primary task of being my self fades into the background, and my preoccupation becomes being the self that I think will earn me the love, esteem, and other reinforcements that appear to lie in the hands of others. I have come to believe that I must be and behave in some specific way. Simply being my body self is no longer enough. It will take a long time and a great deal of hard work for most of us who manage to move beyond this level to again acquire the freedom and simplicity of life associated with the body self. While always looking around to see how we are doing in pleasing the audience that we most value, our movements in life become less spontaneous and more practiced. Viewing our self from an external perspective results in a loss of power—power that we give to those at the other end of that perspective.

All of us know something of this because for all of us, the public self is part of the family of self, even if it is no longer the core of our identity and consciousness. All of us know how easily we can be drawn into compromising our authenticity by worrying about what others think about us. This is just another potential false way of being my true self. For, while it is a developmental gain to be able to view my self from an external perspective, I am not reducible to my image or my performance. Sadly, however, those at this level of development do not know that. Their identity is their image, and their consciousness is now filled with the anxiety that is associated with any performance before an audience that they seek to please.

It says quite a bit about our culture that it is so easy to find examples of this sort of organization of the self in terms of appearance. And those examples are not limited just to Hollywood, the glitterati, or those obsessed with fashion. For lots of people, nothing is more important than how they look to others. Obviously the fashion industry, as well as the entertainment and marketing industries, has tapped into this obsession with great success. Clothes, makeup, cars, and an endless range of other accessories are available to help us shape our image and fashion our selves as we want to be seen. Many people are seduced by these seeming possibilities of creating the self of their desire; thus they live the rest of their life in the relatively superficial space that this public self occupies. Others may allow themselves to periodically, perhaps surreptitiously, glance over their shoulders to see how others are viewing them but no longer equate their self with their image—having moved on to a higher platform. However, this only happens when we genuinely recognize the limitations of the public self. When we realize that our image is not our essence but simply one possible perspective that we or others can take on our self, only then can we move beyond the public self.

The Material Self: "I am My Possessions"

The thing many people most closely identify with is their possessions. No attachment to anything or anyone is as strong as their attachment to the things they assume they possess but that in reality possess them. And, not surprisingly, there is nothing they think about more than these same things.

It is hard to know where exactly to place this in this hierarchy of organizational frameworks of self and consciousness. Because the object of their attachments is inanimate—things like money, cars, books, or something else that might be collected—one could argue that this is an even earlier developmental level of existence than the body-centered self. If one's primary heart attachment is to things rather than anything animate or personal, we might be tempted to understand it in terms of matter and place it as the first level of existence—followed successively by body, mind, soul, and spirit. In some cases this may be appropriate. I have encountered people with serious psychopathology that resulted in an absence of attachments to anything animate but left intact a strong attachment to certain inanimate objects. I think, for example, of a man with a significant cognitive developmental delay who also suffered from chronic schizophrenia and a history of horrendous physical abuse. He had long ago retreated from the confusing, unpredictable, and dangerous world of people and even, as much as was possible, from life itself. However, he had a very strong attachment to a treasured stuffed toy animal that in his regressed state was his most significant link to anything beyond himself.

However, the vast majority of people who have possessions as their primary attachment are no more burdened by psychopathology than those who function at higher levels of self-organization. Charles illustrates this well. He had grown up in a privileged family but after decades of clearly expressed disinterest in his father's business empire, it and much of the family wealth had passed to his older brother who had succeeded his father at the helm of the family business interests. Charles's interests were less materialistic—at least this is what he told his family and what he himself believed. What he meant by that, however, was that the accumulation of wealth was of little interest to him. What was of keen interest however was food and drink.

Charles loved nothing more than good food (which was consumed, not collected) and wine (which formed the core of his most prized possessions). Although he had never married and had few close friends, he was sociable and could be quite generous. That he spent the vast majority of his time alone did not so much reflect a dislike of people as a relative absence of interest in them. When asked, he simply said that the things that interested others were of little or no interest to him.

Living off the family money he had inherited, Charles had never worked a day in his life. Although he seemed to have enough money to live well—at least in financial terms—his world was very small and his life far from rich. He seldom traveled beyond the city in which he lived, dividing his time about equally between his club (where he ate all his meals) and his house (where he slept). He kept his prized and quite extensive wine collection at home, storing a number of cases of whatever he happened to be drinking at any point in time at his club, where he drank only from his own private collection. Occasionally he would share a bottle of wine and a meal with someone he met at the club, but most of his meals were eaten as he lived his life—alone.

Charles's attachment to his wine collection only became apparent if you had a chance to share a meal with him, or if you happened to catch him reading the various wine periodicals he kept at the club and engage him in conversation. He had no interest in politics or world affairs, but get him started on the subject of wine and you couldn't shut him up. He spent his day reading about it and placing orders with his wine broker for cases of wine new on the market. The only thing in which he took pride was this collection and his knowledge of wines that made it possible. It is this knowledge that reveals the way Charles's self-organization anticipates the next major level of self-organization—the mind-centered self. The possession-centered self often reflects significant attachment to mental skills that are taken to be the essence of one's self and that certainly form the person's most significant attachment. Think, for example, of the way people whose wealth is self-made seem to treasure their wealth and their abilities that brought that wealth about equally. Together they form the core of their identity.

The Role Self: "I Am My Role"

There is one other major form of self organization that also serves as a potential transitional place between the body-centered self and the mind-centered self. We see this in those whose identity and

consciousness are centered on what they do (vocationally) or can do
(by virtue of talent, training, or role). Think, for example, of the way
one's identity can easily be organized around being a mother, physician, poet, or comic. While identities based in what we can do leave
us vulnerable when we can no longer perform at our peak, overall the
transition into the role self represents another quantum expansion
of consciousness and identity. Now we shift from identifying our
selves with how we look to identifying our selves with what we can
do. The center of consciousness is still the body because our roles,
at least initially, are still body based. But movement from the public
or material self to the role self involves broadening the perspective
we take on the world and ourselves.

To see the awakening that is involved in this transition, notice how
much background thoughts and awareness shift as we move from
a focus on appearances to a focus on role performance. The most
important feature of this shift is that it represents a return from an
external perspective to an internal one. The question now is "How
am I doing in my role?" But, remember that I now am my role. I have
identified with and begun to internalize the expectations associated
with the role. This is the transformational shift in identity. No longer
am I simply meeting the expectations of others. It is now a question
of how I am doing in being myself, in being my role. This represents
another big shift in the contents of my awareness and in my identity.
I am not simply how I appear to others but how I am doing in a role
that is "me." My self is now centered in my being; even though my
being is still body based, it is perched on the edge of this platform
and is much more ready to transcend it than was the case in the previous substages.

This shift to what we can do opens the doors of self to a much
broader world because while we only have one body, the potential
number of roles that we can play is vastly greater. Roles that begin
within the family can be adapted and played out within the community or other contexts. We also gradually learn that roles are not
just assigned; they also can be created. We can find ways of adding
value to groups and contributing to our communities by the things
we do and the roles we play. And as we do so, the tribe to which
we belong becomes larger and larger. At first we are content with
playing a role in our family. Then we discover that with slight modi-
fication, this role works at least as well in our circle of friends. Soon
we begin to extend it to our way of being in the world. Sometimes

we discover that this way of being has vocational implications, and we begin to move in this direction. But even if it doesn't lead to a career choice, it does provide possibilities for creative adaptation as we look for ways of adding value in our jobs, or in finding new possibilities when we feel stuck in them. This creativity has been at the heart of evolving societies and expanding consciousness and identity of individuals.

Juan was the eldest of five children born to a poor family in a small village in Spain. His mother became ill shortly after the birth of his youngest brother, and although Juan was only eight, he was given the role of taking care of his brother, who was also sick much of the time. This was not something he ever resented. He loved playing with his brother and found it easy to offer him the special care that he seemed to need. Juan enjoyed telling stories and found that he could keep his brother happy and distracted from his pain by singing to him. Unfortunately, his brother needed more than singing and games. He died when he was four years old; at this point, Juan's family assigned him the role of taking care of his mother. With small adaptations of what he had learned to do with his brother, Juan now found ways to be with his mother that helped her cope with her grief and deepening depression. Singing morphed into entertaining as he found that his mother's spirits seemed to lift when he performed pantomimes and acted out family stories and memories. When relatives or neighbors would come to visit, Juan soon also entertained them. You can see where this was headed.

By the time I met him, Juan was an internationally known flamenco artist. He was a world-class entertainer who had learned his craft by adapting a family-assigned role from early childhood. His consciousness seemed to me to still be grounded in the role self. But the creativity he invested in developing these roles showed strong emerging elements of the next major platform of development as he increasingly used his mind, not just his body, to create and live roles that he experienced as himself.

The creativity and adaptability involved in the role self make this such a potentially fertile transitional stage—one that easily prepares us to move into the mind-centered levels of consciousness and identity that are now on the horizon. The reason for this is that once we run out of roles that we can fill based on our body and behavior, we begin to discover that our mind is an incredible resource and opens up many more role possibilities.

Given this adaptability of the role self, you might wonder what loss could be associated with it. That loss is located in the shift from an identity based in being to one based in doing. Both are important. But the treadmill of doing that is not grounded in an identity of being easily leaves people living out of the periphery of their lives, not from their depths. However, as we learn to adapt to the circumstances in which we find ourselves and modify old roles or create new ones, we draw from deeper places within the self. Genuine creativity always emerges from deep places within the self and reconnects us to our being, not simply our doing. This also keeps us open to the continuing invitations of the Spirit to become even more; if this invitation is received with hospitality, it will lead one to a major shift in identity and consciousness. It will lead to a self that is grounded in mind.

Body Centered and Beyond

Not everyone who feels some degree of body preoccupation, self-consciousness, concern about their image, or role sensitivity is at this body-centered stage of development of consciousness and identity. Recall that the issue is the center of gravity. We can identify this in terms of the primary or strongest attachments. If nothing is more central to your consciousness than what is happening in your body or what you can do with your body, you are probably at a body-based level of organization of consciousness and identity. But it is quite possible to have a higher overall level of consciousness and still have frequent awareness of your body, some energy invested in appearances or possessions, or some focus on a significant role. Athletes are good examples of people whose identity could easily be significantly body based. But not all athletes limit their sense of self to what they can do with their bodies. Those who do will face an inevitable crisis of identity as their performance begins to fail and as they reach the outer edge of the age-related window for excellence in their sport.

Also, a body-based identity and consciousness does not mean that the person lacks intelligence or broader life competencies. A good example of this is the management consultant I mentioned earlier whom I treated for a sex addiction. Her identity and consciousness were clearly organized around a body self, but she was highly intelligent, very successful professionally, and much admired by friends and associates. Several aspects of her development were well above level 1. Her cognitive development was highly advanced, as was her aesthetic development, kinesthetic development, and ego development. But her body self was her center of gravity. Consequently it defined her identity and her consciousness. That doesn't mean that she wasn't a good person or a good employee or citizen. It simply describes the platform from which she viewed life and organized her experience. This is very important to keep in mind as we proceed.

However, there are significant implications of having a platform of consciousness that is organized around the body. When the body is the strongest attachment, it functions as a restricting tether on the mind, soul, and spirit, depriving each of the scope necessary to soar in a way that would be possible apart from this preoccupation with bodily existence. This does not mean that there is an absence of mental, soulful, or spiritual life of any sort in the person. Such people might be intellectually active, somewhat soulfully reflective, and possibly even spiritually responsive in a minimal way, but the degree to which this is possible will be seriously limited by their center of gravity. That limitation is most apparent in relation to the levels of consciousness development furthest from the one that is the overall center of gravity. For example, returning once again to the management consultant I mentioned, she was much more invested in her mind than her soul, and even less invested in her spirit. The more remote levels of consciousness are always the most alien to us. If it had been more consistent with her values and of interest, she could have been conventionally religious. But a genuine inner spiritual journey of any significance would be almost impossible. Similarly, she certainly was capable of reflecting on experience, but her inner world was destined to remain quite impoverished until she was able to move beyond a body-based self.

Yet somehow, despite our uneven development, we are sometimes able to discern the call of the Spirit to a higher level of being and prepared to offer our consent to the transition this involves. We have already seen some of the possibilities for this within the body self and with the significant development advance that each level represents over a lower one. Awakening can certainly happen within the body self; when it does, it will be evident in a softer attachment to the body, even though the body remains the organizing framework for identity and consciousness. It will also involve an expanding consciousness and a larger self. When we progress in this manner, the next level that opens itself as a possibility for identity and consciousness is the mind-based self.

Dialogue and Reflection

1. Your first words in this chapter confused me. You said, "The human self is a vaporous and insubstantial thing." I have never thought of the self as so insubstantial. Can you say more about why you see it this way?

> Apart from the body, there is—to borrow a phrase from Milan Kundera—an almost unbearable lightness to being human. This is why we speak more of brain than mind. Mind is too elusive. It lacks physicality. It is just too hard to nail down. Something similar happens with self when we try to make it more substantial by associating it with personality. We can grasp the notion of personality because it is something more objective: a collection of traits or characteristics. But our self is no more reducible to personality than our mind can be reduced to brain. We see this most clearly, however, when we enter the realm of spirit. Christians believe that God is spirit and that we are made in God's image. Spirit is, therefore, essential to our being. But how can we put a spirit under a microscope or weigh it on a scale? The self is unsubstantial, and this is what gives it its lightness of being. So when a self becomes heavy and weighed down, something is wrong. Sensing the vulnerability and fragility of this vaporous thing that is our self, we are often tempted to add substance to it. James Finley describes this as winding experiences around my fragile self in an attempt to make myself perceptible to myself and to the world, almost as if I were an invisible body that could only become visible when something visible covers its surface.[2] It is terrifying to reside within such an insubstantial home. But this is a home that was designed for spirit, and the closer we move toward the spirit-centered levels of being, the more we will feel this vaporous self to be the perfect home for us.

2. You begin with the body, but is there no developmentally earlier platform of consciousness than the body? Doesn't consciousness exist before the identification with the body?

> I am quite sure that consciousness exists in the infant long before one becomes aware of even having a body. But consciousness at this developmental stage appears to be highly

unstable and disorganized and fails to provide sufficiently firm anchors for identification that are necessary to secure an identity. This is the reason why I count the body to be the first focus of consciousness that is stable enough to become a framework for identity.

3. **The example you give of pain in relation to the body self reminded me of Eckhart Tolle's notion of the pain body. Are you speaking of the same thing as him?**

Tolle's understanding of what he calls the pain body represents a very valuable psychological insight.[3] In the simplest terms, the pain body is a repository of remnants of pain left behind from every strong negative emotional experience of early life. These remnants join together and form an energy field that lives in the very cells of our body. Even more serious, like a living organism, this pain body needs to be fed to remain alive, and it does this by seeking out and experiencing more pain. In my view, there is no question that something like this operates. And when it does, it restricts consciousness by orienting it around the pain. So in that sense, his observations fit mine very well. They also fit well when he describes the pain body as the center of the person's identity. But pain is not the only experience that can lead to a primary attachment to one's body. A focus on pleasure or excitement can also reflect the same sort of organization of consciousness. All are ways in which persons can have their identity reduced to their body. So yes, I think I am talking about the same sort of thing that Tolle describes, and I have no serious reservations about his understanding of the pain body. But I do want to make a larger point: what he calls a pain body is just one of at least two possible ways in which our identity and consciousness can be organized around the body.

4. **I didn't hear any spiritual dimensions to life as a body self. Does spiritual development only begin with the spirit-centered self?**

I am so glad you asked that because that is definitely not how I understand spirituality or spiritual development. Spiritual development that does not begin in the body self will always have to work its way backward to integrate the body within

one's spirituality if it is to mature and progress in any meaningful way. The way we relate to our bodies is a matter of
immense spiritual importance. Alienation from our bodies
will always spread into our experience of that which lies beyond our bodies and so will permeate all subsequent spiritual
and psychological development. Our emotions, sexuality, and
vitality are all grounded in the body, and all play an indispensable role in our spirituality. Unquestionably we can begin to
sense the larger horizons of spirit while still functioning in a
body self. But our spiritual awareness and capacity for spiritual response will be limited. However, it is the call of the
Spirit of God that pulls us developmentally forward, so any
response that we offer to whatever spiritual awareness we may
experience at any stage of development provides potential for
further development.

5. But when you suggest that organizing consciousness around the
   body limits the amount of spiritual response that an individual
   can make, are you saying that such people can't have enough
   faith to be a Christian or to grow as a Christian?

No, that certainly isn't what I am saying. Our faith is always
organized in terms of our level of faith development, not
simply our overall level of consciousness. So it might be quite
possible that faith development is higher than consciousness
development. But even if it isn't, faith is still possible for any
human, at any level of development. And as that faith is expressed, it can grow. If that faith is formed and shaped by a
Christian context, there is no question that such an individual
can grow as a Christian. My point, however, is that while they
might become a "good Christian," they will be limited in their
overall spiritual development and limited in their capacity for
awareness of and response to the Spirit.

7

The Mind-Centered Self

The shift from identifying with the body to identifying with the mind is a monumental leap forward for humans. This is where we begin to truly come into our own. Applying our new mental tools, our ability to understand and control the external world takes a quantum leap forward since understanding and control are the primary expression of the drive to mastery that the ego shows when the self is organized around the mind.[1]

Discovering mental capacities to think, plan, imagine, remember, choose, create, anticipate, prioritize, plan, and much more is quite a heady experience. It is no surprise that we begin to identify with these abilities. The new self that emerges from this transition is dramatically different from any of the selves organized around the body. Now I am not simply my body: I am my ability to do all the things that my mind makes possible. The options seem endless. With the body self I have one basic tool; now the range of ways in which I can act on the world and process experience is vast. And because mental processes unfold as they are utilized, the life of the mind becomes increasingly richer as one walks through this portal and begins to engage with the world by means of these new mental resources.

The experiential focus at this level of consciousness development is my mental processes and products. The processes are the tools, such as the capacity to think, feel, choose, evaluate, and so forth; and the products are what we produce by means of this technology, which includes our thoughts, feelings, memories, plans, hopes, beliefs, judgments, and opinions. As we progress through this level, meaning also becomes a central focus of consciousness. As each new mental capacity emerges, it becomes the primary identification and center of consciousness at this level of self-development. This is an important part of the transition to the next overall level of consciousness development.

As important a developmental step as this shift into the mind-based self represents, there is potential loss that can be associated with it. That loss is our attachment to our body. Quickly we move from *being* our body to *having* a body. Preoccupied with the processes and contents of our newly discovered minds, we lose contact with the visceral roots of our being. Many people will never again recover this vitalizing connection with their embodiedness. They will go through life as ungrounded minds, souls, or spirits. Yet this will seriously compromise the further unfolding of their consciousness and identity. They may be able to periodically visit the platforms that mind, soul, and spirit represent, but none of these can become their center of gravity until they reconnect to their bodies.

The Mental Self: "I Am My Thoughts"

The mind is a fascinating thing, and the discovery of what it makes possible presents a powerful opportunity for awakening. The first expression of the mental self is our attachment to our thoughts. Speaking for all who know this attachment, Descartes famously asserted *cogito ergo sum*—"I think therefore I am." Just as I previously attached to my body, and it became the center of my identity, so now I attach to my thoughts, and they define me. They now become my most treasured and wonderfully private possession. I examine my thoughts, review them, and feel the pleasure of identification with them. They are me, and my identity shifts from the public sphere of my role self to this more introspective sphere of my thoughts.

As young children we first attach to our thoughts with little of the reality constraints that will later be present. I describe this as magical thinking, but this label and judgment reflect an external perspective. A more personal perspective would emphasize the power I associate with my thoughts. I discover images and symbols to represent significant experiences and people, and I learn to encode experiences with the external world by means of them. This is an enormously satisfying mental accomplishment, one that will form the basis of much subsequent psychological development. Initially I have no sense of distance between my inner symbols and the external object. Over time, as I deal with external objects, I become aware of their frustrating independence from my representations and cognitive manipulations of them. Hence I begin to develop language, and communication of my thoughts becomes more of a social expression of my identification with the contents of my mind. Now I can identify with my words and my ability to influence the external world by means of what I say. Eventually added to this will be feelings, understandings, plans, and judgments; all these are domains of experience that are available as potential primary identifications. Once again, whatever is in this privileged place of being my primary identification becomes the core of my identity.

Imagination is another dimension of the inner life that becomes available as mental process at this level of consciousness development. With imagination, the self now begins to really unfold—not just in the linear manner that is possible with rational thought but also in fresh and innovative ways that logic can never produce or seldom even understand. With imagination comes play and creativity. Now both the inner and outer worlds become enchanted, and I am filled with wonder and fascination. Creative people manage to retain contact with this part of self and the way it allows them to perceive and engage the world, and we all benefit from the gifts that flow from their life as they cultivate their creativity and share the fruits of their fertile imaginations.

The mental self can take many forms because there is such a broad range of mental processes and products with which we can identify. Consequently, people at this level of consciousness development can appear quite different from each other—and are quite different from each other. The identity of one may be based on his excellent memory, penetrating analytical skills, or seemingly flawless intuition; that of another may be based on her strategic planning abilities, creative writing, or well-informed opinions and beliefs. The common core is identification with what I can do with my mind. For many people, this provides such a powerful grounding of identity that it remains the organizing center of their self for the rest of their life. Their primary identification is with their mind, and the things they can do with it become their greatest treasure.

Morality is another mental product that can become an important potential component of the self and consciousness at this stage of development. This does not mean that it first appears at this stage of development. Morality is a deep part of the human psyche. It may not be as central to spirituality as Christians sometimes assume,[2] but neither is it as superficial and inevitably pathological as Freud assumed.[3] The capacity for rudimentary moral judgments appears to be present in the earliest stages of ego development, and moral reasoning forms one of the primary dimensions of the self from that point forward.[4] Moral development will grind to a halt whenever spirituality is reduced to morality; but as long as morality is merely one dimension of the self and therefore of spirituality, further moral development remains possible.[5]

There is no question that thoughts, judgments, imagination, and other dimensions of mental life can organize the self in a way that expands consciousness and leads to a richer engagement with the external world. But the self that remains mind-centered is a self that is turned in upon itself. This introversive tendency may later be balanced by more extroversive attachments to people and objects beyond one's mental self, but this platform does form the foundation for a lifelong posture of introversion in some who find nothing more interesting or stimulating than their inner mental experience.

This does not mean, however, that all those in the mental-self level of development are introverted or that their worlds are small or uninteresting. Edward Glapthorn, the narrator in Michael Cox's novel *The Meaning of Night*, is an excellent literary example of a character who lives a large and indisputably interesting life but whose overriding passion is the exercise of his mental faculties. Glapthorn is a consummate bibliophile whose attachment to the poetry of John Donne is so deep that he carries a copy of his works in his pocket at all times—even as he commits the murder that is described in the opening sentence of the book. Reflecting on his life later in the story, he comments on the redemptive and transformational nature of mental life, particularly what he calls "those truly divine faculties of intellect and imagination which, when exercised to the utmost, can make gods of us all."[6] He is right. The passionate exercise of mental faculties opens up possibilities for life that are unimaginable from the perspective of the body self.

The Ideological Self: "I Am My Beliefs"

Eventually, thoughts, judgments, feelings, and understandings coalesce into opinions, opinions become beliefs, and, for many people, beliefs begin to form a stable core of a personal framework of meaning. Once again, the nature of their ultimate treasure shifts as they invest their primary attachment to their beliefs. And once again, this becomes the core of their identity. Who am I? I am now my beliefs, not merely my thoughts, imagination, or other mental process or products.

Christians sometimes find their spirituality reinforcing a mind-centered self when their faith has been reduced to beliefs. This has potentially very costly implications since it can impede further un-folding of consciousness and compromise development of important dimensions of self. It does not mean that having beliefs is a bad thing. Beliefs form an important part of our worldview and meaning mak-ing and can have a legitimate and important role in a life-enhancing spirituality. But it is only slightly less sad to see someone reduce their self to their beliefs than it is to see them reduce their self to their body. Growth and transformation can both be limited by an identity that is centered in beliefs. In contrast, however, having beliefs but not simply being them allows one's self to continue to unfold and thrive.

I know personally about the way in which beliefs form a small plat-form for identity and self. For years I defined myself by my theology and clutched my beliefs in a manner that represented an idolatrous substitute for God. This led to a good deal of intellectual dishonesty, as I avoided exploring questions and engaging with issues that seemed certain to lead me outside the bounds of orthodoxy and would, I knew, put me in even more tension with my religious community. Without question this compromised my faith development, but because faith is so central to the self, it also affected the development of other dimensions of my self, of which faith and moral development were the most pronounced.

This began to shift for me as I began to understand the price I was paying for my identification with my impoverished construals of ultimate mystery and as I dared to allow myself to attend to the call of the Spirit to become more than the small self that I was. As my attachment to my beliefs began to loosen, a friend urged caution and expressed concern about what he perceived to be a drift into liberal theology. From his point of view, nothing could be more dangerous. I appreciated his concern for me and told him so, but I also told him that I was not so much abandoning specific beliefs as simply becoming less interested in ensuring that I held true or right beliefs since I felt that at their best, thoughts were limited containers for transcendent mystery. I told him I was simply trying to hold my theology with humility and not confuse my beliefs with Truth. This did nothing to reduce his concern. But it also led him to offer a singularly clear self-definition. He said that he would never change his theological beliefs and that nothing could ever make him anything other than he was—an evangelical. I understand how he felt because I viewed life from the same platform for many years myself. But that is not enough to make me reluctant to describe this platform as small and to regard the self that is organized around the worldview available from it as stunted in its development.

My friend illustrates elements of both the mental self and the next sublevel of the options of a self that is organized around the mind: the communal self. He had the disadvantage of being a very prominent and important leader in a religious community that organized itself around beliefs. Many years later he was able to tell me that he envied my freedom in being able to explore the broader places I had been able to explore. He still disagreed with my theology and felt serious concern about my failure to enthusiastically identify with the bits of orthodox dogma that he felt made one a Christian; but he told me that because of his institutional affiliations, even if he wanted to, he could never explore the things that he saw me exploring. He felt envy and I felt sad. For it is always tragic, in my opinion, to define one's self in a rigid way that limits further becoming. And an inordinate attachment to beliefs certainly qualifies as such a limiting self-definition.

The Communal Self: "I Am My Community"

Although beliefs can be private, once we make them the center of our identity, we generally seek out others who share them. This in turn strengthens and refines our beliefs and opens a portal to a transition from the mental self to the communal self. Passing through this portal, I am no longer simply my beliefs: I am my community.

Because of the diversity of beliefs, many options for belief-based communities exist. Some of these are religious. Most churches involve some degree of shared beliefs, although belief congruence forms a

much more important part of some than others. The same range of
options exists in other religions. But politically organized belief communities also serve many people in the same way by offering an identity
based on membership in a community that holds the same core beliefs.
Social issues also work in the same way, pro-life and pro-choice beliefs
often leading to involvement with communities that share these basic
beliefs and to identification with those communities, which come to
form the core of one's identity. Many other possibilities for belief-
based communities also exist; one can have membership in multiple
communities at the same time, allowing this broader membership
to provide the identification that becomes the core of identity. You
might, for example, identify yourself with progressive Christians who
are social activists, feminists who are pro-choice and antiglobaliza-
tion, and Republican capitalists, allowing your membership in these
informal communities to shape your identity.

But beliefs are not the only mental product that can lead to identification with a community. Value-based communities function in
many of the same ways. Environmentalists are attracted to each other
because of their shared values, and so are artists, humanitarians, nud-
ists, and many others. Once again, it is not simply my values that define
me but also my community. At this stage of consciousness, my sense
of who I am is broader than was the case at the mental-self sublevel
because I do not simply identify with the products of my mind. Those
products lead me outside myself to engagement with others and this
is a tremendously important developmental step.

Meaning making does not begin with the communal self, but it
advances notably at this stage. The making of meaning is such a fundamental human activity that it begins with the earliest body self. There
the meaning that is created as an organizing framework for making
sense of the buzz of experience is the differentiation of me (my body)
from non-self (everything else). This boundary between me and not
me is the central axis of all subsequent developments of meaning
making. Each stage of consciousness development will involve a shift
in the boundary between what I consider to be self and non-self, and
a corresponding shift in the way I understand and make meaning of
my experience in the world. Each broadening of our understanding of who we are precipitates a corresponding shift in the way we
make sense of experience. Meaning is not an objective thing that is
discovered: it is a subjective and provisional way of understanding
reality that develops and changes as our consciousness develops and

expands. An absence of development of meaning making reflects a corresponding absence of transformation.

This, I realize, is not how all Christians understand meaning. Meaning is sometimes presented as something external and fixed that, like truth, needs to be found and then treasured. Any notion of meaning being created and evolving suggests, in such an understanding, that truth might also be personal and not objective. But this understanding confuses meaning and truth. Meaning is the way in which we create coherence for experience. Truth, when confused with meaning, usually means something like veracity or factuality. Meaning may grow out of beliefs and values (this is why the creation of meaning is associated with the mental self), but a robust system of personal meaning will usually be larger, more comprehensive, and more dynamic and evolving than beliefs. Beliefs may have more or less correspondence to reality and could therefore be described as being more or less true, but meaning is neither true nor false. At a given stage of development, it is simply the way we make sense of experience.

Yet the communal self comes with a shadow that, if it is not understood, has the potential to stop further expansion of consciousness and growth of the self. That shadow is the pressure exerted by communities to conform. Formal and informal communities that are based on beliefs and values exist because of belief and value convergence. They all therefore exert some degree of pressure to maintain this convergence. Thus the communal self can devolve into a conformist self. Members who conform to the community's expectations may be oblivious to the fact that there are any such expectations. But generally you will quickly become aware of the implicit or explicit rules of membership once your attachment to those core beliefs or values begins to soften. Healthy communities will always be more tolerant of diversity than nonhealthy ones, but there will always be limits to the tolerance of any community that makes either beliefs or values the ticket to membership.

At its best, however, the communal self is a framework for identity and consciousness that connects the individual to society and orients the self to that larger self that exists in community. At its best, it therefore anticipates elements of the life of the spirit. But there remains a number of other way stations at which the self must rest and organize before it is ready for the soaring of spirit and expansion of the boundaries of the self that are hinted at in the communal self.[7]

The Individual Self: "I Am Myself"

The Spirit is always wooing us to further development. For someone with consciousness and identity organized around a communal self, this might take the form of a growing sense that while I am my community, I am not *just* my community. Increasingly I may have the sense that there are other parts of me that can't be easily explored within my primary community—parts of self that might, for example, be rejected or experienced as a threat. This is one of the reasons why many who sense an invitation to notice and respond to the ways in which their community may be curtailing their further development often hold back from exploring this territory out of fear about where it might lead them.

Yet some feel no option but to walk through the next portal. The parts of them that seem more than their community-based identity press so hard for exploration and expression that they know they must discover what they represent. As they pass through this portal, they discover not a single identity but a seemingly endless range of possibilities. It is dizzying to contemplate all the ways in which I might be myself. And yet I know that I am myself and that my challenge is to live the uniqueness of that self in community and in the world. And so I launch forward on the next great adventure.

As you will by now have noticed, each of the levels and sublevels of consciousness and identity development are based on a truth—an important truth, even if not the ultimate truth of my identity. It is true that I am a unique and individual self: I am more than my body, more than my image, more than my roles, more than my mental products and experiences, and more than my community. I am myself, and nothing is more important than the discovery and actualization of this unique self. Thomas Merton reminds us of the spiritual significance of this discovery in the following words I have already shared but that are worth hearing once again: "There is only one problem on which all my existence, my peace, and my happiness depend: to discover myself in discovering God. If I find him I will find myself and if I find my true self I will find him."[8] Those at the level of the individual self are in no position to understand the spiritual significance of what they feel inevitably drawn toward, but if they are faithful to what they are able to encounter and remain open to their self and to the Spirit, they will be led toward this larger horizon.

Yet this level also has its land mines. That dizzying array of possibilities for my unique self represents a vast range of ways in which I can lose the truth of my being and confuse the truth of my created self, being allured by a self of my own creation. And so in the quest to become my individual self—not defined by family, community, culture, race, or religion—it is almost inevitable that I become seduced by false ways of being. The risks of loss of authenticity are great, but so is the call of the Spirit to discover and be the truth of my self.

It is also very easy to swing too far from the communal self in trying to find one's identity that lies beyond the boundary of one's communities. Individualism has been a seductive siren for those raised in the West. We almost invariably put too much distance between the individual and communal self, despising this lower level of being as soon as we feel our self finally free from its communal constraints. Those in many parts of the East face the opposite challenge, where culture often emphasizes the communal self over the individual self. This is particularly the case in traditional Chinese culture, where unchecked individualism is viewed as disloyalty to the family, community, and society. I recall asking a Chinese friend in Singapore to help me understand the psychology I was encountering but not understanding. My friend gave me a simple formula that children are taught in home and school from the youngest age, a formula that no Southeast Asian person of Chinese origin could fail to know as the framework for their self: "If it's good for the nation, it's good for society; if it's good for society, it's good for the community; if it's good for the community, it's good for the family; and if it's good for the family, it's good for the individual."[9] Unlike the West, things don't start with the individual and work outward toward society. Things move in the other direction—from the largest collective through the smaller ones and finally to the individual. The result is that when people in these communities make the transition to the individual self, they are much less likely to swing so far away from their communal self.

Mind-Centered and Beyond

For all these potential pitfalls, the individual self does represent the transition to the next major framework for organizing self. When we first begin to be aware of true and false ways of being, we have begun a reflective process that engages our souls, not just our minds. Let me tell a story that illustrates this transition.

Maria was raised in a large traditional Italian-Canadian family, her parents having immigrated to Canada just after the birth of her oldest brother. One of her older sisters was a nun; with the family's religious obligations thus being fulfilled, the rest of the children were free to become whatever they wanted—as long as they kept the faith (Roman Catholic) and never forgot the priority of family. Maria had done both well, marrying shortly after graduating from university and having her children dutifully baptized and taught to honor family, the blessed Virgin, and God. If asked to define herself, she first would have said "Italian-Canadian"; second, "Roman Catholic"; and third, "my own person." She told me that she had always found a way to bring something a little different to her way of being in the world. Maria loved nothing more than good traditional Italian cooking but was the first in her family to discover the cuisines of other cultures. She was also the only member of the family to marry a non-Italian—her Afro-Caribbean husband being a bit of a stretch for her family—but they had come to love him as much as he loved them. She was also the only one among the five children to go to university and the only one to consider travel a priority in the spending of disposable income.

At the point where I met her, Maria strongly identified with her ability to live with zest, pizzazz, and individuality. Her appearance was always a bit edgy and frequently changed: her dress and hairstyle usually afforded her a head-turning entrance into a room. She liked to confound expectations about who she was and what she was like, particularly if she sensed that she was being defined by her cultural or religious heritage. Maria held much more progressive social and political views than others in her family or circle of friends, and this too was an important part of her identity. Her friends loved her sparkle, and she received a lot of reinforcement for her persona. There clearly were elements of a role self in this. But she was not simply her role. She was also highly invested in finding her unique self, and this had been the primary expression of her spiritual quest for many years. It was not simply a reaction to her family. It was also her way of being, and it defined her identity and her consciousness and expressed her quest to know and become her true self.

At the point where I first came to know her, she was not very reflective about this process. She lived her life in an impulsive, extroverted manner that left little space for the development of an inner self. However, much of that crashed around her when her husband left her for another man three years after their wedding, telling her that he regretted that he had not been able to be honest with her or with himself but that he was doing neither of them a favor by pretending to be what he was not. The shock waves that this set off began with her shock and hurt at his leaving her but quickly expanded to even more important questions. For reasons that always lie beyond the ability of anyone else to fully understand, she chose to use this crisis to begin something she had never really done before: she began looking reflectively at herself. She couldn't help but wonder if she also had been pretending and, in so doing, fooling herself about who she really was and what she really needed and wanted. Asking this question, she quickly discovered that she really had no idea what she wanted. She also began to question the self she projected to the world. Suddenly it began to feel dreadfully superficial. She realized that her frequent changes of appearance were symptomatic of her inner emptiness: each new persona she created was but another attempt to find her true self. These questions led to an extremely fruitful exploration for her and started a journey that quickly led her to identify with her soul, not simply with her mind. Self-reflection was the transformational portal through which she passed, and what she entered on the other side was a new level of consciousness and identity organization—the soul-centered self.

Dialogue and Reflection

1. **Thinking often seems to get a bad rap in spirituality, and yet you identify it as an important part of the shift from body-self organizations of consciousness to the mental-self platform. Please comment.**

   Thought—along with all the other mental processes we discussed in this chapter—has an important place to play in spirituality. Just as the body needs to be integrated into any full-orbed spiritual response, so does the mind and the soul. So there is no question that thinking and thoughts have an important role in our spiritual response. The reason thought often gets the bad rap you mention is that the mental self-organizations we have been examining in this chapter are so powerful as frameworks for consciousness and life that it is enormously easy to become stuck here. Thought is the great sinkhole of consciousness. Thank God that we are capable of having thoughts. However, we are not reducible to them. How wonderful that we can formulate opinions and hold beliefs. But we are much more than these cognitive products. An inordinate attachment to our thoughts, opinions, and beliefs will always limit spiritual response in the same way that an inordinate attachment to our body does. Spirituality invites us to bring our whole self to the encounter with the Transcendent, but we can only do that when we are ready to release our attachment to an exclusive and primary identification with any one of these dimensions of self. The difficulty in releasing that identification with our thoughts is the reason for the caution spiritual writers often give about thinking and the danger that our attachment to our thoughts represents for awakening and unfolding.

2. **You seem overly critical of people whose identity is grounded in their communities of membership. Might this reflect an overly individualistic bias on your part?**

I have lived much of my life on the periphery of communities and am certainly guilty of having drunk deeply of the individualism that is revered by Western culture. But I don't feel a need to qualify any of my comments about the limiting effects of identity and consciousness that are organized around communal membership. Although our need to belong is fundamental, our penultimate places of belonging should never obscure the fact that our ultimate need to belong points us beyond the ethnic, geographic, familial, friendship, and belief-based places of belonging where we easily settle. Our communities are part of us, but we are not reducible to any of them. They can easily become way stations where we allow comfort to seduce us into an overidentification, and when we do so, we limit our future becoming.

Part of what restricts the growth of the communal self is overidentification with the group that provides the primary reference point for beliefs, values, and identity. This is a form of belonging that gives away too much power and self-responsibility. There is nothing wrong with loyalty to one's family, churches, or roots, but the pressure to conform to the consciousness of the group is always very strong and

ltimately be resisted if you are to grow beyond the
nal self. This is why Jesus spoke such strong words
le at the communal-self level of consciousness and
y: "Whoever comes to me and does not hate his father
and mother, wife and children, brothers and sisters, yes, and
even life itself, cannot be my disciple" (Luke 14:26 NRSV). On
the surface this teaching is very puzzling, even troubling. But
taken in the context of everything else Jesus taught and lived
in terms of love, we can be sure that he does not mean that
we should not love our parents. I believe that the text urges
us to refuse to be locked into a conformity that prevents us
from following Jesus in living the gospel and becoming all we
are meant to be. The unquestioned assimilation of the values
and ideas of one's social group and overidentification with
one's family, ethnic, or religious community—these pressures
to conform can seriously compromise one's awakening and
unfolding. This was, I believe, the point Jesus was making.

3. **When talking about the individual self, you suggested that nothing is more important than finding our unique and true self. Is
there one and only one way of being in our self that is true, and
if so, is everything else a false self? If so, I wonder how anyone
ever makes it past this stage—and whether it truly is essential
for us to discover our true self.**

You have asked several very good questions. First, let me say
that the truth of my self is that I am in Christ, who is my
Source and Destiny. I live that truth as I increasingly allow
all the ways of being that I have created in an effort to be my
own source and destiny to come into the light and warmth
of my relationship with Christ and be woven within the family of self that I am in Christ. The search for the true self
is not, therefore, an exercise in trying on various roles or
ways of being, nor is it a process of self-analysis. These sorts
of attempts simply create new and more sophisticated false
ways of being. I don't think it is helpful to think of the true
and false selves as binary states. They are always intermixed.
Living in truth is not, therefore, so much a state as a direction. That direction is increasingly opening my self to God
in faith and trust since this is how the light and warmth of

God's love flows into my self and produces my awakening, enlightenment, and transformation. Can you get past this stage without having found your one true self? Certainly you can. Perfection is *not* the prerequisite for moving from one level of consciousness development to another. Your job is *not* to find this elusive true self and then grasp it firmly so it won't be lost, but simply to turn toward God in openness and trust as you can. This is all that is asked of you. Turning in openness toward God allows God's life to flow into us. This is how we return to truth and how we increasingly come to live in this place of truth. Remember, living our true self is not living from a place of perfection, or some ideal inner state. It is, in the words of Thomas Keating, "our participation in the divine life manifested in our uniqueness."[10]

4. **I think I might be beginning to get your basic point. Are you saying that at each of these levels of development, the challenge is to embrace the truth of that level without being defined by it?**

That's it exactly. Each level of development must be embraced before it can be transcended. But to embrace it is to recognize it as true while at the same time realizing that it is not the total truth of who I am. I am my mind and the things that I can do with my mind, but that capability is not the essence or totality of who I am. When it is the core or totality of my identity, I am embedded within it. Transcending a level of consciousness organization requires disembedding or differentiation from it, and this is what you describe as avoiding being defined by it.

8

The Soul-Centered Self

The further up the Great Chain of Being we go, the more futile our efforts to define terms become. But this does not mean that we are talking nonsense when we refer to these higher levels of being. Our inability to define a concept with precision does not mean that the concept is meaningless.

Much of the divergence in understandings of "soul" arises from the ways in which the term is used. Theologians and philosophers often approach the concept ontologically, as a way of describing the incorporeal essence of a person or living thing. Some speak of soul more literally as a part of a person, sometimes as that within us that makes us eternal. My own use of the concept is much more metaphorical. Following James Hillman, I understand soul as a perspective rather than a substance, a viewpoint toward things rather than any thing in itself.[1] This perspective is reflective. Soul is the reflective space between a person and the events of his or her life. Soul allows us to transform these events into experience and makes meaning possible. It allows us to be present to ourselves, our world, and our experience. It is the doorway through which we must enter into life if we wish to live it with depth and passion. Soul is the middle ground between body and spirit that connects us to our materiality and to the external world. It is also the place where we learn to hold experience, not simply respond to it. A rich ongoing interaction with this soul is essential if we are to live with groundedness, creativity, and vitality.

Soul thrives in reality but withers when we choose to live in places of illusion or denial. Soul calls us to be so grounded in the ordinary realities of our life that the meaning of our life can be found in these mundane events. Soul finds the extraordinary in the midst of the ordinary because soul is always tethered to life in the world. It can't be separated from the body or from the concrete realities of our relationships and life circumstances. Spirit often calls us to transcend these circumstances and to focus our attention on cosmic issues and universal truths. But soul invites us to find the transcendent in the mundane, the sacred in the shadow. Soul calls us to pay attention and live life where we actually are, not where we might want to be. Soulful living helps us engage with these realities in ways that are life enhancing for ourselves and others. This means we learn to relate to self and the world with love, for without love, life can never be genuinely full and fulfilling.

Soul is more expansive than either the body or the mind, and the framework that it provides for the organization of the self is also much vaster. Soul is grounded in body and mind but moves us beyond both, reaching out and seeking meaningful connections with others. The mental self can be quite content with its own company, whereas the soul is nourished by communal engagement. Soul translates the rhythms of ordinary life into the liturgy of a richly meaningful existence that is created within the community and shared by all who participate in it. Just as soul food is meant to be eaten with others and soul music meant to be enjoyed with others, so too soulful living is a way of being in relationship with others who open themselves to life and to its gifts.

Soulful living[2] is living with sufficient reflection on experience to ensure that it is woven within the fabric of self in a coherent and meaningfully way. It is living with attentiveness to the gifts of the moment found in the simple, the routine, and the ordinary. It is living with hospitality to the otherness of strangers and intimates alike, allowing these bearers of otherness to challenge our ways of being in the world. It is living with openness to life in a way that makes that living meaningful. It is saying yes to the invitation of the Spirit to immerse our self in the moment and open our self to its experiences—regardless of whether or not we recognize the Spirit as the source of the invitation or even discern an invitation apart from our response. It is saying yes to the Spirit's invitation to soften our willful existence and allow our selves to enter the flow of life that we can never control. It is saying yes to the Spirit's invitation to surrender: this is the way in which the soul-centered stage of development represents a potential preparation for a spirit-centered one.

This invitation to surrender also helps us understand the cul-de-sac that we can enter at this level of development, which often makes it hard to move on. Surrender that emerges only in response to a movement down and into experience and that lacks a self-transcendent reference point is ultimately incapable of allowing the spirit to soar in the ways invited by the Spirit. When this happens, what we have surrendered to is simply experience. But experience, no matter how rich, is never enough to support the human spirit.

The Reflective Self: "I Am My Experience"

The first face of the soul-centered self that we encounter is the reflective self. First and foremost, this reflection is built on attention. Attention is our connection to experience. It is the connection between us and what happens to us. But, far from being automatic, this connection must be cultivated. Therefore the practice of attentiveness is the foundation of soulful living. However, because attention to anything opens a window to the transcendent, it is also foundational to spirituality. Attention makes reflection meaningful. Reflection in the absence of attention is empty and meaningless. Attention brings experience into focus. Without reflection, we are simply being carried along by the flow of life. Attention momentarily introduces a short pause in that flow, marking an experience with a soul flag that allows us later to come back to it if we choose to reflect on it.

Reflection is as profoundly new and important a step in the development of consciousness as were the first steps associated with the cultivation of mental life. Reflection involves the mind and cannot be undertaken apart from thought; yet because reflection is thought turned back upon experience, it represents a higher-order cognitive process that is more characteristic of the soul than the mind. This does not mean that it demands higher levels of intelligence. I know some extremely bright people who live life without any soulful reflection. They analyze objects and classify people or things but do not create the space for their experience that genuine reflection demands.

Reflection is a form of inner dialogue. Like any genuine dialogue, it requires listening, not just speaking. To allow encounter and knowing, it also demands sufficient silence and stillness in the interaction. Thus, it is not as direct or purposive as analysis.

Reflection is a gentle action of holding experience in hospitality and openness. We hold experience when we simply allow it to be rather than demand what or how it should be. This is why I describe it as an act of hospitality. Reflection starts with the act of making space for the experience and then spending time with it, allowing it to reveal itself to you. This process is more passive than many people can easily tolerate. Their impatience and need for control make it hard for them to offer this gentle act of hospitality to their experience. But apart from doing so, Socrates suggests that life is not worth living. That goes further than I myself would argue; yet I maintain that without reflection there can be no depth to life because reflection cultivates the interior space that is shaped by experience.

The focus of reflection is not simply experience but *my* experience: thus the object of reflection is *my* self because at this stage of consciousness development, I am *my* experience. Being my experience is not the same as being what happens to me. Identification with what happens to me, whether trauma or bliss, is a body-self way of organizing consciousness. Experience is not simply what happens but how I sense the event: how it registers on my body in my emotions, and how I process it in my mind. This is quite personal. No one but the individual can speak for the experience of an event; it is this experience, much more than the actual event, that is crucial in determining the impact of an event. This we learned from Freud; despite the fact that he overemphasized experience at the expense of what actually happened, he did help us understand just how powerful the interpretation that we give to the event really is. This is why two or more people can experience the same event—say, for example, a plane crash or car accident—and each can respond to it in highly unique ways.

I serve as the consulting psychologist for a global adventure tourism company and witnessed this when their expedition ship suddenly hit an iceberg and sank in the Southern Ocean off Antarctica a few years ago. All 154 passengers and crew experienced the same middle-of-the night event: awakening to the sound of distress alarms, quickly boarding lifeboats with nothing more than the night clothes in which they had been sleeping, and then spending two hours bobbing in icy waters before being picked up by a Norwegian cruise ship. Thankfully no one drowned or was even seriously injured. Once ashore in Argentina and given a chance to tell their story, the diverse ways they had experienced the incident became apparent. Not surprisingly, some found the event terrifying; a few of these later sued the company for the trauma they experienced. The majority, however, took the event in stride and, even though they lost all their possessions and the expedition was suddenly terminated, were not unhappy with the overall experience and gave the company and the cruise very positive ratings. A notable number responded to the experience even more enthusiastically, asking what next adventure the company offered that might match the thrill of this one! Just as beauty is in the eye of the beholder, so too is experience in the soul of the individual. Events happen to us, but consciously and unconsciously we shape them into the experiences that become, at this level of development, our primary identifications.

Because at this stage of development I am my experience, all reflection is also self-reflection. Thus, as we saw in an anticipatory way for the individual self ("I am myself"), the reflective self is also concerned with existential issues such as being myself with integrity and authenticity. Questions of actualization ("How do I become who I most truly am?") and fulfillment ("How should I be in order to experience the greatest degree of happiness and well-being?") also become important. In this stage we encounter the first clear expression of a desire to be and to become all one can be. This is clearly a spiritual desire, and the response to this desire forms an important part of the resulting spirituality. Any spirituality that does not emerge out of this soil will always lack soulfulness and will consequently remain too ethereal to be truly transformational.

Unfortunately it is quite possible to become lost in this soulful reflection rather than allowing it to be a platform on which we can stand to view the vistas of an even larger self and world. This happens whenever we accept a penultimate identity with too much rigidity. One such possible identity that emerges at this stage of development results from identify with the soul work I'm doing. The identity that results from this is "I am my issues." Although it is important to work on these issues if I am to become all I most truly am, my transformation will be blocked if I allow myself to be reduced to my issues.

But I do not want to rush too quickly past the importance of doing this work if my development is to continue. Working on our issues is an extremely rich component of soulful living in that it frees us up to become more than our issues. The person who has never been reflective about one's easy slide into anger, tendency to harbor resentment, or vulnerability to depression is unable to ever become more than these issues. The same is true of all the other dimensions of soul work that are crucial if we are to become more than we are.

Someone who had been working with me on her shame and inferiority issues recently said that she wondered how her parents—who had never had therapy and seemed to have lived without the sort of self-reflection that had characterized the last decade or so of her life—had been as happy as they seemed to be. But happiness does not depend on the expansion of consciousness. I saw this in my own parents, who were simple people who lived lives of deep fulfillment apart from the benefits of intense self-reflection. They were rather typical of their generation, of those whose basic adult formation occurred before the rise of the therapeutic culture of the last four or five decades. I feel no regret for them. I am not sorry that they did not have an opportunity for psychotherapy, nor that they did not avail themselves more than they did of the soul-work resources that were available to them. I pass no judgment on their level of consciousness development, nor do I do so with anyone else. My patient need not feel regret that her parents did not do the work she was doing. She should only feel gratified that she had the chance to do this work and was able to experience the awakening that came from it.

The face of the reflective self that we are most used to seeing is rather serious and intense. At this stage of development, people often become caught up in a good deal of self-preoccupation. They can easily lose sight of the fact that reflection should be in the service of life, not the other way around. The purpose of reflection is to deepen engagement with others and the world. Reflection should not be an alternative to this engagement. Sometimes I have to remind people that soul work is *preparation* for life, not life itself. Working on our issues is important if we are to be free enough to step outside of the self-preoccupation that our unresolved psychological issues set up. As self-reflection does thus free us, it begins to lose some of its intensity and starts to fit within the flow of normal life, not requiring that we step outside of life and try—always unsuccessfully—to stop its flow.

Mature self-reflection gives depth to life. Because it is built around presence to self, it helps us be more present to others and to what is going on around us. The most aware and attentive people I know are all, without exception, people who have learned to open up the space for others and the world that exists within them by means of self-reflection. The moments of self-reflection that now routinely form part of their life ground them in the present moment and make them more alive and open to life as it exists in the present.

The path to this mature self-reflection leads, however, through a dark and potentially quite frightening valley of shadows. Unless we have the courage to continue into this potentially frightening terrain, we will forever be caught in the less mature forms of self-reflection characterized by self-preoccupation.

The Shadow Self: "I Am My Shadow"

One of the most important matters that we will inevitably encounter as we reflect on experience is our shadow: the disowned parts of self that we are unwilling to acknowledge as "me" because they are either too negative or too positive. Since we have denied and disowned these shadow parts, we project them onto others and encounter them as things about other people that disturb us. When we are ready to begin to recognize our shadow and get to know it, the first place to look is always to the things in other people that we find most annoying, irritating, or upsetting.

A failure to embrace one's shadow compromises all subsequent developmental possibilities. But this is the hardest challenge that we encounter on the journey to this point. Many who confront this challenge do not ever move beyond it because they seek only to eliminate the troublesome experiences and are unwilling to acknowledge them as parts of their self. Most people, however, know nothing of their shadow self. Even if they develop a reflective self, they remain distracted by the myriad of easier personal issues that become their focus and fail to recognize how these issues represent parts of themselves, not merely problems they keep running up against. Until they do recognize their shadow parts, they continue to struggle with their anger, depression, or other painful symptoms that are simply the unrecognized face of their disowned self and the consequences of this ongoing investment in denial and avoidance.

Christians are sometimes aided in their avoidance of an honest encounter with these disowned parts of self by unhelpfully labeling them as sin. Often they are quite dark and can appear to be frightening, even evil. But Carl Jung—who first identified the shadow and its importance in psychological development—reminds us that its darkness is the result of its being deprived of the light of consciousness.[3] No part of self is inherently evil, although humans clearly are capable of doing great evil. Evil gains its power within us in many ways; one of the most important ways is when we deny the existence of inner realities that frighten us. Repressing these inner realities does not bring escape from their devilish aspects but leads us unknowingly to fall victim to them. Denying the reality of the shadow is not to know one's self, and not to know one's self is to risk becoming possessed by that which we have ignored.

Another reason why we often avoid an honest encounter with these disowned parts of self is that we fear their strength and worry that we will become them rather than simply allowing them a place within our self. A man struggling with depression tells me how much he fears that if he dared to welcome the aggressive self that he encounters in his reactions and dreams, he might become a monster—potentially even a homicidal one. His anger terrifies him, and so he has cultivated a persona that is so excessively nice as to make others sometimes feel that they are drowning in sugar syrup. Even he finds his niceness tiresome and inauthentic, but his fear of his more assertive and potentially aggressive self terrifies him and keeps him from offering any hospitality to his shadow. He suffers from both all-or-none thinking and a misunderstanding of hospitality. He fears that any hospitality to his shadow self will immediately and automatically lead to his becoming that which he fears. But genuine hospitality is never like that. If we are hospitable to a stranger, we may slowly get to know that person, but we never suddenly become that other person. Hospitality does not lead to inevitable all-or-none identification and fusion. In terms of our shadow, hospitality simply gives us a chance to get to know a part of self that we think we know but which we only view with prejudice—we keep it in the dark and repressed parts of our hidden self. Hospitality to our shadow is our willingness to kiss the leper and in so doing discover that the leper is us.[4] It is being willing to embrace the prodigal son or daughter and discover that he or she is also us.

Embracing our shadow is essential if we are truly to know ourselves. Until we do this, we will never escape the enormous disruptive influence that these lost fragments of self play in our lives when we try to keep them locked up in the cellar of our unconscious. But when we are finally able to receive them with hospitality as parts of our family-of-self, they can then be integrated with the other part selves, and as a result we can become our whole and true self.

The first step in embracing our shadow is openness to the possibility
that what we encounter in others might also be in us. I recall a woman
who told me how upset she was by an opinionated colleague who was
always drawing attention to himself with his pontifications and who
always stubbornly insisted on being right even when he was clearly
wrong. Sensing the possibility of a lurking shadow, I asked her if she
felt that her reaction might carry any information about herself, not
just about him. She became indignant and said she was in no way like
him. I didn't know him, but I did know her reasonably well. I knew
how strongly she held her beliefs and judgments and how stubborn
she could be in defending against anything that felt like a challenge
to them. Although she was not yet ready to meet any disowned parts
of self, she was a reflective woman and, apart from this blind spot,
did have a good deal of self-knowledge. And she was committed to
being honest with what she encountered in her reflection on experience. And so, allowing my question to remain at the fringes of her
consciousness, over time she began to notice that she was bothered by
her reaction to this man, not just by him. This was a very important
discovery, and it quickly led to a softening of her defensiveness and
openness to the possibility that she and he were actually much more
similar than she had realized. This identification with him quickly led
to identification with her shadow. She told me that she felt horrified
to see how blind she had been to a part of herself, a part that she now
began to totalize and relate to as if it were the whole of her self. It
wasn't. It was just a lost part of self that had come in from the cold.

"I am my shadow" is a distortion of the truth that "my shadow
is part of me." It may feel that my shadow and I are interchangeable
because the shadow will often feel quite overwhelming. It will be hard
to imagine that it could be merely one among many parts of me. But,
brought into daylight, it inevitably shrinks and can be seen for what
it is: a lost fragment of self that was set aside because it didn't seem
to fit with who I thought I should be. Although I never really am my
shadow, this is the illusion that we easily slip into when we identity
with our shadow.

Identification with our shadow is a place of powerlessness. There
is nothing pleasant about it. But shadow work is essential if we are
to move to higher levels of consciousness. In calling it work, I should
be clear that this does not mean that it is something we need to accomplish. It will *feel* like work because we resist reclaiming these parts
of self that we have sent into exile, but what we have to do here is the

same as what we have to do in each developmental stage. What we must do is offer our consent to the growth and transformation that is ours if we dare to be open to life and to the Spirit who meets us in it, calling us to become more than we' are.

Soul work might be hard and certainly demands intentionality, but we ruin it when we turn it into a project. We do not have to fix our shadow or resolve all our inner issues to continue to grow. What we have to do is simply be open to the truths of our inner self. This is what we do when we acknowledge something to be a part of us. Doing so is much more a process than a project; it is a process of allowing our self to establish deep roots in the truth of who we in reality are, a process in which we consent to our becoming a larger and more authentic self rather than fashioning that self in the shape of who we want to be seen to be.

The Divided Self: "I Am Not Always My True Self"

Our shadow is simply one of the many part selves that confront us with the reality that we are a kingdom divided. We try to appear to be the single self we wish to be, but all of us are a family of different selves, and some of these part selves are inevitably in conflict with others. We are not the consistent self we try to present to the world. That persona is but one face of the multiplicity that we are. Until we are willing to welcome the other part selves into the family, we will never be whole.

Becoming aware of our dividedness is a mark of entering this next substage of consciousness development. Now our dividedness becomes a central feature of our consciousness: growing awareness of our lack of wholeness forms a prominent part of background awareness as we gather hints of what it is to live our truth and yet be surrounded by evidence of how little we do so. Although the way of being my truth is now on the horizon and I have touched it enough to know its singularly integral taste, much more of the time my experience is of being other than this wholeness and truth. My self therefore is the one who is not always living the truth of my self.

The author of the New Testament book of James understood this self-pathology when he urged his readers to no longer be of two minds (1:8). Suggesting that purity of heart is to will one thing,[5] Kierkegaard argued that the self can become whole only when it embraces the tensions within its constituent parts. This anticipated the insights of the depth psychology that emerged in the following decades and captures precisely the challenge of becoming who we truly and more deeply are.

Awareness of being a divided self does not make its first appearance at this stage. As early as the reflective self, we will be aware that we are fragmented and pulled in different directions. Our experience may be that, as Jesus said, the spirit is often willing, but the flesh is weak (Matt. 26:41). Or we may be aware that we both want and do not want a certain thing, or want two things that are mutually exclusive. In short, we will be aware that we are far from single in our desiring and that, not surprisingly, our motives are seldom pure. Reflection on our inconsistencies is always valuable, although the ideal response to this is usually not the default one. The default response is often to try to eliminate the inconsistency as a way to hopefully become more whole. But wholeness never comes from this sort of aggression, which only strengthens our false self. A more healthy response to the inconsistency is to feel the tension that it involves and live that tension, allowing each voice in the sometimes cacophonous dialogue to be heard. When all parts of self are included in the family gathering, the conversation will be richer and life will be fuller because we will actually be more whole.

The dislocation that begins to appear in this substage I am calling the divided self is more specific than this general sense of being pulled in different directions. The reference point for the sense of dividedness at the level of a self organized around soul is an awareness of the possibility of alignment, authenticity, and being in a way that is deeply truthful. After experiencing even brief moments of such oneness within my self and alignment with the truth of my being, I begin to notice the difference between these moments and the many more when I am not true to my self. Even brief brushes with this state of at-oneness produce a lingering memory that will serve as a reference point and will allow me to know the difference between true and false ways of being. Almost always such moments will lead to a longing for more.

Sometimes the true self is presented as if it is hidden in the larger false self and only discovered by peeling away the levels of untruth, much as one might peel away the rings of an onion. Unfortunately, the results are about the same; when the last ring is peeled away, what you are left with is a lot of tears, but not much more. Our truth does not lie in some hidden or lost part of us that must be uncovered: it lies in a way of being. This is why I prefer to speak of true and false ways of being.

Being and living our truth is being and living at one within our self and within our Source. The problem of the false self is a spiritual problem, not simply a psychological one: it is a problem that cannot be solved apart from spiritual response. Our truest self and most authentic way of being cannot be found apart from our being in the larger whole I call God. The good news is that we are already in God. Like the fish desperately swimming around in the ocean searching for the sea, we discover that as we search for a way of being in truth, we are already in the truth we seek. We are already in God. All that is missing is awareness. At this level of self-organization (the divided self), we may not yet recognize the transcendent nature of the truth in which we have our being, but we will experience a deep existential sigh when we notice that we are already within that which we seek. This sigh becomes the reference point for the sense of being a divided self.

Many turn the quest for their true self into an exercise in self-discovery or self-actualization. It should be both of these things, but unless it is also a response to a taste of what actually is—an encounter with their larger self as it exists in something that is transcendent to the self—it will never be more than a project of the false self. The transcendent is lurking in the background during all stages of the unfolding self, but it comes closer to the edges of consciousness as we move closer to the spirit-centered self. There is always a spiritual component to any genuine self-discovery and self-actualization. Thomas Merton understood this quest for the truth of our self to be at the center of the spiritual journey.[6] But what makes it a spiritual quest is when it is a response to the Spirit, who invites us to live out of the center of our being in God.

Abraham Maslow called these moments "peak experiences," times when we feel connected and experience a deep-seated sense of well-being, belonging, and alignment.[7] He recognized the spiritual nature of these moments and suggested that they are characterized by a sense of alignment with something larger than and beyond the self. Such moments also produce feelings of integration and affirm the meaning and value of existence. But this doesn't mean that they are spectacular; although I believe they are quite common, they are easily overlooked. However, when people are asked about them, many are able to identify such moments of alignment and at-oneness, moments that leave a memory and serve as a basis for a longing to know more deeply this place of belonging and self transcendence.

Soul-Centered and Beyond

Although there is tension in the divided self, it is quite different from the tension of the shadow self. This tension is more bearable and much less likely to be overwhelming because there has been at least a brush with a way of being that is vastly more expansive, true, and integral than how I normally live my small life. The motivation for a fuller living of the truth of my being thus is not simply an expression of a quest for perfection or personality development; more basically, it is a response to a gift. It comes from having had a peek into a world of possibilities that could never be known and never created by a willful and striving self that is seeking fulfillment. This is why the divided self is such a place of grace. It means that we are right at the portal into the Spirit-centered ways of organizing self and living.

Life centered in the soul will, if lived faithfully and fully, present many invitations to a life grounded in the spirit. Recall the way in which spirit is nested in soul, which is nested in mind, which in turn is nested in body. Spirit is present in all but comes closer to the surface of consciousness as the journey of awakening moves us up through the progressively broader and more expansive regions of the Great Nest of Being. Spiritual awareness and response is possible at any stage, but the call of spirit can be discerned more clearly in the soul-centered stage of development than at any previous level of development. As we have seen, the fullest living of a soul-centered life demands spiritual response and invites us to the realm of the spirit-centered life, which is lurking on the horizon.

Dialogue and Reflection

1. **I found this chapter extremely helpful. Unless I am fooling myself, I suspect that more of us now are somewhere in this soul level of consciousness and identity development than might have been the case a generation or two ago. Any thoughts on that?**

   You are probably right that many of the thoughtful, educated people in our age and culture are somewhere in this third level of consciousness formation. To one degree or another, most of us in the West are products of the therapeutic culture of the late twentieth century and its emphasis on knowing and working on our issues. Many of us have reasonable space, freedom, and support to engage in these ways of living. Yet, whenever I talk to individuals, I quickly become aware of how misleading generalizations like this can be. There is great variability in levels of consciousness. Though there is some reason to believe that there are more people at this level than would have been the case a century or two ago, it is quite clear that education and participation in a postmodern culture does not automatically translate into movement to these so-called higher levels of consciousness.

2. I know you have said that the movement through these substages of development is not sequential, but I keep hearing something linear in your presentation that I find troubling. Can you offer anything to help me further with this?

What I have been describing in these chapters is the general shape of each of the four major levels of consciousness organization and identity, not the way we move between them. That I will do in chapter 12, where I will present a model of our progression from one level to another that I think you will see is definitely nonlinear. But I do understand how it is easy to hear the implication of sequential movement as I describe these levels. Although I do not think that our development unfolds as neatly as these levels, I do think that the levels suggested by the Great Chain (or Nest) of Being that I am describing do represent progressively broadening frameworks for consciousness and identity. So, quite apart from the question of how we move from a body-centered self to a mind-centered, soul-centered self, or spirit-centered self, I do believe that these represent the major available options for organizing identity and consciousness and that they represent a progressive expansion of self. In my view the overall contours of the journey of awakening thus involve a movement toward larger and more inclusive perspectives that are progressively more and more attuned to that which is transcendent to one's self. But the journey is, as you correctly recognize, far from linear.

3. I wonder if what you call the shadow is what Christian theologians call sin.

> Some people would certainly think of the shadow in terms of sin, but I do not think that this is helpful. Such labeling confuses something that is merely outside the light of awareness with evil. Though I would certainly not deny the capacity for human evil, I think that our greatest vulnerability to it comes from a failure to face the things about our self that we fear or are unwilling to acknowledge. I also recognize that theological and psychological languages differ from each other, and consequently I am not proposing that the theological concept of sin is synonymous with the psychological concept of the shadow. But neither do I confuse these few brief comments with the comprehensive mapping of the two terms (shadow and sin) that might be warranted; I will have to leave that to someone else more interested in sin and more competent to deal with it theologically.

4. I found your discussion of the reference point for the divided self helpful. I think you said that this point was not simply one's lack of wholeness but especially moments of alignment, authenticity, and being in a way that is deeply truthful. I have struggled with becoming my true self, but if I am honest, I have hardly bothered to notice whether I have ever experienced such moments of alignment. My focus has been more on trying to make myself something more than I am. Can you say anything further about this to help me focus more on what I may have already tasted but not noticed?

> You have put your finger on something very important. We can only progress so far on this journey of awakening by means of the sort of soul work you describe. Eventually we discover that we must be drawn into the larger spaces associated with higher levels of consciousness, not simply push ourselves forward as part of some kind of self-development project. Two things can draw us forward. The first is desire. Our deepest desires point us beyond our selves and therefore are deeply spiritual. Our desire to be more than we presently are thus is a desire that is always worth attending to, and doing so is one important way in which we open our self to the Spirit. The second is

awareness, particularly awareness of our momentary brushes with the Divine that we simply fail to notice. I am convinced that we all have had these moments of being touched by the Spirit or having tasted the eternal water for which we thirst but simply swallowed it without noticing. Noticing these moments—either in the present or, with prayerful stillness and attentiveness, in the past—offers us the possibility of discrimination. Now we have a reference point against which we can judge the substitute gratifications we accept for our deepest longings. Notice the moments of alignment between Spirit and your deepest self. Pay attention to what they feel like, and notice how they differ from the way you normally live your life. And then keep this in mind as you seek to open your self to the Spirit. The Spirit will do the rest, and you will be drawn toward the spirit-centered self that you long to be.

9

The Spirit-Centered Self

If soul is the reflective space that transforms events into meaning-ful experience, spirit is the dynamic force that makes us yearn to transcend experience. While soul calls us down and into the details of our life, spirit calls us up and out, toward that which tran-scends us and the circumstances of our life. Spirit is the fire in the belly that kindles passions and vitalizes life. It calls us to be more than we are, urging us beyond the small safe places where we make our abode and inviting us to find our true home in relationship to the self-transcendent. A life aligned with this transcendent reference point allows the spirit-centered self to soar in realms unimaginably broader than anything encountered to this point.

The journey of spirit helps us transcend the particulars of our own small and often cramped lives. We discover a self that includes so much more than what we previously thought of as "me." As we have seen at earlier levels, each new organization of the self involves expanding the sense of what is me and what is not me—something that Robert Kegan describes as a renegotiation of the boundary of self and non-self.[1] This can be quite disorienting. Yet it is not confusing just for the one experiencing this new ground of being; it will also be almost impossible for anyone else to understand.

People who live in these realms sometimes speak of loneliness associated with learning they had to keep their experience private.

137

One woman told me that, after marrying for the first time in her early forties, she quickly discovered that even her husband—a minister and someone she considered to be very spiritual—could not understand her sense of deep communion with trees and animals, or her keen awareness of God in all things and all people. His theology limited his ability to receive and hold experience that did not readily fit—something that happens to all of us quite easily. This is why our understandings should always be held with humility and constantly updated.

Perhaps this need for caution about sharing deep spiritual experiences was part of what Jesus was referring to in Matthew 6:6: "But when you pray, go to your private room and, when you have shut your door, pray to your Father who is in that secret place." Or think of the many times Jesus urged those he healed to tell no one of their experience. There may well have been more than one reason for this injunction, yet possibly Jesus was aware that not all spiritual experience should be shared. Some encounters are simply too precious to be communicated; they should simply be cherished. This is also the teaching of Hafiz, the fourteenth-century Sufi mystic who encouraged followers to find God everywhere, but keep it a secret.[2] While this may be hard advice to understand in our age of promiscuous self-disclosure, it does reflect deep spiritual wisdom.

These higher levels of awakening that saints and mystics describe are increasingly hard for us to understand apart from personal experience. Added to this is the problem that inevitably comes when trying to describe experiences and forms of knowing that cannot be reduced to words. But, as I have suggested earlier, just because something is transrational does not make it irrational. And because something remains unknowable by normal mental processes does not mean that it is unknowable. The prayer of the apostle Paul for the Christians in Ephesus was that they might know the love of Christ, which is beyond all knowing (Eph. 3:14–19). Many spiritual mysteries and blessings are rationally unknowable but experientially knowable to those who are open and ready to receive them as gifts of grace. Let us therefore explore the gifts of consciousness and identity that are associated with the spirit-centered self.

The Essential Self: "I Am"

The experiential focus of people whose consciousness and identity is organized at the level of the essential self is being. We have seen hints of this in the soul-centered self, where being true to one's self (authenticity) and being at one with one's self (integrity) are not simply values but are central planks of consciousness. But now that focus becomes not being in a particular way as much as simply being.

It is highly significant that when Moses asked by what name he should be known, God self-revealed as the "I AM WHO I AM" (Exod. 3:14), sometimes translated as "I AM HE WHO IS." Jewish and Christian theologians have plumbed the mysteries of this name for millennia, but one thing is clear; it reflects an identity that is based in being. This terse statement of being requires no predicate. "I AM" requires no qualification. It tolerates no limits. It marks the Deity as eternal, unbound being.

It therefore is very striking that Jesus adopts the same language. Nine times in the Gospel of John, Jesus self-identifies by means of the phrase "I am"—*egō eimi* in Greek—without any predicate, such as saying: "I who am speaking to you, . . . I am he [*egō eimi*]" (John 4:26); "It is I [*egō eimi*]; do not be afraid" (6:20 NRSV); "When you have lifted up the Son of Man, then you will realize that I am he [*egō eimi*]" (8:28 (NRSV); and "I tell you most solemnly, before Abraham was, I am [*egō eimi*]" (8:58). Jesus was intentionally using language that his Jewish audience would clearly recognize. They did. And they responded to this clear identification with the one they knew as "I AM WHO I AM" by trying to stone Jesus for blasphemy (8:59).

Jesus was not simply being provocative. He was declaring his identity and his essence as he had come to understand and know it. Even when his "I am" statements include a predicate, what was added to the statement pointed to being and life itself. Using the same "I am [*egō eimi*]" construction, he added such things as "the bread of life" (John 6:35 KJV), "the light of the world . . . the light of life" (8:12 KJV), and "the Way, the Truth, and the Life" (John 14:6). None of these things qualifies or limits Jesus's identity as being; they simply unpack what a life grounded in being involves: life.

But there is no reason to assume that this essential self is unique to Jesus, or to the one he called his Father. We too can know what it is to have our identity grounded and centered in our being, to have our self distilled to its essence and to know our self as an "I am." But notice how naked this stands in relation to all the other "I am" statements we have encountered at each of the previous levels of consciousness development. Up to this point each of the selves we have encountered limit our being by equating it with some object, experience, or state:

I am my body, my image, my possessions, my role, my thoughts, my beliefs, my community, myself, my experience, my shadow, or my dividedness. The essential self recognizes that while all of these things may be true, they do not define me. I am much, much more than any of them. I am. My being is not constrained by my characteristics, history, possession, abilities, or experiences. I simply am. And in realizing this, I am filled with the wonder and the simple joy of being.

It is quite remarkable how something so fundamental to our existence can be so far from awareness. Modern psychology has certainly largely lost sight of it, focusing instead on such dimensions of human personhood as doing, thinking, feeling, willing, choosing, and many others. Unfortunately, Christian spirituality has often fallen prey to the same oversight. Here the focus has been on spiritual practices and too often has tended to treat human beings as human doings. Or listen in on the sorts of things that we tend to thank God for. We might express gratitude for good health, for friends and family, for spiritual blessings, but how often do we recognize that the most basic gift that we all experience is the gift of our being? It therefore is a great awakening when this focus on being suddenly emerges from the hazy background and comes front and center to consciousness.

The awareness that I am not simply a male, a psychologist, a writer, a husband, a Caucasian, my body, my thoughts and feelings, or my experience but that "I am" represents a radical change of perspective. For once I begin to notice my essential being, I also begin to notice the essential being of all others. And once I begin to be aware that life itself is my greatest gift, life itself—wherever it appears—becomes fundamentally precious. Treasuring this most basic gift leads to a treasuring of others and of life. How can I fail to value life wherever it appears when my own life now pulsates with previously unknown vitality? The "me" who observes this is a larger self that identifies with life wherever it appears. This self that I am has been both distilled and expanded. This is the paradox of the essential self.

There is a noticeable vitality and presence to those who live out of this essential center. The vital presence that they are able to offer others arises from their presence to themselves and from their at-one-ness within themselves. This does not mean that they are thoroughly consistent or completely integrated. But it does mean that there is a simplicity to their being—a kind of elegance and ease of being that comes from living out of a place of such centeredness and distilled essence. I think, for example, of the simplicity, vitality, and joy that characterized Francis of Assisi. It is no wonder that he is the most loved of the Christian saints. As recorded in the legends of his life, even the birds and animals could not resist his charm. As the story is told, one day, while traveling with his companions, Francis noticed a place where birds filled the trees on both sides. He told the others to wait for him while he went and preached to his sisters the birds. Francis approached the birds and, drawn by the sound of his voice, they quickly settled down; not a single one flew from the tree while he proceeded to remind them of the gratitude they owed to God for their life and blessings and how much they could count on God to take care of their needs.[3] His love and pastoral care for all of life sprang from the essential nature of his own being.

Although I have identified losses as well as gains associated with movement into previous levels of being, I am unaware of any losses associated with any of these spirit-centered levels of consciousness and self-organization. Everything is gathered up and brought along; nothing is left behind. If it were otherwise, it would be impossible to move into this realm of being. But this does not mean that there is not yet more scope for further unfolding. I propose that at least two levels of further development can be identified beyond this essential self.

The Divine Self: "I Am One with God"

The next manifestation of awakening is that of the divine self. This we see with singular clarity in Jesus when he repeatedly speaks of being one with the Father. His alignment with the Spirit of God is so profound that the apostle Paul describes him as the visible image of the invisible God (Col. 1:15). Jesus didn't simply try to practice a life of alignment with the Father; he lived out of a deep knowing that he and the Father were one.

One of the occasions when he spoke clearly of this was when he was confronted at the Feast of Dedication and asked to plainly declare his identity. When asked if he was the Christ, Jesus replied, "The Father and I are one" (John 10:30 NRSV). As opponents were preparing to stone him for blasphemy (on the charge "You are only a man and you claim to be God" [10:33]), Jesus answered:

> Is it not written in your law:
> "I said, you are gods?"

So the law uses the word "gods"
for those to whom the word of God was addressed,
and scripture cannot be rejected.
Yet you say to someone the Father has consecrated and sent
    into the world,
"You are blaspheming,"
because he says, "I am the Son of God."
If I am not doing my Father's work,
there is no need to believe in me,
but at least believe in the work I do;
then you will know for sure
that the Father is in me and I am in the Father. (10:34–38)

Being one with the Father seems to have been central to the consciousness of Jesus. His whole life flowed out of this fundamental
awareness. I am quite convinced that this was an awareness that had
to be cultivated. It makes a mockery of his humanity to think that
as an infant he knew he was God. His humanity demanded that he
grow physically, psychologically, and spiritually; central to that growth
was for him, as it is for us, the development of one's own identity
and consciousness.

Without understanding it, I believe that the oneness with the Father
that Jesus experienced and continues to experience as the risen Christ
is unique. However, I also believe that his own teachings assure us
that we also can and are meant to know a similar oneness. This is the
testimony of those who have encountered their divine self. Those who
have traveled into the realms of the spirit-centered self on the journey
of awakening tell us that the further they proceed on this journey, the
more the boundary between them and God becomes fuzzy for them.
They also speak of it being increasingly impossible to fail to see God
in all humans, and indeed in all that is.

In chapter 5 I referred to the experience of someone who told me
that she found herself less and less clear about the boundaries between
herself and God—or anyone and God. Seeing God in everything and
everyone had initially been confusing for her, but she had come to
find great comfort in this secret that she knew, a secret that few others
seemed to be aware of. She had given up speaking of it because she
had quickly come to discover how troubled people tended to be when
they heard of her experience. In one particularly upsetting encounter
with her minister, she shared her secret with him, and he responded
by lecturing her on the importance of never losing sight of the huge

chasm between God and humans. That had never been her experience, and the further her journey of awakening took her, the less it fit with what she knew in her depths even if she felt incapable of adequately articulating that experience.

Mystics love the Divine so much that they no longer see any boundaries between God and mortals. This is the shared experience of mystics across all religions and spiritual traditions. They point to a single center of their deepest knowing—that they are one with the Beloved, and that the further they go in this journey of love into the Beloved, the less clear any boundaries between God and self become. Cynthia Bourgeault states, "As we move toward our center, our own being and the divine being become more and more mysteriously interwoven."[4] Meister Eckhart speaks of a place in the depths of our soul in which God alone can dwell and in which we dwell in God. Meeting God in this place, we are invited to sink into what he calls "the eternity of the Divine essence." Doing so, however, we never become the Divine essence. This, he says, is because "God has left a little point wherein the soul turns back upon itself and finds itself, and knows itself to be a creature."[5] The Christian mystics do not confuse themselves and God. They know that in union with God, human personality is neither lost nor converted into divine personality. But they also know the profound inadequacy of language to either hold or communicate these deep mysteries.

I have been blessed to have the opportunity to know well several people for whom union with God was not just a momentary experience but a relatively stable part of their ongoing journey. Although I wasn't seeing any of them as a psychologist, I couldn't entirely set aside a psychological perspective as I responded to their invitations to accompany them as a spiritual guide. I was, for example, interested to learn what exactly this sense of increasingly blurry boundaries between them and God meant in terms of their sense of their self. I also wondered whether I would find any signs of psychotic or delusional features, and about the overall effect of this sort of journey into God was on their mental health.

What I discovered was that these people were definitely not psychotic. In fact, they were very different from psychotic patients I have worked with—patients whose psychopathology manifested itself, in part, in the form of delusions of being God. Sadly, their experiences of God were being processed through the same distorting filters of mental illness as all their other experiences. I am in no position to say that they did not have mystical experiences. What I can say was that their illness led them to interpret any such experiences in the same unreliable way in which they interpreted all other experiences.

The modern mystics I am speaking of showed a high level of mental health and psychological maturity. That doesn't mean that they didn't have problems. They were human, but they were far from psychotic. One of the most consistent things I encountered was the fact that rather than having a disintegrating effect on their psychic organization, their life in this place of blurred boundaries with the Divine consistently served as a force of ever-deepening integration and wholeness. Though language failed them in efforts to describe their experience, none of them confused themselves with God. They had never been confused about who they were, nor had any of them ever lacked a full and complete sense of continuity of self over the course of their life. It was simply that their sense of who that self was and what it included had expanded—and kept expanding. And God now was on the inside of that self-boundary, not the outside.

What most struck me as I related to them over time was that their ever-deepening journey into God made them more deeply human, not less human. None showed anything like a flight from their humanity or a quest to be God rather than human. Instead, what I encountered were people who become more and more fully and naturally human, more relaxed within themselves and in their experience in the world. None showed an avoidance of the realities of life, and none seemed to use their spiritual experience as an escape. Although by this point they all had established a contemplative dimension to their life, they all were active in serving others in the world. This, they knew, was their home, and it was here that they had learned to meet God.

The Cosmic Self: "I Am One with Everything"

There is yet one more level of spirit-centered awakening. The cosmic self reminds us that oneness with God is not intended to be a private experience. Because all people live and move and have their being in God (Acts 17:28), it is not just me and God that are one. Even beyond this, because everything that exists is held in the unity that is Christ (Col. 1:15–17), everything that exists is one in Christ. The old joke about the mystic who walks up to the hotdog vendor and says, "Make me one with everything," misses the point. I am already one with everything. All that is absent is awareness. This awareness is the gift of the cosmic self.

Once again, this is not life in a psychotic fog of enmeshment. It does not involve a regressive return to a developmental state before differentiation of self from others. Instead, it involves transcendence through awareness that the apparent separateness of the one from the many is an illusion. Slowly we begin to see that both the one and the many are held together in the One—the Eternal Godhead. And as we come to know our self within this One, we also come to know our oneness with all that is held by the One.

The medieval Flemish Christian mystic John of Ruysbroeck described this knowing of our self as one with everything as being grounded in the first and supreme unity of knowing our self as in God. "All creatures," he declared, "are immanent in this unity, and if they were to be separated from God, they would be annihilated, and would become nothing. This unity is essential in us according to nature, whether we are good or bad. And without our co-operation it makes us neither holy nor blessed."[6] Ruysbroeck was not articulating some arcane point of theology. He was describing something he came to know through a life of contemplation—that he was one with everything that is and that this union, grounded in his union with God, was the reality of everyone and everything, perhaps not realized but nonetheless real. Awareness allows us to know this reality, and our cooperation with the Spirit allows this awareness to become transformational.

This knowing is often called enlightenment because it involves seeing what is. Obviously the eyes that are enlightened are not our physical eyes. The eyes with which we see are the eyes of the One. Meister Eckhart puts it this way: "The eye with which I see God is the same eye with which He sees me. Mine eye and God's eye are one eye and one sight and one knowledge and one love."[7] But this reminds us that it is not just our minds that are enlightened on this journey of awakening; it is also our hearts. For if we are to see God, we must see not simply through the eyes of the mind but also through the eyes of the heart.

To be one with everything is to have overcome the fundamental optical illusion of our separateness. We establish boundaries to try to reinforce individuality, but what we get is isolation and alienation. We think we *have* bodies instead of *being* our bodies, and the result is alienation from our bodies. We distinguish between our self and the natural world, and we end up exploiting the environment from which we feel estranged. We think we are separate from other people, and the result is a breach in our knowing of our underlying shared humanity. Boundaries disrupt the flow of participative energy between elements of creation that can be distinguished but that are intimately interrelated. Raimon Panikkar captures this well: "I am one with the source insofar as I too act as a source by making everything I have received flow again."[8] To realize that we are already one with everything is to have restored the flow of creation and allowed ourselves unqualified participation in the life of God.

Buddhists and Hindus talk more about becoming one with everything than Christians, but I am convinced that this sense of solidarity with all things and the ability to see all existence as held together in Christ are parts of the journey of the spirit-centered self for all humans. Its place within Christian spirituality has been most clearly understood and articulated by three people: Hildegard of Bingen, Teilhard de Chardin, and Matthew Fox.

Witnesses to the Cosmic Christ

Hildegard of Bingen (1098–1179) was a woman who experienced a life-transforming enlightenment and whose life has continued to help others see through the eyes of the One in whom we are all held. One day when she was forty-two years old, a bright light suddenly filled her body and soul. She described it as a flame that inflamed her heart and mind. All of a sudden she knew what she had previously only believed—particularly the truths of Scriptures as they pointed to the life of her Lord. After this, her most common way of referring to her Lord was as the Cosmic Christ. This Christ, whom she had long known from the Bible (encountered in such places as John 1:1–3; Acts 17:23–31; 1 Cor. 8:6–7; Col. 1:15–20; Heb. 1:1–3), she now encountered in her heart and mind. This Cosmic Christ became the center of her mystical theology and spirituality and was implicit if not explicit in much of her legacy: books on medicine, biology, and social policy and justice; morality plays and opera; a great volume of music, art, and poetry; and her still immensely relevant writings on mystical theology and spirituality.[9]

Hildegard regarded herself as a prophet, as did her contemporaries both within and outside the church. Her call was to restoring a creation-centered spirituality and theology, following the Cosmic

Christ into the world, and participating as God makes all things new in Christ. Her vision allowed her to see the deep unity of art, science, and spirituality. It allowed her to unite "vision with doctrine, religion with science, charismatic jubilation with prophetic indignation, and longing for social order with quest for social justice,"[10] and she did this as a medieval woman outside all the power structures of the day. She did it, she said, following the Cosmic Christ, in whom all was already held and everything belonged.

Pierre Teilhard de Chardin (1881–1955) was a French philosopher and Jesuit priest who trained and worked as a paleontologist and geologist. He also saw a unity to all of life, a unity that he was convinced came from the Cosmic Christ, who holds all things and shapes their becoming. He taught that humanity was evolving in the direction of an increased collective consciousness. Arguing that "all that arises, converges," he described this point of convergence and higher consciousness as Christ consciousness.[11]

This vision of evolutionary spirituality has been picked up by many others since de Chardin, but by none with more eloquence and force than Matthew Fox (b. 1940), a contemporary American Episcopal priest, mystic, and theologian. Fox also draws together things that others see as quite apart. For him, creation, spirituality, science, art, and mysticism are inseparably linked. And right at the center once again is his understanding and experience of the Cosmic Christ.[12]

Fox's mystical quest is for the divine pattern that connects all things—things seen in science, imagined in art and literature, described in theology, and lived in the experience of humans. His answer is that the Cosmic Christ—grounded in the life, death, and resurrection of the historical Jesus—connects and holds everything together. Once again, this is the Christ of Colossians, "the firstborn of all creation, . . . [who] holds all things in unity" (Col. 1:15–17); and "the radiant light of God's glory and the perfect copy of God's nature" (Heb. 1:3), sustaining the universe by God's powerful command. Only the quest for such a Cosmic Christ, Fox believes, can free the church from its captivity to a truncated and anthropocentric Christianity and engage with the world as it is and as it is becoming.

Cosmic Christ, Cosmic Self

The reason I have written of the Cosmic Christ in as much detail as I have is to show the legitimate and important place that a cosmic vision has in Christian spirituality. Although this cosmic vision is far from the center of contemporary Christianity, it is an important part of the Christian tradition that provides a spiritual and theological context for the journey of the cosmic self.

The life of the cosmic self is meaningless apart from love. You cannot see creation as being held and sustained in Christ and not begin to care for it as you would care for anything or anyone being held by God. Similarly, you cannot see others in God and God in others without an opening of your heart; when this happens, love leads you to know your deep solidarity with all humans as you and they are held in God. As you live in God and increasingly see others through eyes of love, you discover that the ways in which we normally categorize people and set ourselves apart from others are less and less meaningful. Although distinctions can surely be made, they are a distraction because they take our attention off the much more fundamental sameness.

We see this in the mystics who often become uncomfortable with customary religious classification. Hafiz, the fourteenth-century Sufi mystic, speaks of his journey into God's love having made it impossible for him to call himself a Christian, a Hindu, a Buddhist, a Jew, or even a Muslim. Love, he says, ruined him for this sort of classification and freed him from all such concepts.[13] Distinctions can still be made. Certainly there are differences between Christians, Muslims, Buddhists, and Jews; between males and females; between young and old. But in the Cosmic Christ, all these divisions are obliterated and we are one in Christ (Gal. 3:28).

Plutarch tells the story of how Alexander the Great came upon the philosopher Diogenes examining a pile of human bones. "What are you looking for?" asked Alexander. Diogenes answered, "Something I cannot find." "And what is that?" "The difference between your father's bones and those of his slaves." Retelling this story, Anthony De Mello adds: "The following are just as indistinguishable: Catholic bones from Protestant bones. Hindu bones from Muslim bones. Arab bones from Israeli bones. Russian bones from American bones. The enlightened fail to see the difference even when the bones are clothed in flesh!"[14]

When we focus on the externals and the distinctions we can make based on them, we miss the fact that the other is both a face of self and a face of Christ. We also miss the common journey that we share as humans who dare to follow the Spirit on the journey of human awakening and unfolding. And we miss the fact that we are all children of God (Acts 17:23–29).

Spirit Centered and Beyond

I have no idea what, if anything, might exist beyond the spirit-centered self. The best available maps of the journey of awakening simply give us no meaningful hints of what may lie beyond. This does not mean, however, that there is not a beyond. The God of all becoming cannot be limited by any conceptual map as crude and limited as this one necessarily is. The mystics give us no reliable hints of what beyond might be. Nor do theologians, transpersonal psychologists, or spiritual writers.

I personally suspect that the spirit-centered self is as awakened and unfolded as it gets. For most of us, this still leaves lots of room for the journey to continue! My own experience of these possibilities gives me only hints, not a steady-state ongoing experience, of these spirit-centered ways of being. Yet the hints carry such striking confirmation that this is indeed a journey into God that I know I am headed toward my true home. Every moment spent in the freedom of these spirit-centered ways of being spoils me for any petty concerns, inferior quests, lesser gods, or smaller selves.

Dialogue and Reflection

1. **Your references to higher levels of consciousness suggest a spirituality of ascent rather than one of descent, which is how your previous books seemed to present the journey of Christian spirituality. I also dislike the implicit elitism that seems present in these rankings of levels of consciousness and self-development. Any comments?**

   Your first comment about ascent versus descent brings us right to the heart of the paradox that this journey into God represents. Like the journey of Jesus, it is one that begins with a long, seemingly endless descent but that ends with ascent into the presence of God. Each successive letting go of ego attachments results in a self that is less and less overinflated. But paradoxically, we become less so that we may become more. Or in the language of Jesus, we lose our self so that we may find it. But the self we find is no overinflated ego-self that must be deflated and dethroned. It is a self that is aligned with the Spirit of God because the self is so fully rooted in the Spirit that the self's truth is the very truth of God. This self is both broader, deeper, firmer, truer, larger, and higher than any other self we have examined to this point because it is a spirit-centered self. But it is not a self that we can achieve in some sort of journey of ascent by striving and successive approximations at perfection. No, it is a self that comes to us only by losing the self we already have. That self we must voluntarily surrender if we are ever to receive the gift of our true self-in-Christ.

Regarding the elitist overtones from ranking levels of development that you sense, I start by saying that I don't think the way to avoid elitism is to pretend that people are equal in anything other than inherent value. Obviously humans differ physically, and this is equally true in terms of psychospiritual development. But to say that one person has more complete development of consciousness and self than another is not to say that this person is a better human being, or a better Christian. Nor is it to say that this person is of more value. It is simply what it is: a statement of where they are on the human journey of awakening and unfolding, a journey that we all make at varying speeds and to varying degrees.

2. **I don't think I understand what you mean when you suggest that each stage of awakening represents a renegotiation of the boundary of self and non-self. Can you explain this further?**

Each of the levels of consciousness development represents one way in which we can and do answer the question, who am I? However you answer that question tells us something about where you place the boundary between what you consider to be your self and what you consider to be non-self. The body self sets the boundary between self and non-self at what we might call the skin boundary. Everything on the inside of that skin boundary I take to be "me," and everything outside my skin is "not me." The mental self includes this but expands the understanding of self by pushing the boundary beyond the skin to include not simply my physicality but also my mind. The soulful self pushes this boundary even further, now also including the possibilities of living with deep connection to others, the world, and life itself when we live out of our depths. This boundary expansion is pushed even further—right to the point of extinction—when boundaries dissolve and we begin to live with the awareness that we are one with everything that we have, at various points in our journey, previously defined as non-self. This does not mean that there are no meaningful distinctions that can be appropriately made between elements of the larger whole; it means simply that we know our place within this larger harmonious whole and that our identity is no longer based on the small bit we previously tried to carve out of it and stake as "mine" and "me." With each successive level of consciousness development, there are fewer aspects of the universe that feel external to the self. The person still retains a sense of being an "I," but everything else that exists is so integrally connected that the line between me and these larger horizons for self is not a boundary but simply a line. A line becomes a boundary when we think of that which is on each side of the line as separate and unrelated. In truth, however, the boundaries that become renegotiated and eventually dissolve on the journey of awakening are simply lines that distinguish but should never fragment the larger whole and the unity that exists within it.

3. **I find your language of the essential self a bit confusing. What do you mean by "essential"?**

"Essential" is based on the same root word as "essence," and I chose it simply to suggest that the self at this level is now down to its essence. It is stripped of much of the protective shroud in which it wrapped itself at earlier levels of development. No longer is it clutching to the body, mind, or even soul for its identity. Instead, it stands quite naked and vulnerable, grounded simply in its being. Thus there is a considerable lightness of being at this level, and this is why the spirit can soar in response to the invitations of the Spirit.

4. **If the Cosmic Christ is so evident in the New Testament, why is the concept so foreign to most contemporary Christianity?**

> Fox's answer to this question makes good sense to me: the Enlightenment. The individualism that was introduced into society and the desacralization of the universe experienced during the Enlightenment led Christian theologians to set aside the big-picture cosmology symbolized by the Cosmic Christ and focus instead on personal salvation. Suddenly the world that was interesting wasn't the cosmos viewed through eyes of wonder but the world that could be studied by science. And with the rise of humanism, people in the West became more interested in themselves than in God. Interest in the fate of nonhuman creation declined even more precipitously. But these developments in the West were not shared by the East, as even a brief visit to an Eastern Orthodox cathedral makes clear. The Cosmic Christ retained a central place in their tradition. But this Christ has never been entirely unknown in the West. The rise of interest in ecospirituality and creation spiritualities and the hunger for a truly transcendent Christ, not merely the Jesus who is my best friend, reminds us that, for both humans and the world, nothing less than the Cosmic Christ is big enough to either hold us or address our deepest longings and problems.

5. **Thank you for speaking positively of Hildegard of Bingen and Teilhard de Chardin. Hildegard's music melts everything within me and assures me of the reality of life in the Cosmic Christ, and Teilhard's words inspire me to follow this Christ into the world and participate in God's care for the cosmos and restoration of it. It is so good to hear someone I respect offering respect to others I deeply value.**

> Thank you. I am very glad I gave these people as much discussion as I did. Doing so, however, I was keenly aware that some people who have been journeying with me over recent years will be distressed by some of the ideas I present in this chapter. Some readers won't even get that far in this book! But these people and the other mystics I cite throughout this book have been speaking to me deeply for a long time. Discerning readers have sometimes noticed their lurking presence. I recall

someone writing to me after reading *Surrender to Love* and telling me how much of Teilhard de Chardin he saw in that book. I was quite astounded. I certainly didn't quote him and wasn't even sure I understood him. But I have been spending a considerable amount of time with these mystics for many years now, and no doubt their spirit has influenced mine in deeper ways than I know. So I am happy to be able to bring them front and center in this book, and to be able to affirm my solidarity with their vision of life. If religion is to have any future, I am convinced that it must be a religion that is shaped by the mystics. As noted by Thomas Merton, the spiritual anguish of humans has no cure apart from mysticism.[15] Or in the words of Karl Rahner, "Tomorrow's devout person will either be a mystic—someone who has 'experienced' something—or else they will no longer be devout at all."[16]

10

Spirituality and Awakening

Every step on the journey we have been considering over the last four chapters is full of spiritual significance. The spiritual dimension of life does not wait backstage until we have entered into the higher levels of consciousness. Spirituality is the way we live our life in relation to that which is transcendent to our self. At any point in our journey of awakening, we will relate to this transcendent reference point through the consciousness that characterizes our present level of development. We cannot do otherwise. Consciousness mediates how we perceive and relate to everything beyond the self. It frames the only self that we have, and consequently we have no alternative but to perceive and respond from the platform on which we stand.

The young child has no alternative but to think of God through parental and other authority-figure-colored glasses.[1] Hence there is nothing mysteriously wholly other about God in the eyes of a child. God is simply a powerful human, even more powerful than parents or authority figures. This does not mean that the child is incapable of making a spiritual response. Spiritual response can be made from any developmental platform. But the person operating from within a lower level of consciousness will relate to the Divine in quite different ways than what is possible at later stages of development.

At all times the Spirit is inviting us to be more than we are by calling our attention to that which lies beyond the boundary of our present sense of self. Any awakening is, in effect, a response to an awareness of realities beyond our present self-organization. Such awareness of these realities calls us to redefine and realign our self in relationship to transcendent realities that exist beyond our present awareness.

For example, when consciousness is organized at the level of the body self, the horizon of self-transcendence that is most figural is the mind. It is a step of spiritual response to discover and begin to enter the life of the mind because it presents a larger horizon for the self than that presented in the body. This prepares one for later—at least potentially—making the same shift to the life of the soul and the spirit. These shifts in the organization of consciousness involve a spiritual response. They are not merely the result of the passage of time. The spiritual nature of these responses is seen in the fact that they are acts of openness to something larger than and beyond our self as it presently exists. In each case this involves a posture of willingness (rather than willfulness), faith and trust (as opposed to fear and caution), surrender (rather than an attempt at control), and consent to awakening (rather than a return to sleep). It means offering a fullhearted *yes!* to life, to love, to others, to the world—to that which is beyond or transcendent to our self. By responding in these ways, we open ourselves to the possibility of becoming more than we presently are.

At each point of development, the alternate choice to becoming more than we are is trying to hold on to the life we have. This is also full of spiritual significance. However, the implications of this choice are much less life giving. Life is like breath. It isn't meant to be held, but to be expended and then drawn in with a fresh inhalation. Settling for where one is on the journey of becoming isn't contentment. It is saying no to the invitation of the unceasing invitation of God's Spirit to become more than we are. And any persistent rejection of becoming more than we are ultimately becomes a choice that leads to becoming less. Ultimately it is as stark a choice as that which Moses gave the ancient Israelites: the choice between life and death (Deut. 30:19).

So at any particular point on our journey, the way we choose life will depend on our stage of self-development. We first say *yes!* to life by saying *yes!* to our bodies. At this stage the spiritual is encountered in the embrace of materiality. Trying to rush too quickly beyond this—or failing to ever embrace it and trying to skip over this level of existence—leads to being doomed to a truncated spiritual response and a diminished mind, soul, and spirit. This is one of the great problems with religion. Too easily religion rushes past these foundational steps and tries to take people immediately to the realm of spirit. But there will never be any spiritual depth that is greater than the embrace of all three earlier levels of existence. Only after we first learn to fully embrace body can we then transcend it and move into an equally full embrace of mind. And only after we fully embrace mind can we transcend it and move into an equally full embrace of soul. The same pattern plays itself out with soul and spirit. In order for any stage of the journey to be transcended, it must first be fully embraced.

Each step on the journey of the awakening self is a response to the Spirit and a movement toward transcendence. However, each step can be undertaken in a healthy fashion as it differentiates and integrates the elements of that level, or in a pathological fashion as it either fails to differentiate (and thus remains in fusion and fixation) or fails to integrate (which results in repression, alienation, and dissociation). Ken Wilber points out that healthy development and transcendence are the same thing, since healthy development is always based on transcending while including.[2] Anything that we try to leave behind results in denial, and denial is an expression of pathology, not of transcendence. Every step of genuine transcendence gathers up everything that I am and carries it forward as I become more.

Apart from genuine transcendence, all we have is flirting with higher levels of existence that we are not yet prepared to truly enter. Flirting with these higher levels isn't necessarily a bad thing as long as we don't confuse looking at something from the outside with letting it be our reality. Some flirting can even be helpful when it awakens longings to become. Think, for example, back to John, the foreign affairs correspondent, whom we first met in chapter 3. John's openness to growth and to becoming more than he presently was had been nurtured by his Christian spiritual journey. It would have been tremendously easy for him to confuse the ideal he had come to value with his present reality. But his honesty indicated his openness and thus was an important part of what made his modest involvement in Christian community and its processes of spiritual formation an authentically spiritual response. I recall him saying to me at one point that he had read one of my books that his wife had suggested he read, but had done so quickly because he wasn't yet ready to engage with it fully. I was struck by this degree of self-awareness and honesty. It kept him grounded and allowed him eventually to move deeper into the journey of becoming that he desired.

Yet it is alarmingly easy to loosen one's embrace of reality and confuse flirting with surrender. The ones who have the courage of honesty not to be confused in this way, and who have the willingness to hold the tension of not being where they want to be, these are the ones whose response show openness, faith, and willingness—the hallmarks of authentic spirituality.

Initiative and Consent

Most essentially, spirituality is openness to the Spirit. The Spirit is the engine behind all human becoming. This is why it is more accurate to describe the journey of awakening and unfolding as involving steps of response rather than steps of initiative—response to the initiatives of the Spirit, who continuously invites, woos, supports, sustains, and enables our becoming. Or, if I may change the metaphor, the whole thing is a dance. Your partner is the Spirit, who has already entered the dance floor and is calling for you to come. The Spirit will lead the dance. You only need to follow. Don't hold back from trying to first learn the dance steps. Just get out onto the floor and trust your partner to teach you everything you need to know and to give you everything you need to receive.

One of the great paradoxes of the transformational journey is that effort and initiative are both counterproductive. All that is required of you is consent that is offered in openness and faith. Effort may sometimes be enough to change behavior, but it is never enough to awaken a self. But do not read this limitation of effort in awakening as suggesting that our role is simply to passively await awakening. The offering of consent involves an active response. Awakening is always an active response to the Spirit, and if what we offer is not a response to Spirit, it is not a spiritual response.

Contemporary understandings of Christian spirituality miss this truth much more often than they recognize it. So often the spiritual journey is presented in terms of what we must do. And what we are told we must do is to be faithful in our effort and discipline. This is a recipe for spiritual disaster because what it does is strengthen the false self. When the spiritual journey is my own self-improvement project, the major product will be an ego that is in even more control than before the journey began.

Even the notion of seeking God seems misguided. Describing her own spiritual journey, Simone Weil stated that she had never understood all the talk about seeking God because never once in her life had she sought after God.[3] God found her even without her seeking. We are like the fish in the Sufi tale that was swimming around madly, seeking the sea, only to be confronted by the wise old fish who told the mad swimmer that it could now relax because it was already in the sea; we too do not need to seek the God in whom we exist. Instead, we need to awaken to the truth and reality of our existence. Awakening is not an achievement; it is a grace, a gift that we can receive if we are willing to accept it in openness and faith.

We do not need to engineer our own awakening. Anthony De Mello tells a story of a person sitting by a river seeking enlightenment. The river noticed this person striving to attain something that he could not produce and said: "Does one really have to fret about enlightenment? No matter which way I turn, I'm homeward bound."[4] We too are homeward bound when we notice and then respond to the invitations of Spirit to become all we are meant to be.

Barriers to Becoming

But why would anyone ever say anything other than a fullhearted *yes* in response to the invitation of Spirit to return to our Source? What is so frightening about consent to becoming? Why do we both long for transformation and fear it?

The taproot of our fear of change is our fear of death. If, as argued by Ernest Becker,[5] both personality and civilization are unconsciously shaped by the denial of death, it is clear that we will go to almost any length to protect our selves not just from death but also from awareness of how much it terrifies us. And so, successfully distancing our selves from this core fear of death, we become anxious around anything that threatens our sense of stability and the illusions of permanence we manage to create in life. Instead of learning how to die well, we focus on minimizing change and consequently live and die poorly.

Have no doubt about just how big a change is presented by the transitions between the levels of self-organization. Fear of death makes us want to hold on to whatever we feel we possess, and what we identify with, we easily assume we possess. So "I am my body" easily becomes "My body is mine." The same temptation to shift from identity to possession presents itself at each of the later levels of awakening, although because the self becomes lighter and more expansive at each stage of development, the temptation is lessened. This segue from "me" to "mine" is pernicious, not just because my possessions soon possess me, but also because the emptiness that the self experiences as it lets go of one level of consciousness and consents to the next quickly becomes fullness as I greedily grasp that which I view as mine.

Consent to the invitation of Spirit to become more than I presently am always involves letting go of something safe and secure before I have a firm grasp of anything to replace it. It involves stepping off the platform on which I stand before I have my feet firmly planted anywhere else. Often what follows after stepping off that platform is free fall. But just as we must let go of others to know that we are held, so too we must step off that edge to know that what feels like falling is simply our transition into a more spacious state of being.

At each awakening we stand at a threshold to the next room in this ever-expanding mansion of self that we are becoming. But each threshold feels like a chasm. De Mello tells a story about a conversation between a spiritual master and someone standing at such a chasm, full of fear, but longing for transformation: "Make a clean break with your past and you will be Enlightened," said the master. "I am doing that by degrees." "Growth is achieved by degrees. Enlightenment is instantaneous. Take the leap! You cannot cross a chasm in little jumps."[6]

Growth is more incremental than transformation. This is why so many people settle for working away at their self-improvement projects but shun the letting go that is involved in stepping into the chasm that they find themselves on the edge of at various points in their life. Stepping back from a physical chasm may be understandable, but stepping back from an invitation of the Spirit to openness and trust will always result in a truncation of development.

This brings us, however, to another barrier to becoming that is associated with growth: the parts of our self that have not kept up with the rest in terms of development. In general, the more dimensions of our being that remain stuck at levels beneath the overall level of our consciousness and self-organization, the more our advance to higher levels will be compromised. The highest levels are possible only when the lines of development are increasingly centered in the stage where we are. But we all leave psychological and spiritual resources at lower levels of development and, with somewhat depleted resources, are then at a disadvantage in terms of further developmental advances. Eventually this will hold us back, even though we may be sufficiently ready for advance that it might be possible to creep ahead in terms of substages within a level.

This helps us better understand how growth and transformation are related to each other. Transformation is not the direct result of growth, but failure to mature and grow in the major lines of development compromises transformational possibilities. Every line of development that remains below our overall center of gravity is like a weight holding us back. And conversely, every line on which our level of development is above our overall center of gravity represents a pull toward a higher overall developmental platform.

Psychopathology operates in the same way. If we had to be free of all psychopathology for any advancement of consciousness and identity, none of us would have any possibility of advance beyond the body self. But psychopathology does serve as a transformational impediment; in general, the more serious the pathology, the greater the impediment. We have already seen, for example, how certain psychopathologies can keep our awareness and identity tied to our bodies. Others may not lead to a specific body focus but simply keep us internally preoccupied and reduce our capacity for transcendence.

Readiness to move ahead, however, is not simply a matter of either relative freedom from debilitating psychopathology or developmental lags. The spiritual posture of openness and trust that I have described involves a readiness to come to the edge and then let go. It thus involves trusting openness to that which is beyond the self. Transcendence always requires a relationship to the self-transcendent, and in order for us to experience authentic transformation, this relationship must be characterized by faith that is expressed in trust. We cannot pull ourselves up to higher levels of consciousness by our own bootstraps. Genuine transformation always involves a cooperative response to the initiative of the Spirit. What makes us ready for it is simply our willing consent.

Such consent does not have to be total. We can only be as open and trusting as we can be in any moment. Any measure of faith is enough to start the process moving. Each expression of openness and trust produces its own rewards. Each involves an awakening and leads to a less obstructed flow of life through us.

Jesus said that an unobstructed eye results in a body that is full of light (Matt. 6:22). But similarly, an unobstructed mind results in a person that is full of wisdom, and an unobstructed heart results in a person that is full of love. Removing obstructions lets the river of life flow through us. Living waters flow into us and then pass through us, bringing nourishment and growth to all whose life touches ours. In short, we become unobstructed channels of Spirit.

Every genuine opening of the self in trust leads to a more unobstructed self and furthers the journey of the awakening self. Awareness is the fruit of such an unobstructed opening of self. But the openness that is required for awareness involves a great deal of vulnerability. The risk of openness is that we might be hurt. The risk of awareness is that we might have to change. But this risk is why awareness is so essential to transformation. And the risk is why we so easily settle for oblivion rather than the genuine presence to life that awareness involves.

Spirituality is indispensable to any journey of human becoming. The spirituality that supports the awakening and unfolding of the self will always involve more than beliefs. Although we shall see in a moment how important practice is to any authentic spirituality, transformational spirituality will always involve more than things we do. More fundamental than what we do or think is our openness to the Spirit. This and this alone can produce a transformation of consciousness that then flows into the rest of our existence.

Spiritual Practices

Spiritual practices that contribute to transformation are those that offer opportunities to practice openness, surrender, and willingness. This immediately eliminates much of what we often do when we follow the so-called disciplines of the spiritual life. It is alarmingly easy for practices to simply strengthen willfulness, and when they do, they further reinforce us against transformation. However, most spiritual practices can be offered in a spirit of openness, surrender, and willingness, and when they do, they prepare us for saying *yes!* to the Spirit when next we are presented with a choice of backing away from the chasm or stepping into it.

Think, for example, of a devotional reading of the Scriptures. We can come to the Scriptures out of either duty or desire, and we can engage them either seeking to find words and concepts that will reinforce what we already know or with openness to encountering the Living Word that will raise us from our slumber and self-preoccupation. Approaching the Bible not as a book of helpful spiritual teachings or theological truths but as the Word through which the Spirit can breathe life is approaching it in a way that helps us cultivate openness and prepares us for a response of willing surrender.

Prayer should also be an opening of our self to God.[7] Even though Christians believe that God is both beyond and within us, the Divine encounter is always internal. We don't have to leave our self and go to a church or for a walk in nature to meet God. Instead, we meet God within our self. Each dimension of self that we learn to open to God is a place of encounter with the Spirit of transformation. Properly understood, holistic prayer is an opening of the totality of self so that we might encounter God in the totality of our being. This is why holistic prayer includes not just the conscious mind (words and thoughts) but also our bodies, emotions, imagination, unconscious, and much more. Prayer as an opening of our self to God is prayer as a spiritual practice with enormous transformational potential.

The spiritual practices of any tradition that have the most transformational potential are those with a contemplative dimension. This is because they are the ones that are most firmly grounded in stillness before self and the Divine. It is in this stillness that we best learn true openness, and thus it is here that the Spirit has the most opportunity to work in our depths in ways that can prepare us for further becoming.

I speak of a contemplative dimension to our spiritual practices rather than simply the practice of meditation or contemplative prayer because, properly understood, contemplation is a way of living, not simply a form of praying. Prayer is much more than praying. Prayer can be our whole life, just as our whole life can be a prayer. But if it is to become this, we must learn prayer as being, not simply prayer as doing. The contemplative dimension of any spiritual practice helps us step back from doing to being. It recognizes that the essence of prayer is an encounter of being with Being. It is, we could say, a knowing of our being-in-Being. It is standing naked before Ultimate Reality in the reality of our own being.

Authentic spirituality will always involve direct experience of Living Reality that is disclosed immediately but recognized gradually by awareness that will emerge from spiritual practice. Contemplative stillness is the place of deep transformational encounter with our own self and with the Spirit. This is the hearth in which the alchemy of transformation makes us more than we are. Without regular times of such stillness, we will remain caught up in our psychospiritual self-improvement projects and our growth will have little transformational potential. With such times, we will become more than we are. It is as simple as that.

Contemplative stillness is essential because it allows us to step back from the ordinary background noise of consciousness at our respective level of self-development and organization. It allows us to notice our preoccupations and identifications and set them aside in an act of surrender. The goal is not to eliminate anything but to release everything. For only then do we discover that we are not defined by what we hold, but by whom we are held.

Jacob Böhme tells the story of a spiritual seeker (whom, in sixteenth-century language, he calls a scholar) and a spiritual master that illustrates the process and fruit of stepping back from the preoccupations of ordinary consciousness:

> The scholar said to his master: How may I come to the supersensual life, that I may see God and hear Him speak? The master said: When thou canst throw thyself but for a moment into that place where no creature dwelleth, then thou hearest what God speaketh. The scholar asked: Is that near or far off? The master replied: It is in thee, and if thou canst for a while cease from all thy thinking and willing, thou shalt hear unspeakable words of God. The scholar said: How can I hear, when I stand still from thinking and willing? The master answered: When thou standest still from the thinking and willing of self, the eternal hearing, seeing, and speaking will be revealed to thee, and so God heareth and seeth through thee.[8]

Stepping back from the din of ordinary consciousness allows us to become aware of the things we identify with and to which we attach ourselves. This awareness then presents us with the option of gently releasing whatever it is that is in our awareness.[9] We become aware of a thought and gently release it. We become aware of an emotion or a sensation and we gently release it. We become aware of God's presence and gently release even that. We become aware even of our awareness, and we release that. This is not the time to savor the contents of awareness but rather the time to release them so that, in the nakedness of our being, we might encounter Ultimate Being. Spending regular time in this place is the most important single way in which we can express our consent to Spirit. It therefore is the foundation of any transformational spiritual practice. (See appendix 2 for a fuller discussion of meditation and its role in awakening.)

Spiritual Development

One important question about spirituality that we have not addressed to this point is whether it is one dimension of development along with many others (emotional, faith, cognitive, interpersonal, etc.), or whether it is a quality of the development of the whole person. Arguments have been made for both positions although, since the early church fathers, the bulk of those who have thought about this issue have come down on the side of spirituality being a unique dimension of development. I thought of it just this way myself for a long time. However, as I look more at the whole person that makes the journey of transformational awakening, I have come to think of our spirituality as a characteristic of that whole self—something that is potentially integral to the development of every other dimension of self and definitely essential to the transformation of the whole.

Daniel Helminiak argues that "spiritual development is nothing other than human development viewed from a particular perspective."[10] The reason I am convinced that this is right is that spirituality is itself a perspective on life. Recall that I defined it as the way we live in relationship to that which is transcendent to the self. The relationship to the Transcendent is the perspective from which we view people if we seek to understand their spirituality. And if we seek to understand their spiritual development, we view them from this perspective over time and watch how this relationship to the Transcendent influences their development.

If spiritual development is the development of the whole person, then the levels of existence we have used to chart the journey of the awakening self provide us with one way of mapping spiritual development. Other people have mapped this in different ways, but the names of the stages are not as important as an understanding of what things change in our relationship to the Transcendent as we make this journey. In reflecting on this, I will not try to explain, either metaphysically or theologically, the great mystery of our relationship to the Transcendent. But well short of this, let me draw several helpful insights from the understanding of spiritual development offered by Daniel Helminiak,[11] whose work on this topic I find very helpful.

Helminiak begins his attempt to understand spiritual development with the human spirit. Following Bernard Lonergan, he defines human spirit as our radical drive for self-transcending authenticity. By starting with the human spirit, not a self-transcendent divine Spirit, he offers a nontheistic transcendent principle that he suggests must be central to any understanding of spiritual development. The drive of the human spirit toward authentic self-transcendence may, as I have argued earlier, be understood as a response to the constantly outpouring life of the Spirit; but it is also an intrinsic part of being human. This quest for authenticity is such a fundamental part of the human spirit that a commitment to authenticity (not simply self-transcendence) is, in my view, necessary but not sufficient for all development beyond the mental self.

Self-transcending authenticity always involves a cost; we, like the person in the parable of the pearl told by Jesus (Matt. 13:45–46), must have our eyes and heart so set on the pearl of inestimable value that we will be prepared to do anything to get it. Because of the immense value of the pearl of authenticity and self-transcendence that we seek, no price is too high. This is the motive behind our openness. But our whole person must be involved; because the whole person is at stake in spiritual development, nothing less will do.

The result of this seeking and desiring openness is that the person will become increasingly authentic, increasingly at one within his or her self, and increasingly anchored in a place that is transcendent to the small self that begins the journey. These characterizations of self-actualization, self-consistency, and self-transcendence are characterizations of the whole person, not descriptions of some spiritual parts of the individual or their relationship to the Divine. Spiritual development involves growth of the whole person, and this will be noticed across the lines of development that we considered in chapter 3.

Spiritual development is a human phenomenon, not a religious one. It is human development organized around the quest for authenticity and self-transcendence. The content of one's faith can either block this development or facilitate it. Religion therefore can either be part of the problem or part of the solution.

Religion and Transformation

Religion's power to inspire people to live authentically and orient themselves toward the self-transcendent is immense. At its best, it puts us in touch with the mythic and archetypal mysteries that shape our lives and serves as a powerful force to move us along the path of ever-self-transcending human becoming. It also provides a framework that allows us to be in contact with the transcendent while remaining grounded in the realities of ordinary life. Religion also provides us with stories that have the potential to be big enough to make life meaningful, regardless of whatever comes our way. It teaches us what it means to be human and how to live with authenticity, purpose, and meaning. And religion shows us how to live in a trusting and open relationship with that which is beyond the self while at the same time connecting us back to the roots of our existence and of our shared humanity.

Religion holds unique potential to teach us how to journey through the great mysteries of life—such things as love, loss, sex, failure, suffering, and death. But it can also eliminate the mystery and transformational potency of these life experiences. And while nothing has the power of religion to transform and expand consciousness, it can also freeze development in the early stages of the journey and keep people in small places. This is always at the expense of the human spirit, which must be anesthetized to become comfortable with absence of self-transcendence. But that too is the power of religion: it can be a force either for good or for bad.

Ken Wilber suggests two extremely important and unique contributions that religion can make to the transformational journey. The first is that religion provides the only credible source of authority that can sanction the higher stages of human development for those within any given spiritual tradition.[12] Christianity, for example, can pronounce such things as being at one with God and at one with all of creation as integral parts of the Christian vision of the journey into God and by doing so make the spirit-centered levels of consciousness and self-organization legitimate and sacred. The second crucially important contribution that religion can make is to support contemplative spiritual practices. Religion is the most legitimate context for these practices; recognizing their unique potential to aid transformation through the expansion of consciousness, Wilber states: "No other single practice or technique—not therapy, not breathwork, not transformative workshops, not role-taking, not hatha yoga—has been empirically demonstrated to do this. Meditation alone has done so."[13] Transformation apart from a religious context will, therefore, be limited—this according to Ken Wilber, a person who has not always been a friend to religion.

But religion does not accomplish any of this in some generic way. Religion displays its potency when it provides a living tradition that can become meaningful to people as they are embedded in a community that is grounded in a spiritual tradition; that encourages growth, change, and transformation; and that provides a theological context to understand it. The possibilities for this are all present and readily accessible within Christianity. Authentic Christianity already clearly includes a vision of how humans can enjoy a growing participation in God. This is more than what it is often reduced to—a relationship with God. It is a real participation in the very life of God, a participation that is validated by the Scriptures and testified to by the mystics of our tradition. Daniel Helminiak states: "Belief in human divinization is at the core of Christianity. This belief is inextricably linked with belief in Jesus Christ as the Eternally Begotten of God who became human and in his humanity attained divine glory through his resurrection and so introduced into history a new goal for human fulfillment. In his resurrection, Jesus thus becomes the paradigm of human divinization. Others' attainments of divinization in Christ depends on the gift of the Holy Spirit."[14]

Spirituality therefore is indispensible to the journey of awakening, and nonreligious spirituality operates at a distinct disadvantage in relationship to spirituality that is nourished by its embeddedness within a living tradition and a meaningful communal context. In the next chapter, we turn to a more careful consideration of this communal and interpersonal context of awakening.

Dialogue and Reflection

1. I was interested in your suggestion that the face of the transcendent is different at each of the levels of development. Are you saying that God is experienced differently at each level, or am I reading too much into this?

    That wasn't quite the point I was making, but I would say that God is experienced differently as our consciousness expands.

This is one of the reasons why our personal theology has to be updated as our consciousness and self-organization develops. The body-centered self, for example, cannot conceive of a self that is not embodied. Because ghosts are the most readily available selves without bodies in Western culture, God therefore becomes ghostlike, this made all the easier because the Spirit of God is referred to as the Holy Ghost. Similarly, to the mind-centered self, God is pure intelligence and rationality. Scholastic theology and much contemporary systematic theology reflect this sort of overly intellectual way of approaching God. To the soul-centered self, God is met in reflection, introspection, and intuition, not merely in reason. God correspondingly becomes bigger as the self becomes bigger. This culminates in the experience of the spirit-centered self where the person discovers that their very existence is in God and that God holds them and everything else within the Divine self. So yes, God is indeed experienced quite differently at each level of consciousness.

2. **What do you mean by flirting with higher levels of development, and why is it a potentially good thing to do?**

What I mean by flirting is exploring things that I am not ready to truly make my own. I began reading the mystics while still in university, decades before I was ready to make contemplative stillness a meaningful part of my own life. Something deep within my spirit drew me to Thomas Merton, John of the Cross, Teresa of Avila, and others whom I couldn't really understand but kept reading for reasons that I also didn't fully understand. Now I believe that this was the response of my spirit to God's Spirit's calling me to deeper places. I call it flirtation because I kept my engagement with the things I was encountering safely superficial. I was getting ideas, but none of what I encountered was getting me. Why do I say that this can be good as long as you don't confuse what you read about as your own experience? Simply because I was responding to my questing spirit as it responded to the invitations to deeper life offered by God's Spirit. All we can do is all we can do, and at that stage and for many years afterward, all I could offer was my mind. My spirit longed for more, but I kept it safely constrained by my mind. But we must start where we are and offer what we can, and that is how I now, in retrospect, understand this part of my own journey.

3. **You suggest that we are all homeward bound. Are we really? I thought many were heading in quite the opposite direction.**

This is a big question, and my answer must be small and necessarily quite limited—not just by space and focus but also by virtue of being a psychologist, not a theologian. I do believe that we are all homeward bound. I can come to no other conclusion when I recall that our origin is God and that it is God's intention that no one be lost, regardless of how far we wander or what path we take. I simply do not believe that God's love and redemptive intentions will fail. We are in the river that is flowing back to its source. We are in God, and one day we will know that truth more fully and clearly than now. But I do recognize that many Christians do not see it this way. I take comfort, however, in knowing that my own position is far from fringe and that I am not alone in leaning into God with the confidence that I do in this regard.

4. **I didn't like the sound of an invitation to the edge of a chasm, then being asked to step off and let go. Any additional comments on this?**

This may not be the way you or I would arrange existence if we were God and putting this whole thing together ourselves. But let me ask you a question. Think back to the moments on your own journey that were most transformational. Is it not true that these were times when you were no longer in control? And did not the deep changes in you that resulted come from trusting and going ahead and stepping out, regardless of your fear and uncertainty? I suspect that it did because that is how it has been for anyone who has ever talked with me about their journey. This is what makes it a journey of faith. If we could see where we were going, and if we could have our feet planted on the next platform, being asked to step off the one we are on wouldn't require faith. But from beginning to end, the journey of awakening and becoming is a journey of faith.

5. **The special place that you suggest for contemplative spiritual practices in transformation sounds elitist to me. Any comment?**

Suggesting that contemplative practices have distinctive transformational potential would only be elitist if these practices were available to only a small number of spiritual giants. But this is simply not true. Far from being the most advanced practices, I count the contemplative ones to be the most basic and natural. Children know how to step outside themselves and their preoccupations by immersing themselves in contemplative engagement with things. Just watch a four-year-old play with a fluff ball or watch in fascination as a butterfly flits by. It is only adults who need to relearn this posture of an absorbing openness in stillness. When we do, we learn that this posture is not a retreat from life but a way of living life more fiercely. It isn't an alternative to action but preparation for action that distills the buzz of distracting noise and brings one into the present moment. I reject that this is elitist because I affirm that it is accessible by everyone, regardless of personality, gender, age, or maturity. Contemplation is a way of knowing and a way of being in the world, not just a spiritual practice or discipline. Contemplative prayer can therefore be a way of life, not just a form of prayer.

6. **Earlier you said that despite all its rhetoric, most religion is hostile to transformation. And yet in this chapter you suggest important contributions that religion can make to transformation. How do these statements fit together?**

The short answer is that despite the ambivalence that many religious authorities have about genuine transformation that they do not control, religion retains an absolutely indispensable role in transformation. Sadly, the people who talk most about transformation are often the ones most resistant to releasing the reins of control and allowing the Spirit to guide this process. Religious institutions and communities that may value transformation in theory easily become invested in controlling the spiritual experiences of their members. They fear that those who respond to the Spirit in a way that is not mediated by them might wander away; hence, acting in an alarmingly parental way, they sometimes try to protect us from what they think might harm us. But self-interest clouds their judgment, and the consequences are disastrous for genuine transformation and growth. Yet this does not change the fact that these same people have enormous potential to contribute positively to the growth and transformation of those within their communities. This is what I will talk more about in the next chapter.

11

The Communal Context
of Transformation

Carl Jung argued—correctly, I think—that it is impossible to become conscious without a relationship with another person. He expands on this: "The unrelated human being lacks wholeness, for he can achieve wholeness only through the soul, and the soul cannot exist without its other side, which is always found in a You. Wholeness is a combination of I and You, and these show themselves to be parts of a transcendent unity."[1]

Consciousness always arises in the interplay of a self and something beyond the self, and it develops in the same context. It is not something that we create. Rather, consciousness forms in response to the dynamic interactions of relationship. The same is true of the self. Psychoanalytic object-relations theory has shed considerable light on the formation and development of the self, a process that we now know is interpersonal to the very core. Most psychoanalysts no longer think of the constituent parts of the self as intrapsychic dynamisms such as id, ego, or superego. Rather, we understand that what we experience as our self is a collection of internalized representations of significant interpersonal relationships combined with some basic ego structures, functions, and dynamics. If the formation of both the self and consciousness are, therefore, as much an interpersonal process as this suggests, how obvious it should be that the re-formation and transformation of both self and consciousness will necessarily also have a significant interpersonal context.

Up to this point I have written about the transformational journey as if it were something we undertake on our own. Too often this is how we think of it, as something we work out within ourselves. But this is far from the truth. Although moments of awakening are certainly possible apart from the presence of anyone else, it is impossible to separate out the interpersonal experiences that prepare the person for these moments. However, a moment of awakening is, as we have seen, not necessarily enough for the individual to stay awake and continue the quest toward authenticity and self-transcendence that we have seen to be indispensable to transformation. That commitment and continuing quest develop within an interpersonal context, and the journey that they lead to, if it is to result in transformation, will always unfold within and between communities of others who either facilitate or impede awakening and unfolding.

Holding and Unfolding

We gain our first glimpse of the developmental importance of a person's psychosocial environment in infants. Observing the interactions of mothers and their young children, the English pediatrician and psychoanalyst Donald Winnicott argued that what caretakers provide is not just care but also what he called a "holding environment."[2] Holding is everything that mothers do for their infant that produces a sense of wholeness and well-being. It includes both the coming together of their bodies as well as the times when they are apart because its most essential feature involves the way mothers (or other caretakers) attune themselves to and respond to the infant. An ideal holding environment provides continuity with the holding that was experienced in the womb and allows the infant to develop the foundation of basic trust that is essential for all future development.

The importance of this concept is, however, far from limited to infants and their interactions with caretakers. Understood most broadly, an optimal holding environment is intrinsic to all human unfolding at every stage of the journey. Throughout life we are held by a succession of environments that either support our continued growth and development or hinder it. Our family, in both its primary and extended forms, represents for many the most important of these environments. But the secondary communities within which we participate and belong also hold us at various stages of our journey. Some of these communal contexts remain with us for our entire life; others are an important environment for only a stage of the journey. Often they overlap with each other, one decreasing in importance as another increases. Sometimes our transition out of a community that is providing more constraint than support for our growth is difficult—on occasions, even traumatic. Other transitions are smoother. And a fortunate few find themselves in a community that evolves as they evolve, and hence they are able to remain within it for much of their life.

I have already suggested that this journey of spiritual unfolding happens best within a communal context. Most people on an intentional spiritual journey are within communities of fellow seekers of some sort or another. I know many people whose community of reference and significance is on their bookshelf. Many of those whose lives have most influenced me and whose companionship on my own journey of awakening has been most significant are people whom I have encountered only through their books. With increasing technological developments, the primary spiritual community of many more people is in cyberspace, where they connect with others by means of Twitter, Facebook, email, Internet forums, blogs, wikis, podcasts, virtual game worlds, and virtual communities—to name but a few of these ever-evolving e-communities. While technology can certainly isolate, there is no question that these and other social media provide many people with a form of community. It used to be that people who stopped going to church sometimes spoke of TV evangelists as providing their church replacement, but now the options are much greater and are much more genuinely communal.

Humans are more than individuals. Robert Kegan states that the very word *individual* refers only to those dimensions of a person that are individuated or differentiated from others.[3] But there will always be dimensions of the person that remain embedded in one's own communal contexts. Kegan suggests that to reflect this fact, rather than speaking of individuals, we should speak of persons as "embedduals." There is never just a you: "At this very moment your own buoyancy or lack of it, your own sense of wholeness or lack of it, is in large part a function of how your own current embeddedness culture is holding you."[4]

Knowing When to Let Go

Life is a succession of holding environments and cultures of embeddedness. Environments that support growth, transformation, and human becoming must do three things: They must hold, they must then let go, and they must stick around long enough so that we can be reintegrated in the next community that will hold us.

The first thing a holding environment must do is hold, but it must do this in a way that does not confine. Holding refers to supporting, not controlling. To hold without constraining is the first requirement of care. Pathological holding environments always fail first at this level, and this makes it impossible for them ever to progress to the second and third tasks.

Holding is allowing the other to attach to you. You must first allow embeddedness to develop if there is to be subsequent differentiation. Just as the mother (or caretaker) must allow attachment, so too subsequent holding environments must do the same. In later stages of life, this will manifest itself in terms of identification—"I am my community"—but the core of the attachment remains the same. I feel connected to and a part of something larger than myself, with which I am fused. I belong. I am part of something that supports my existence.

Yet that holding must always anticipate letting go. If it does not, it is clutching, something that arises from the needs of the individual or community that is doing the holding. A good holding environment—whether it is an individual, a family, or a social group or community of some sort—will always be a good host, and this means avoiding tightening the holding in such a way as to create dependence.

The prototype of all human holding is the womb. Here the fetus is supported and nourished as it develops. But when gestation is complete, the womb releases the newborn and delivers the infant to a new environment. If the womb didn't let go, it would have exercised a fatal constraint.

The second function of a holding environment is that it must let go. Or better, it should prepare the person for a timely process in which he or she outgrows the need for the sort of holding that is initially offered. Good parents prepare their children for independence, and good communities should do the same.

A few years ago I was asked to assist a large church in exploring how they might introduce a contemplative component to their communal life. I was surprised by the invitation because, from what

I knew of them by reputation, their culture was quite distant from anything contemplative. While spending some time with their leadership, I discovered that they were primarily interested in contemplative practices because they were losing significant numbers of their most spiritually mature adherents to liturgical churches that had a more contemplative tradition. When I asked why they wouldn't feel gratified that they had been able to help people move to the stage of their journey where they could now benefit from something a little different, one of the senior pastors said, "I hate to use business terms, but the short answer is that we are concerned that we are losing our market share." Covering for him, another quickly added that of course they were concerned about the continuing spiritual growth of their members, not just market share, and that they really believed that they were in the best position in their city to give people what they needed—and to give them everything that they needed for every stage of their spiritual journey. I was quite taken aback by the arrogance this displayed but on reflection realized how typical their possessiveness of adherents probably was. Perhaps what made them different from most other churches was simply their success in keeping as many people dependent on them for as long as they did. But many other churches undoubtedly share their assumption that they have everything their members and adherents could ever need spiritually.

Letting go supports differentiation. We need to belong, but we are more than our communities. Ideally, therefore, we need to be able to experience the embeddedness but also experience support for disembedding. This does not have to mean disidentifying; it simply means seeing myself as more than my holding environment. This is what it means to differentiate myself from my environment. Dis-identification always reveals the absence of a smooth process of letting go and subsequent differentiation. The world is filled with people who not only no longer attend church but who also actively disidentify with their religious past. All lacked the support of a church environment that was able to help them move on. Those who have the good fortune of such support do not need to be against religion, Christianity, fundamentalism, or whatever particular face of religion they found constraining and nonsupportive of their journey of becoming. They can simply continue their journey of finding their faith and footing in the ways they need to do so.

In addition to holding and then letting go, the third task of a culture of embeddedness is remaining in place during the period of transition. When this happens, that which was me, and over time became merely an important part of me, can now gradually become part of my story. Growth that involves genuine transcendence of earlier positions demands that we reconcile with those places of holding and the associated identifications. Apart from this we merely move on but fail to move beyond. Growth requires that we reconcile our self with what we previously identified with as self. This is the way in which we develop an ever more encompassing meaning for our selves, our lives, and the world. As H. Richard Niebuhr puts it, "We understand what we remember, remember what we forgot and make familiar what before seemed alien."[5]

Speaking of how this happens within families, Robert Kegan explains, "It takes a special wisdom for the family of an adolescent to understand that by remaining in place so that the adolescent can have the family there to ignore and reject, the family is providing something very important, and is still, in a new way, intimately and importantly involved in the child's development."[6] But I also think it takes a very special spiritual community or church to do the same. It takes a big perspective and firm trust in the possibilities of the Spirit's operating outside the bounds of our community not to interpret someone moving on as our failure. But what a gift we give when we can stay involved long enough to help them with the transition and ensure that by doing so, they truly do move beyond, not simply on.

Nothing is harder for communities than to support members who feel a need to move beyond the community. The healthiest communities of belonging do this well and therefore always remain an important part of the person who needs to move beyond them. The unhealthiest are those who perceive as failure the fact that they do not have everything that members need at every stage of their journey. But this is simply taking the matter too personally. It is tribal functioning rather than truly communal functioning. Such groups need to get over themselves and see that communities exist for the support of others, not their control. Like enmeshed families or codependent marriages and partnerships, such communities fail to see the other as separate from themselves and to celebrate this fact and then help people achieve this differentiation in a healthy manner.

Robert Kegan summarizes three faces of the holding that we need as our journey of unfolding occurs within and between communal contexts. They are confirmation, contradiction, and continuity.[7] We confirm the existence of another person by providing a warm, close, emotionally supportive presence that is attuned to them and affirms their uniqueness and presence. We contradict (or challenge) the existence of this person when we nudge them out of the comfortable nest when it seems time for them to disembed and find their life beyond the place it has provided. And we then provide continuity when we remain in relationship in order to allow the person to move through the transition into this new embeddedness. At any given moment the question in a person's development is how well their culture of embeddedness is performing these three functions. Each time a particular culture holds securely, it ensures the integrity of the person and of itself as a community that genuinely exists to aid the development of people. Each time it assists in letting go, it attests to the community's greater loyalty to the person-who-is-becoming than to the person-who-is. Performed well, these things assure the person that he or she can continue to grow, and they assure the community of the person's continued relationship to them in some form or another.[8]

Healthy and Unhealthy Transitions

The families and communities that provide our support and identification have a crucial role in our success in navigating the transitions between the developmental plateaus on the journey of awakening and unfolding. Unhealthy holding leads us to separate ourselves not only from our old meanings but also from the people and commitments that have formed us. This is always a tragic outcome. It results in a disruption of development that leaves many people stuck for the rest of their life in postures of dis-identification (being against beliefs and practices that previously defined them). One has only to look at the former fundamentalists and other religionists whose passions are now directed against the beliefs and values that were previously theirs to see the magnitude of this tragedy. This is an extremely costly life course. But it is preventable. All that is required is long-term support for people who will necessarily change and grow on their journey of becoming. Holding them before, during, and after their transitions will help the person who moves beyond their community acknowledge and grieve the losses that are associated with this transition while at the same time acknowledging and celebrating all they learned and became during their period of close identification with it.

Let me illustrate these two possibilities by means of two people, Erin and Bas. Many aspects of their personalities and histories are similar. The differences are primarily in their cultures of embeddedness and how these communal contexts managed their points of transition.

Erin was born into a fundamentalist Christian family in the Bible Belt of the United States. Her family was not as legalistic as her church, but her religious community was at least as formative in her development as her parents. And that influence was not as benign. Erin grew up believing that the only Christians were those within her Bible church tradition. She was also taught that science and the world (meaning "secular" culture) were the enemies of faith. The church also had a distinct anti-intellectual bias. Questions were seen as expressions of doubt. This puzzled Erin since she had a fertile mind and endless intellectual curiosity, but quickly she learned to keep this part of her life private. Unfortunately, however, her intellect also became isolated from her faith, which increasingly became simply a matter of unthinking compliance with things that made less and less sense to her. It wasn't doubt that bothered her. It was that she felt she was being asked to leave her mind at the door when she came to church. Her parents never discouraged her questions, but neither did they affirm them. Erin often wondered if they had brought the wrong baby home from the hospital because she felt so different from the rest of her family. But she was a compliant child, and over time few seemed to notice her uniqueness.

One thing her family and friends did notice, however, was that, as her mother described it, Erin always had her head in a book. She had been a voracious reader since she was seven or eight years old. In contrast, most of her teenage friends didn't read for pleasure, and if they did, it was limited to magazines. But Erin constantly had at least one novel on the go, devoured the daily newspaper, and every week would come back from the library with an armful of books on whatever subjects had caught her attention. Everything she read broadened her world. But it also made her feel that the world she had absorbed from family and church was too small. It wasn't that she had trouble with any of the specific teachings of the church. It was simply that her spirit was calling her to larger places.

As she was approaching graduation from high school, her church friends pursuing higher education all headed to the nearby Christian college. Erin felt that this was her chance to branch out into the world that had been beckoning her. She told her parents that she wanted to study at the state university. Although they were nervous about her going to a "secular" college, they somehow found it within themselves to support her decision. It actually represented something of a shift for them. Although they spent the rest of their lives happily with the same church, it was at that point that they were finally able to acknowledge that Erin was destined to leave it. As Erin was leaving for college her father told her that they recognized that their world was not a good fit for her and that although it scared them, they were excited to see her reach out and find her own way.

The next few years were wonderful for Erin and very important for her development. She quickly connected with other Christians through a campus ministry and was excited to discover a broader faith tradition that seemed to warmly embrace her mind. She also found herself sharing much more of her journey and discoveries with her parents. Although she was living away from home, she never felt closer to them. Increasingly they expressed interest in what she was reading, thinking, and learning. They almost never expressed disagreement with any of the ideas she found herself entertaining, although she could tell that they were often uncomfortable with where it was leading her. Erin's parents told her that they trusted her and were just happy that she remained a committed Christian, even if she chose to attend an evangelical church.

A few years later, when Erin was living in another part of the country and told her parents that she was attending a more liturgical church and finding it really nourishing for her faith, once again they were able to offer the same support. Her former church took this transition fairly well. Her pastor warned her about the dangers of attending a "liberal" church and told her she couldn't expect the same close fellowship he knew she had appreciated in their evangelical community, but he was able to affirm her quest to deepen her faith by pursuing her interest in a more contemplative approach to worship. Some of her church friends, however, had trouble understanding her decision to leave their church. They seemed to take it as a personal rejection. One close friend told her that she was troubled by her talk of a spiritual journey. She said that she didn't understand why being a good Christian was not enough. She had found faith and belonging, and Erin's questing spirit was a challenge to her way of being in the world. But by this point Erin had come to realize that her own journey was more important to her than any specific friendship. She also realized that a failure to respond to the yearnings of her spirit would do irrevocable damage to her soul.

Once again the holding of her family and the support of both her former and current churches allowed Erin to make this transition well. At the point where I met her, she showed little or no reactivity to her very conservative past. She was convinced that the questing spirit and fertile mind that God had given her were gifts, not curses. And she continued to follow the Spirit, using her own deep longings to lead her forward. The most recent of these longings came in the form of an attraction to silence and to using it as a means of deeper knowing of herself and God. She had also been reading about meditation and felt that this was something she wanted to explore for herself. She didn't know where this would lead her, but she had come to know that she needed to follow this sense of calling. She felt supported in this by her present church, but she also trusted that she would always be able to find some people who understood and shared the most important parts of her journey, wherever that might take her. She did not simply unfold on her own. The communities that held her were sufficiently successful in each of the three tasks of any good holding environment so that she was able to move ahead and become more than she was.

Bas was raised in an equally conservative and religious home of second-generation Dutch immigrants. But his unfolding was much more constrained by his communities of support. His childhood church had a strong ethnic quality that grounded his identity in being a Dutch neo-Calvinist. Not surprisingly, this was not a big-enough identity for him as an adolescent, and as soon as his unfolding began to reflect a unique path, he ran into conflict with his authoritarian father. The conflicts were around rather typical adolescent issues: his friends and how he spent his time. Yet the friends in question were other Christians his age who were also in Christian families and who attended church regularly. The problem was that they were from another church, one that his father called "Canadian," in contrast to their own. His father was extremely upset that Bas, now eighteen years old, couldn't seem to find good-enough friends within his own church, and even worse, that he wanted to go with his friends to their church's youth group. At this point his father contacted his pastor, and his pastor, sensing an intractable conflict, contacted me, asking if I could help the family.

Unfortunately, I wasn't able to be of much help. I was involved with the family off and on for nearly a year, but one conflict was simply followed by another. His father was as committed to keeping

Bas within the fold as Bas was committed to finding his own way. And so, by the time Bas turned nineteen, I began to work with him alone, hoping to help him secure as healthy an independence from his family as was possible.

A number of things impressed me about Bas. He was a reflective and very creative young man who was full of potential and who displayed a good deal of maturity. The hurts he had experienced at the hands of his father were real and significant, but as he worked through them, he showed a surprising willingness to let go of the resentment. He told me how he realized that his father was a victim of his own upbringing, and he vowed he would not be similarly victimized. I was also struck by his spiritual openness, something I would not have expected after the religious pressure he had experienced. He moved out of his home, began to live with one of his friends, and seemed to find life in the church that he began attending with this friend. One day, with tremendous excitement, he told me that he had become a Christian. I was a little surprised at this since I assumed that he had been a Christian all along, but this conversion in an evangelical church felt to him like the start of his spiritual journey, not its next stage. I understood the sense of being a new person and his excitement about this awakening. His parents, however, were much less excited. On hearing this news, his father took it as the last nail in the coffin of their relationship and informed Bas that he was no son to him, nor would he ever be until he reclaimed the faith of his baptism.

This was a blow he had not expected, and it set him back. Not only did it make it harder for Bas to move beyond and not simply away from his family, but it also made it hard for him to integrate his early religious heritage in any healthy way before transcending it. He was more successful in forgiving his father than in finding a healthy way to deal with his religious upbringing. Bas was extremely upset when his former pastor contacted him and tried to convince him that he had been a Christian all along and that his more recent "conversion" was a step away from God because it had taken him away from his heritage and the baptismal vows that were made on his behalf as an infant. Years of conditioned response to the authority that a pastor carried in their tradition made it even harder to deal with the former pastor than it had been with his father. He didn't feel anger as much as confusion. He began to wonder if what he needed to do was get away from the church entirely and make a clean break with his past. This is exactly what he did, but the break was not as clean as he had hoped.

I lost touch with Bas soon after this and didn't hear from him again for several years. He next contacted me for a character reference when he went to university as a mature student in his late twenties. He told me he was now an atheist and was much happier. However, he didn't seem happy to me. Bas seemed quite angry. Those in his new community of support seemed to be as defined as he was by anger at the religious communities that had hurt and oppressed them. I next saw Bas nearly twenty years later, when he came up to speak to me after I had given a public lecture in the city where he was now living. I was struck by the fact that he was much more at peace than I had ever seen him. He told me he had been married and divorced and now had custody of two children from that marriage. Somehow he had managed to become a better father to his children than his father had been to him.

Nevertheless, his unfolding had been seriously compromised. I recalled a young man full of passion and idealism, and what I saw now was a middle-aged man who had settled down in life but who had lost the fire in the belly that had once been so striking in him. When I had worked with him, Bas often shared poems and other things he wrote, and so I asked him if he was still writing. He told me that his creativity had dried up and that he hadn't written anything for years. But it was more than his creativity that had dried up. His soul had atrophied. I felt sad to see the compromises he had made to the quest to become all he could be, the quest that I had seen in his early twenties. He hadn't really transcended the early levels of consciousness that I had encountered earlier. In some ways he had actually regressed. He was less reflective, less expressive, and less emotionally buoyant. He told me that neither religion nor spirituality held any interest for him. But of even more concern, nothing much held interest beyond his work. He had spent the intervening years working in a bookstore. Initially he had loved being around the books because they helped him stay intellectually alive. Now he said it was just a job. He described himself as living on the edge of communities, not within them, and declared that he had never experienced a community that brought him anything but grief.

Transformational Communities

Although it is all too common that a person's unfolding is curtailed by early communal patterns of holding, this is far from inevitable.

I have known many people who, despite unhelpful early family and community experiences, have been able later in life to find healthier communities that genuinely supported their development. We do not need to be victims of our past, but the myth of self-made persons who pull themselves up by their own bootstraps is, at least in terms of spiritual unfolding, sadly just a myth.

Communities that support transformation in their members and adherents are communities that are themselves open to transformation. Rather than trying to preserve what they have always been, they embrace change and have learned to continuously evolve. They know that the most basic lesson of life is that brittle things are either dying or have died; flexible things are growing. Communities that find a way to stay molten help their adherents and members also to stay molten. But sadly, individuals and organizations that may begin in a molten state usually quickly cool down and ossify.

Transformational communities embrace diversity as a way of honoring otherness. They recognize that the other is a face of the self and a face of the Ultimate Other. This is the motive for the hospitality to diversity and otherness that they offer. They make no demands that everyone be the same. They recognize that their strength lies in diversity. The greater the variety welcomed, the healthier the community and the more capable it is of supporting transformation. For example, a club that welcomes both males and females but beyond this is limited in its tolerance of diversity is definitely more capable of supporting growth and transformation than one with single-gendered membership. But it still falls desperately short of the potential that resides in one that also welcomes diversity in terms of ethnicity, sexual orientation, economic and social status, political beliefs, and so forth.

Finally, a transformational culture will always be one that encourages seeking rather than self-contented finding. Questions—all questions—will always be welcome because these communities are continuously open to further change and evolution. This is what allows them to support, rather than fear, the same sort of change and evolution in people.

No single thing could make a bigger positive change in the growth and development of persons than an increase in the number of communities that understand the first rule of care to be holding without constraining and that learn to celebrate when members are ready to move beyond the community. The coherence of the self is enhanced when we are able to live within social groups for a considerable period of time, but this only happens when communities learn the rhythm of holding, releasing, and then staying involved with those who leave until they are well embedded in the next community. This allows us to move beyond old communities of belonging but still remain attached to them. Separation from old places of belonging is always grievous because it involves separation from old meanings and previously significant relationships. Robert Kegan declares: "This is an extremely costly life course. Its amelioration requires supports which have a longitudinal basis—that is, they know and hold persons before, during, and after their transitions; they acknowledge and grieve the losses, acknowledge and celebrate the gains, and help the person (or family) to acknowledge them."[9]

Dialogue and Reflection

1. I am happy to hear you argue that our development is always either facilitated or impeded by the communal contexts within which we function. But I was also surprised to hear you argue this point from a psychological perspective, not simply a spiritual one or even a sociological one. How atypical is this point of view in psychology?

   Psychology is slowly recovering from its limiting view of persons as individuals. The person I quoted throughout this chapter, Robert Kegan, has played a major role in bringing about that correction within developmental psychology, but others have also done the same in clinical psychology. I mentioned object-relations theory and the way it has introduced a more interpersonal perspective to psychoanalytic psychology, but its influence is more pervasive than that and has now spread to many other approaches to psychotherapy. So I am happy to be able to say that the days of myopically viewing people as isolated psyches seem finally behind us.

2. You said that the first rule of care for another person is to hold without constraining. Can you say anything more about this?

   If we are honest, we have to acknowledge that this is often much harder than it looks. It is so easy to relate to others in terms of our own needs. Both communities and individuals do this. Although they don't always realize it, communities often "need" their members to stay within the shared world-view that holds the group together, and this is often built around a shared level of consciousness. When this is the case, the community will act to keep people within its framework for understanding and relating to the world (its level of con-sciousness), and those actions will be ones of constraint, not simply holding. But individuals do the same. We may think that we care for another person, but the measure of that care will be reflected in how willing we are to help them grow in ways that we haven't grown and move within themselves to places we have never explored nor inhabited. This takes a great deal of courage and trust, not just in the individual but more importantly in the Spirit and in the human capacity to follow the Spirit on a journey that is not always mediated by those who provide their care and support. This is hard, but it is the true measure of love. True love is love for the person in terms of who they may become, not simply who they are. This is not conditional love; it is visionary, trusting love that seeks to hold but never constrain.

3. Do churches ever achieve this balance of holding without constraining?

Without question they do. But generally the ones that do are the ones with the broadest theology. When "conservative" is used as an adjective to qualify anything, part of what it is describing is a desire to conserve. In churches, the focus of that conservative instinct is usually theology, and so tight boundaries are placed around theological understandings that are considered to be orthodox, and everything outside this is marked as heretical or liberal. This means that what you think and how you approach certain questions are either within this boundary or outside it. Consequently it is not surprising that the community constrains members to stay within this boundary, or why someone who moves outside this boundary is viewed as a threat. But many churches exist with a more inclusive framework of belonging. The follow-ing statement is prominently displayed in the service bulletin of one: "As a community we welcome and celebrate human diversity—including spirituality, ethnicity, gender, and sexual orientation. We aim to create a space where people of any faith or none can question and discover the sacred in life through openness, struggle, and prayer, and in common commitment to be in solidarity with the poor and marginalized, and to cherish Creation. We don't always succeed, but we do keep trying." Not surprisingly, this church does not do much constraining. It seems very successful in allowing people the freedom to be able to grow and change and still find a place of belonging. So it can be done, and many churches do manage very successfully to hold without constraining.

4. **You have spoken more about how communities hold people than about how individuals do this. Can you say more about how individuals can support the growth of those they care for?**

Briefly, I suggest several important things that anyone can do. These are as applicable to psychotherapists, counselors, or spiritual directors as they are to friends, neighbors, teachers, or anyone else—and they are not hard to do. They will, however, ensure that you are not just someone who fixes things that need to be fixed, or offers support when there is nothing else that can be done, but one who nurtures growth and transformation.

The most important thing that you can do to help others be open to growth and transformation is to avoid giving more support than is needed or reinforcing immature levels of development, coping strategies, or defense mechanisms. Typically these unhelpful ways of responding arise from excessive identification with the other person or simply seeing them as an extension of your self. Genuine care involves acting in ways that are best for the other person, not simply those that leave you comfortable. Support can often camouflage your own discomfort with growth, freedom, and release of control, just as reinforcing immature levels of development or coping usually reflects a discomfort with someone's moving to places of more health or freedom than you yourself possess. Remember rule number one: hold but don't constrain.

The second thing is to help others watch for the transitional moments, where they stand at a threshold and face the possibility of moving beyond the limits of what they are toward what they might become. Often these moments lie between separation from something and reincorporation into something else. Frequently they involve disruptions of coherence. This can come from a crisis or unwelcome event, but it could equally be from a brush with the Transcendent that leaves the person with what Rudolf Otto has described as a shudder of the soul. Great suffering and great love also offer the same possibilities, as does aging. Ask those with whom you work or support to notice opportunities for new ways of being in the world that may be presenting themselves in this situation. These transitional places are tremendously fertile moments in human becoming but are easily missed or ignored by the person in the midst of them. The affirmation of others about the potential of the moment and the encouragement to live its tension and hold its potential with patience—these responses can often make all the difference.

Third, if someone feels stuck and unable to move ahead, invite them to consider where trust and openness might lead them. Encourage them to pay particular attention to what they feel may be evolving, opening, moving, or new—and to keep watching until they notice this usually very small bit of movement amid sameness and stuckness. This is where the Spirit is in their life, and consequently this is a liminal space. Even if everything seems dark, encourage them to stare into that darkness until they see the light. It is there.

It does not take special training to be able to do any of these things. However, it does require that the individual doing the holding have experienced a holding community that knows how to hold, how to let go, and how to remain present during periods of transition. It also helps if individuals who are caring for others are themselves part of such communities as they seek to hold others. If they are not, they are less likely to encourage those they help to experience belonging and growing within a community, or to believe that it is even possible to do so.

12

Transformation and Transcendence

Earlier I suggested that the essential dynamic of the human spirit is a radical drive for self-transcendence: a longing to be more than we are, to be all we can be. At some deep level we seem to recognize that this "more" is not simply more of the same but that it demands deep transformation. It involves a reorganization of the self so radical that our old self must be released before our new and larger life can unfold. We must, as Jesus taught, be prepared to lose our life if we wish to truly gain it. Transformation always involves a continuing series of surrenders of the smaller selves to which we attach our selves as we become our larger and most authentic self. These acts of letting go form the transitional moments on the journey—the moments where our response to the inner call to the self-transcendent results in the quantum shifts in our center of gravity that I have described as the movement from one level of consciousness to another. It is these moments that I want to examine more closely in this chapter. But before we get to this, we need to first take a more careful look at the overall shape of the journey.

The Shape of the Journey

The best-known metaphor of the journey of human unfolding is that of the transformation of the caterpillar to a butterfly. It is easy—but misleading—to assume that human development unfolds in a similar, sequential manner through discrete stages of development with firm and clear boundaries between them. In reality, however, the lines between levels of consciousness are much less distinct than what I have implied and present in summary fashion in figure 12.1.

Figure 12.1
Levels of Consciousness Development

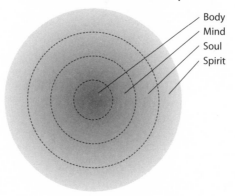

The dashes are intended to indicate that these boundaries are indistinct. It is seldom apparent in the moment that you are crossing a threshold of unfolding. You are much more likely to notice such transitions when you look back on your life. Then you may catch glimpses of a shift in your way of thinking and being that is usually indiscernible in the moment. Looking back, you might be quite astounded by the magnitude of the change. As we have noted, this shift will always include a change in identity and a change in the normal background of consciousness. But it will also include a change in how you relate to others and to the world. Consciousness is not simply a private mental experience. It is you who have changed, not just your inner experience. So, as your consciousness expands, you change in fundamental ways, which can even include changes in your body and its chemistry. However, these changes will usually appear gradually, and as the ground on which you stand broadens, movement back and forth across this borderland between major levels of consciousness will be frequent.

A second way in which the shape of the journey of human awakening is misrepresented by the life stages of the butterfly is that our journey is not nearly as linear as that of the butterfly. Steadily the butterfly progresses through four stages: from egg, to larva (caterpillar), to pupa (chrysalis), and finally to the adult butterfly. Human movement through the levels of development is less regular, and the stages do not unfold in as neat and ordered a fashion as figure 12.1 suggests. The levels point to the possibilities of our unfolding, but progress is usually interwoven with regress, expansion with contraction, and broadening and opening with retreat to narrower and safer places.

One way to capture this nonlinear movement is to think of the journey of unfolding in terms of a series of spirals. Rotating figure 12.1 on its horizontal axis and adding spirals around and through it gives us figure 12.2.

FIGURE 12.2
The Spiral Dynamics of Awakening

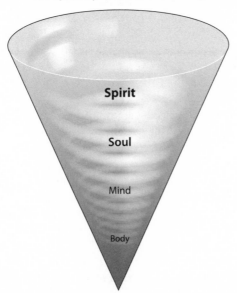

This perspective allows us to see more clearly the expansion of self and consciousness that represents the general direction of awakening. To better reflect the open and fluid nature of the journey, I have also removed the boundaries between the levels. Thinking of the journey in terms of an ever-widening series of spirals helps us take into account regress as well as progress. Whether we think of it as going back instead of forward or down instead of up, clearly the journey of the unfolding self sometimes involves movements in a direction that seems opposite to where we thought we were heading. But this is not something to be regretted or avoided. Such regress is essential if we are to gather up all the parts of self that are not yet quite at the level associated with our center of gravity. Transformation may reverse arrested development and release repressed structures, but to do so, it requires that the looping series of spirals take us backward as well as forward. Though it can also involve a leap ahead that, at least temporarily, appears to bypass certain stages, we will always have to go back and reclaim the territory we appear to have skipped over. This makes it possible for us first to stably inhabit the platform associated with that center of gravity, and second to subsequently move beyond it.

However, even an image of a series of spirals is overly simplistic because the movement is not always as steadily forward as this implies. As I have mentioned earlier, we often spend our whole life at the level of consciousness that we inhabit in early adulthood. If that level is the body self or mental self, there may be little evidence of a series of ever-widening spirals. However, if there is movement, it will not be linear, and the image of the spiral probably serves us better than an image of a straight line.

Most people have at least one significant awakening during the course of their life. They discover their separateness from their family, or they realize the possibilities of further unfolding associated with claiming or releasing their image or role, the power of their thoughts, the joy of belonging within a community, or the enrichment of their inner life that comes from reflection on experience. This may not feel momentous at the time but will leave them changed in a way that is clearly discernable in retrospect. They will be viewing life from a higher platform, and their sense of self and the world will be filtered through a broader perspective. This perspective may not be permanent. But once you have stood on a higher platform, it is easier to find your way back to it again.

Let me illustrate this by means of two case studies, each focusing on key transitional moments and the role they played in the person's transformation.

Transcending Image

Alex was a twenty-six-year-old advertising executive who came to me for help related to his struggles with homosexuality. He was involved in a church that viewed homosexuality as sinful and taught celibacy as the only acceptable way to manage his desires. He wanted me to help him do this—or even better, he said, to help him eliminate his sexual desires entirely. I told him that by virtue of both my theological and psychological convictions, I could not help him try to eliminate his sexuality, as I counted it to be too fundamental to his personhood. He then asked what help I *could* offer him. I answered that, if he chose to work with me, my approach would be to assist him in gaining inner freedom through expanding self-awareness. After some thought, he said that he would give this a try, and we agreed to work together.

At the point where I met Alex, his self and consciousness were both firmly grounded in his body. Extremely fit and always something of a fashion plate, he was heavily invested in his appearance and image. In terms of the framework presented earlier and summarized in table 12.3, his self-organization was at the general level of the body self—more specifically, the substage I have called the public self. He equated himself with his image. Furthermore, he did not just view himself from an external perspective; he related to himself from this vantage point. His knowing of himself was not so much personal as objective, and that almost exclusively from a visual perspective. Alex knew himself as he appeared to others. Although he was curious enough to be attracted to a deeper knowing of the truth of his self, initially he had trouble moving beyond this external, visual perspective on himself.

Alex's curiosity about what might lie beyond being his image was, however, a good sign. I didn't tell him, but I understood it as an openness to the Spirit, who was calling him to become more than he was, and consequently, I encouraged it whenever I saw it manifest. Frequently he asked me how I saw him. Initially he meant this quite literally, but over time, that literal request was replaced by a desire to learn how I encountered and experienced him. This external perspective to knowing himself as he was known was natural to his level of self-organization, but it was at the same time a response to this nudging of Spirit for deeper knowing and more authentic being. I sought to respond to his repeated requests for information about how I experienced him by telling him exactly how, in that moment, I was actually experiencing him. I didn't treat this as a request for information as much as a request for contact. His homosexual encounters had always been casual and unsatisfying, and in none of them had he ever found the deep connection that he sought. But he did respond very positively to my engagement with him. More than

TABLE 12.3
Levels of Unfolding and Awakening

Level	Self	Identity
BODY	Body self	I am my body.
	Public self	I am my image.
	Material self	I am my possessions.
	Role self	I am my role.
MIND	Mental self	I am my thoughts.
	Ideological self	I am my beliefs.
	Communal self	I am my community.
	Individual self	I am myself.
SOUL	Reflective self	I am my experience.
	Shadow self	I am my shadow.
	Divided self	I am not always my true self.
SPIRIT	Essential self	I am.
	Divine self	I am one with God.
	Cosmic self	I am one with everything.

just a sexual encounter, he sought contact—deep, authentic human contact. He told me of a recurring dream of reaching out to touch his father, who in the dream and in life was always walking away from him and beyond reach. But it wasn't even simply contact that he wanted from me. Alex was asking me to be a mirror for him so that he could see and know himself as he was known, and this is exactly what I tried to offer him. I sought to meet him where he was and give him what he needed to help him become more than he was.

I am sure it wasn't his first awakening, but I recall the point in our work together when I saw the first signs of awareness of the cramped nature of the platform on which he had built his identity. He commented on his noticing that he apparently needed to see himself from my perspective and wondered why this was so. I asked him for his own thoughts about this. Alex said that it struck him how important it was that he knew how I saw him and that he always felt that his identity was validated when I saw him in a way that matched how he experienced himself. He then went on to wonder out loud how this might be related to the emphasis he placed on image. This was the first time he had commented on his investment in image; when I again invited elaboration, I was surprised to hear his sense of embarrassment that something he said so clearly revealed his superficiality. I encouraged him to hold off passing judgment on himself or demanding to immediately understand the meaning of any of these things but simply continue to explore the questions he was raising since they seemed to me to be potentially quite fruitful.

Alex began the next session by telling me that he had thought a lot during the previous week about our discussion and had come to see that his whole life was organized around creating and managing impressions. He said that he had suddenly recognized how even his work fit this pattern and that he found it really depressing to realize how petty and limiting his investment in image was. Alex said that he was aware that he was selling himself short with this approach to life, and that it was keeping his relationships with others in a superficial place. He said he knew he was much more than what others saw in him, particularly because all he had really been caring about was whether or not they saw him as physically attractive. Alex realized that my seeing of him and knowing of him went deeper than image, and he felt a deep gratification in connecting at this level and wanted more of the same.

This was the beginning of the first of several significant transition points in Alex's journey. It was the earliest sign of his emerging readiness to move beyond a body-centered self. That movement didn't happen immediately. As he began to explore how he was much more than his physical attractiveness, the first thing that he identified was his competency and creativity in his work. What was emerging was a role self, in which he equated himself with what he could do. But because his creativity was not simply a role or even something he did but was instead a mental competency, this was simply a stepping-stone to the mind-centered self. Slowly he became as attached to his creativity as he had been to his body. Although physical appearance remained important to him, he increasingly began to identify with his inner life—not just with the products of his creativity but also with the process of creative expression. He had long been interested in photography but had never done anything more than take snapshots. Feeling that it was time to do more, he bought a digital SLR camera and signed up for a continuing education course at a community college. His instructors told him that his photographs showed a lot of potential, and he found a great deal of fulfillment in taking them. But even more noteworthy, he reported feeling a degree of authenticity in his being when he was taking and working with his pictures that had not been present when all he sought was admiration for his body. He was still working with images, but they were not simply images of himself. He was exploring and developing his creative abilities and was discovering that he was not simply his body: he was also his mind. The world that began to reveal itself to him was much vaster than the one he had inhabited in his body-centered self. Both his inner and outer worlds were richer and more enriching as his consciousness, identity, and ways of relating to that which was beyond him began to expand.

During this time Alex began to find his work increasingly unfulfilling. Even much stronger than this, he said he found it detestable. He felt appalled at what he had previously settled for, viewing his work in advertising as manipulation. He wanted to find a way to bring the authenticity to his creative work that he was discovering in his avocational pursuit of photography. Alex wanted his creativity to do more than sell products. He didn't know exactly what this more would be or how to find or express it, but he knew the next step was that he simply had to quit his job and go back to school to study photography. Most of his friends told him he had lost his mind. He said that he was simply coming to his senses. Alex turned out to be right, and this step proved to be a response to his awakening that helped him shift his consciousness and his self-organization to another plateau, that of the mind-centered self.

During the first year or so of our work together, Alex's issues around sexuality formed a major part of our focus. After this they slowly faded into the background and were replaced by a primary focus on his awakening and his life. I was aware that he was struggling less with his homosexuality and had come increasingly to accept it, but his sexuality was far from the center of either his focus or ours as we worked together. Any issue we explored would inevitably have a sexual component to it; when I noticed this, I would encourage him to circle back and connect the dots between whatever we were presently exploring and these underlying issues associated with his sexuality and identity. But increasingly, his focus was on who he was becoming, not simply who he was. Even after the point of his coming out as a gay male, I recall him telling me that while this was a crucially important part of his identity, it was far from all of who he was. He resisted being defined by his sexual orientation. Yet he needed to embrace that part of his identity if it was to be integrated within the fabric of the self he was becoming. Over time, this is exactly what he was able to do. In order to transcend his body self, he had to accept it and integrate it. And similarly, in order to transcend his sexual orientation as a base of identity, he had to fully accept it and integrate it within the larger family of self that he was. Alex had begun to know that he was more than any one of his abilities or attributes. He was a human becoming, not merely a human being.

Alex's journey illustrates the way in which transcendence and transformation are related. Yet as we have seen, there are several other important elements in this relationship. The first of these is an embrace of the realities of one's existence. Neither transformation nor any genuine transcendence of present realities can emerge apart from a full embrace of them. We have to start where we are—where we really are. Alex had to start with his primary identification with image if he was ever to transcend this as a basis of identity and consciousness. There are no shortcuts to transformation.

Alex's unfolding also illustrates the way in which transformation always involves differentiation (the masculine principle) and integration (the feminine principle). Transcendence cannot happen apart from the presence of both. We see differentiation in Alex's story in the way in which he noticed and was later able to emerge from his embeddedness in image. But if differentiation allows us to emerge from embeddedness, it is to prepare us for a new embeddedness in a larger place in the world. For Alex, this was his embeddedness in the life of the mind—specifically, in his creativity. At the end of our work together, the world in which he was embedded was larger than the one he inhabited when we began. His movement from the one to the other was based on spiritual awakening—even though God was only very minimally present in his consciousness during this process of awakening and unfolding.

Grounding Spirit

Paula's story of unfolding is a bit more complex because aspects of her life and inner experience made it look as though she was already living at a spirit-centered level of consciousness when I first met her. Her journey allows us to examine more closely the way in which stable transcendence requires gathering up and integrating everything within the self as it is transformed.

If I had met Paula as a child, I think I might have been tempted to abandon the framework of unfolding that we have been examining in this book. So I am glad I didn't meet her until she was a little older and I could then gather a bigger picture of her functioning and development. Paula was born in Colombia (South America), an only child in a traditional Latin American Roman Catholic family. Her parents ran a very successful group of family businesses related to coffee production and export, and she was raised primarily by a live-in nanny and her grandmother. Although she seldom spent time with other children outside of school hours, she said that her childhood was blissfully happy. She would wander the grounds of the large gated estate on which they lived, talking to the trees, birds, butterflies, and anything else living that she encountered. Looking back on this time, she said she knew she was surrounded by God and was often so struck by God's being present in everything she encountered that she wondered if she must somehow be inside God. This thought came to her when she was six years old. It would be followed by many more similar ones. Paula was a child mystic.

A few years later, when she began to have more contact with other children, she was shocked to discover that they, unlike her, did not sense God everywhere and in all things. This was quite distressing for her and left her rather disoriented. Paula never talked with her parents about these things, nor did they ever talk with her about spirituality or religion. Neither did her nanny, who took her to Mass each week. But she did occasionally tell her grandmother some of her thoughts and experiences; her grandmother told her not to tell anyone else because what she had was a special spiritual gift that few could ever understand. She also told her grandmother that sometimes she thought she must be God because otherwise she didn't understand how God could be so close to her and how she could feel God's joy and see things through God's eyes. Again, her grandmother simply smiled and told her to keep these things to herself, adding, "You are very special to God, but God is much bigger than we can ever understand." This lessened Paula's need to try to either understand or talk about these things with others. And so she continued to grow up in this God-saturated world that from an external perspective appeared lonely and unhealthily devoid of other children, but which gave her the best years of her life.

Things changed suddenly one day when she was thirteen. The driver dropped her home from school only to be met at the gate by her mother, who was sobbing and informing her that her father had died from a sudden, massive heart attack. Paula didn't feel sad. She was never really close to either of her parents, and although she said she loved them, her actual attachment to them was minimal. She did, however, feel fear. Paula worried that things would never be the same again, that she might have to leave this place where she and God spent such wonderful time walking and playing, and she wondered if God would still be in her, or if she would still be in God, even if she had to move. It wasn't as clear whether God was with her at school, this being the only other place apart from her home where she ever was. She did very well in her work, but she didn't enjoy it. Paula didn't sense God with her nearly as clearly when she was there—sometimes hardly at all. She suspected that this wasn't because God wasn't there but because she was somehow distracted. That, she said, was why she liked it so much in the forests on their estate, for there she could be open to God without distraction.

Things did change for Paula, but not in the ways she expected. Not long after her father's death, her mother agreed to go to church with a Pentecostal friend. That night she came back home and told Paula that she had become a Christian and that she wanted Paula to come to a special service the next night so she also could become a Christian. This confused Paula since she thought she was already a Christian, but she didn't argue. And so, after dutifully going forward to the altar at the end of the service the next evening, Paula came home a new kind of Christian. Now their world was filled with church, and now her mother became a much more important part of her life. They went to church several times each week and also spent much of Sundays at various services. She liked much of what she was learning, but immediately she noticed that God was not as close to her anymore. This saddened her, but she resolved to try harder to do the things she was being taught to do in this church, with the hope that she would again know God as she had before she started attending there. But year followed upon year, and her inner spirit only became drier. She tried harder and harder to be a good Christian, but the joy had all gone from her life. She had friends—although she spoke nothing of her inner spirit to any of them—but she so missed the simple times of just being with God. When she managed to be alone, and even if she went back out into the forest on the property where they continued to live, God seemed to have left for some other neighborhood.

Paula and her mother moved to the United States when it was time for her to go to college. Her mother sold the family home and businesses, and they settled into a comfortable, although much less affluent, life in a large urban center. Paula attended a Christian college in this city; even though she was exposed to good Christian teaching and many other wonderful young Christian friends, her capacity to enjoy God's company and sense God's presence in everything around her became even more a thing of the past. She began to think of it as a function of childhood, something that must be released as she continued her escalating movement into adulthood.

College years were, however, good for Paula. She continued to excel academically, and she began to thrive intellectually. But she never lost contact with her interior, secret self. Through high school she had filled book after book with her poems, and at college she also began to write children's fiction. Several of these stories were published by the student union, and out of this came a surprising and quite remarkable invitation from a book publisher to consider a book-length work of children's fiction. By now she was in a pre-med program and busy with studies, so she put this project on the back burner for a later point when she might have more time. But she did continue to offer rich reflective space for her experiences, often praying through her day before going to bed at night as a way of committing the day and all her experiences and the people in them to God. Although she was happy with her life, including her friends and church, the one thing she missed was solitude. Everything was so full and busy: she missed the emptiness, stillness, and lightness of being that she had known in her childhood. Sometimes Paula wondered if this was why she was so much less close to God. The summer after she was admitted to medical school and just before she was to start these studies, she decided to do something for herself. She told no one she was thinking about it but simply tracked down a nearby Catholic retreat center and booked herself in for a one-week directed retreat. Once again her life was about to change dramatically.

The short account of this retreat—which she gave me shortly after it ended—was that it was extraordinary. She felt like she was on her way back to the places of stillness and presence to the God who was present to her in her childhood. But at the same time, she was filled with excitement about the contours of the path ahead, one she sensed from these days of stillness, prayer, and conversation with the nun who had served as her director. This director honored the practices of Paula's evangelical culture but also encouraged her to attend to God's Spirit. She encouraged Paula to notice whether she felt drawn to explore any of the newer spiritual practices that she had sampled in those days of retreat. *Lectio divina* and centering prayer[1] both held a sense of invitation for her, and she was excited to discover where they might lead her. Her director had also introduced her to some books on the contemplative dimension of Christian spirituality—several of mine included. This was why she contacted me after the retreat ended and before she began her medical school studies. She said she wanted someone to accompany her as she moved forward, yet hopefully as she also somehow found her way back to the closeness to God she had known as a child.

This sense of what she needed turned out to be quite prescient. Over the next few years, Paula's journey involved a series of spiraling loops back through the levels of consciousness and self-organization that she had never stably transcended. Without question she was a deeply spiritual young woman. Her attunement to spiritual realities was a very special gift. But she had been unable to carry it with her as she grew up and moved out from the shelter of her childhood home because she lacked the maturity of the other dimensions of her self that were necessary to do so. Over the next few years I saw what at times looked like two separate journeys, but which I knew and told her were really just one.

The journey of soul took her down and into herself as she came to know herself more fully and then learn to be present to herself in stillness. The most important part of this journey of descent was that she had to learn to inhabit her body. Her relationship with her body had always been rather limited; at least in part, her life in her spirit had been a defense against engagement with her body. Paula had cultivated a degree of soulful reflection, and her rich inner life also included a reasonably healthy mental life, but her distance from her emotions and discomfort with her sexuality betrayed the fact that none of the higher functioning of the realms of mind, soul, and spirit were adequately grounded in her body. She was honest enough to be able to tell me that she was both attracted to silence and stillness and frightened by it. They confronted her with dimensions of her body self with which she was quite uncomfortable. But that she still felt an invitation to stillness and silence despite this ambivalence was a tremendously good sign. For it was here that she met and finally came to peace with her body.

The journey of spirit also took her up and beyond her self as she encountered ever more deeply and fully the God whom she knew once again to be present to her as she was increasingly present to her self.

And Paula did this through the busy years of medical school and the early years of medical practice. Both movements were essential parts of the whole as she continued her journey into God.

Nearly ten years after I first began to work with her, Paula's life is so filled with God that she tells me that she can't tell where God ends and she begins or what in her depths is God and what is her. This is not psychotic rambling. She is very careful to communicate this awareness to only a very small number of people since she is well aware how easily her sharing could be misunderstood. But her words, as limited and imperfect as she knows them to be, do communicate something of her experience. For the greatest part of most days, she says, her consciousness includes God, and her identity is grounded in being one with God. Often she again feels the oneness with everything that she knew as a child, although this is not present all the time. Remarkably, she is able to keep this openness of her consciousness and self to God even as she now works as a busy family-practice physician. She feels no desire to leave her work and the world and retreat to some mountaintop where she and God can be alone— or to move into work that might be perceived to be more explicitly "spiritual." God is with her, and she is where she knows she is supposed to be: in the world, living out her life in God in a way that allows God to live through her. This is indeed a spirit-centered and Spirit-filled life.

I said that if I had met Paula when she was still a young girl in Colombia, I might have assumed that she was already living in a spirit-centered level of consciousness. I think I would have been correct in that judgment. However, it was an unstable state of consciousness, not an enduring one. Her self-development simply did not support a spirit-centered level of consciousness as her ongoing state. By virtue of a particularly sensitive, open, and responsive spirit, she was enjoying swimming in deep and extraordinarily rich waters spiritually even when she was a young child. But she was not able to stay there without further development, nor could she float in those waters with the surrender that was possible when she reentered them later in life. Now she brings body, mind, and soul with her as she plunges into the river that is Spirit. And now, because she can be one with herself, she can now be one with everything else.

Movement from one stage of consciousness to the next always involves a movement toward and in response to the transcendent Spirit of God. The cases we have examined in this chapter illustrate healthy transcendence. What allows the person to continue to move forward is not simply their openness and faith; but it is also their acceptance and inclusion in self of that which is, in truth, part of their experience. Ultimately transcendence, transformation, and healthy development are the same thing, since healthy development is always based on transcendence that emerges from the prior act of including, and this movement toward transcendence is always transformational. Each of the three starts where we truly are because that which is excluded from the self will always be projected onto others and will sabotage any future transcendence or development. Transcendence therefore demands an embrace of the truths of my existence and openness to allowing them to be woven anew into the new self I am becoming. Margaret Silf understands this well. Let me close with a story she tells—really more of a word picture that she paints—to illustrate this:

> I see myself standing on the banks of a fast-flowing river. I know I must cross, but there is no bridge. Then a figure, a Christ-figure, comes to me carrying a large boulder, and places it in front of me, in the river, inviting me to take a step out onto it. Every day he brings another boulder, another stepping stone. Every day I move farther into the waters, balancing precariously on my fragile faith. One day he is late. I turn around, mid-river, and only then do I see where the boulders are coming from. He is systematically deconstructing my cozy little cottage on the shore, in order to turn it into stepping stones for my onward journey. He is using my past to create my future. He is asking me to reach out with both hands—one to let go of all I thought I couldn't live without, and one to reach toward everything I thought I could never attain.[2]

Transcendence demands a deconstruction of my past so everything can be included and be put together in a new way. Ultimately I don't need to leave any part of my self behind as all things become new. And paradoxically, just as Jesus said, this only happens when I let go of the self I presently am—even to the point of being willing to lose that self. For only then do I discover and become more fully the true and full self that I am in Christ.

The Point of Transformation

As we have seen, awakening is a process, not a onetime event. This is why I have referred to it as a journey of awakening. But, after emphasizing the process to this point, let me gather up some of the things we have noticed or that I can now say about the outcome. What would the totally awake person look like? What changes as consciousness expands and identity becomes more inclusive? And why is this important?

To be totally awake is to be totally present. Thus increasing presence to self, others, and God is an important marker of progress on the journey of awakening and transformation. Jesus was described as one who taught with authority (Mark 1:21–28). I believe that, first and foremost, this is a comment on his steady-state presence. The basis of his authority was his recognized presence to others. This arose out of his steady-state presence to God and expressed the total alignment of his being with that of God. This alignment of the totality of his being began with his consciousness. He knew that his life was meaningful only in relationship to his Father. And this relationship—this state of being one with the Father—was the basis of the integration of his head and heart.

The presence that we are able to both offer and experience as we become more awake is increasingly vulnerable and naked. Our capacity for openness increases with each step of increasing wakefulness. The two are not synonymous, but they are mutually reinforcing. Awakening both invites openness and is nurtured by it. Another dependable marker of the journey of awakening is, therefore, increasing vulnerability in relation to one's self, others, and God. This will be reflected in a tempering of one's knee-jerk judgments and polarized thinking. It will also be reflected in an increasing ability to avoid the creation of false dichotomies to comfort one's ego.

Awakening will also be reflected in a looser attachment to things that previously shaped our identity. As we have seen, this includes our thoughts, opinions, and beliefs. These will not be eliminated, but we will hold them more lightly. The only sure way to eliminate cognition is the closing of consciousness through death. The opening or expansion of consciousness does not eliminate cognition but loosens our attachment to our mental products. Opinions and beliefs are held with more humility. Though they are useful and even important ways of organizing experience, they are recognized to be extremely limited containers for holding the ultimate mysteries of existence. This softening of attachment to one's thoughts is, as we have seen, also reflected in a softening of attachment to all small, ego-bound ways of defining self and organizing consciousness. Everything is held more loosely; as we do so, in the depths of our being we increasingly know that we ourselves are held. Releasing our grasping allows us to know what we could never know but which we most deeply need to know if we are to be well: a oneness within our self and with all that is beyond our self.

We will know this, and increasingly all things, in both our heads and hearts. Hence this integration of head and heart is another important marker of increasing awakening and transformation. Head and heart are perceptual organs, ways of knowing and ways of engaging with reality. Both open us to the worlds within and beyond us. As they do so, what we increasingly notice is the transformation of boundaries into lines of distinction. As our small ego-self is replaced by a larger self that is increasingly at one with everything, both our consciousness and identity broaden and become aligned and integrated. Fragmentation of our being is replaced by an increasing at-oneness. We see the illusion of our separateness from that which is beyond, and we experience a healing of our alienation from our Source and Destiny.

Ultimately transformation is not even really about me. It is about an increasing recognition of the reality of the me-in-God and the God-in-me. Self-engineered attempts at transformation are far too self-focused to truly allow my ego-self to die and my spirit-centered self to emerge. This is why I have described the journey we have been examining as a journey into God. The whole point of this journey is a return to our true home. It is a return to our Source so that we might fully participate in the divine life.

As we journey deeper and deeper into God, the me-in-God and the God-in-me become more and more inextricably intertwined. This is what the mystics are referring to when they speak of union with God. But becoming one with God does not mean that we become God. Nor does participation in the life of God mean that we lay siege to and take some sort of exclusively personal possession of God. It means that our identity is centered in the Spirit, and our consciousness is dominated by the experience of being at one with the Spirit and therefore at one with everything that is.

Participation in the life of the Spirit means that we become more like God without becoming less human. We could even say that this goal is a fulfillment of our humanity by restoring our spiritual alignment with God. This is the point of transformation. Yet here we must take special care to guard against facile, overly anthropomorphized characterizations of God. God is qualitatively different from any and all finite beings. God is the "totally other." The reality of God lies beyond all human ideas, concepts, and language; if we forget this, our God-talk quickly degenerates into idol (and idle) talk. But Christians are not left guessing what God is like because we believe that God is uniquely revealed in the person of Jesus. Expansion of consciousness does not come from simply trying to be like Jesus by imitating his behavior. His personality was unique, just as ours should be. But in Jesus we do see a way of relating to others, to life, and to God that can be ours—and does become ours as we travel into God on this journey of awakening and becoming.

Participation in the life of the Spirit is also participation in the Spirit's life and activity in the world. God's agenda in the world becomes mine. But this requires that I am able to discern God's agenda, presence, and activity as they really are, not as I might assume them to be when I view them through the eyes of my communal self or through the perspective of my religious or spiritual tradition. Despite what we often assume, God's activity and presence in the world is not limited to our tribe and our community, or even to the church. The point of transformation is alignment with the Spirit and with the Spirit's work and play in the world, making all things new in Christ.

Transformation is about my alignment with God and my alignment with all that God has created and is making new. It is about more fully entering the stream of life and going with the flow. It is about me becoming more than I was and more than I am as I participate in the divine generative act of the becoming of all of creation. It is about me becoming a better conduit for the life of God, which is primarily manifested in terms of love. Our unfolding is part of the unfolding of creation. Both are an expression of the constantly outpouring life of God.

If we can think of this journey of awakening as movement toward enlightenment, the purpose of enlightenment is transpersonal, not merely personal. Enlightenment is not a possession but a privilege. Seeing my place in the larger whole more clearly allows me to move out into the cosmos and become more capable of offering loving service. As in the bodhisattva vow of Buddhism, where an enlightened being voluntarily renounces an attained status and chooses to remain on earth to assist his or her fellow beings, so too should all of us understand that our becoming more than we are is for the purpose of others and the world. Our freedom comes from being servants of all those not yet ready to live in the freedom of truth and love. The Spirit of

God—the source of all generativity, all creativity, and all life—invites us to participate in the grand adventure of cosmic becoming. This participation, not perfection or fulfillment, is the point of human growth, transformation, and becoming. But in such participation, not in perfection or in our own ideas of fulfillment, lies our ultimate fulfillment and completion.

Dialogue and Reflection

1. You suggested that holding beliefs—in fact everything—more lightly is a marker of progress on this journey of awakening. I can understand holding my beliefs about God more lightly, but are you also implying that I should soften my attachment to God?

> When you cling to God, you can never be sure how firmly God has a hold on you. If you are truly in God and God in you—which I firmly believe is the truth of all humans—your clinging does nothing to draw God closer. Your relationship with God does not depend on your holding on to God—however you may be doing that. Let go and discover that God is in you and you are in God, that this reality is not dependent on your clutching.

2. Please comment on the understanding of the spiritual journey as primarily involving growth in Christlikeness.

> If Christlikeness is not reduced to behavior but involves taking on both the mind and heart of Christ—not just the behavior of Jesus—this exactly describes what I think unfolding involves. But it cannot simply be a matter of conformity. We must understand that the Christ-in-me will always look different from the Christ-in-you. Also, we need to be clear to distinguish this from a journey of increasingly sinless perfection. Holiness may or may not accompany an expanding consciousness. But let me return to what I mean when I say taking on the mind and heart of Christ is, not just conforming to a pattern of behavior. Taking on the mind of Christ is not the same as adopting a set of beliefs. It is enlightenment. It is attunement to God. It is seeing God

as God is actively present and at work in all circumstances, in all places, at all times, making all things new in Christ. Taking on the heart of Christ is not simply a matter of consciousness. It involves experiencing and responding to the world through the heart of God. Together these describe the spirit-centered self.

3. **These case studies are really interesting, but I suspect that most people don't experience changes of this magnitude during their life. Do you agree?**

Sadly, I think you are right. Most people seem to find a level of consciousness and self-organization sometime in early life—perhaps in their twenties or thirties—and then settle there for the rest of their life. My guess is that something like 40 percent of the population of the Western world settles in a body-centered self, about the same in a mind-centered self, about 20 percent in a soul-centered self, and perhaps 1 percent in a spirit-centered self. Awakenings can and do happen later in life, and transformation is possible, as these case studies illustrate. But I do not believe that it is as common as is often thought or claimed.

4. **I was glad to hear you comment on markers of the transformational journey. But can you say anything more about our inner experience of transformation, what it feels like and what we will sense?**

If we are in an authentically transformational process, what we will notice will often be quite surprising. Unlike growth, which often feels like a satisfying gain, transformation will often be experienced as an unwelcome loss. We might sense the absence of the familiar framework that has been our identity and mourn the loss of this. We may even feel disoriented. Sometimes we will feel that we are in free fall or possibly in exile. So don't expect a blissful state of pleasurable progress. But, that being said, we will also experience a healing of our alienation and a release of our sense of estrangement. As we move from the isolation of our individuality to deeper belonging and union, we will sense an at-oneness within our self and between our self and everything that still feels beyond our self. We will also feel an increasing sense of being at peace with life, with the world, and with all that is. This certainly does not mean that we will passively accept what is and simply go with the flow. Instead, what it means is that we will allow life to flow through us as we participate in it—or to use more religious language, as we allow God's life to flow into and through us.

5. What is the connection between integration and transformation?

Integration is as ambiguous a term as *transformation*. Often it implies a goal that is elusive and not even desirable: the complete synthesis of all the disparate elements of self. To be human means living with tensions that emerge from the very core of our existence as humans. These tensions cannot be eliminated, at least not without destroying our humanity, because they are rooted in our ontology—in our being dust and breath, participating in the finite and infinite, caught forever between necessity and freedom, and so on. Being human demands holding the many tensions of our existence that can never be fully reconciled. Kierkegaard argued, I think correctly, that the self is not the synthesis of these elements but is found in the relationship we establish between them. It operates in and through the tensions created by opposing forces. Kierkegaard believed that the self is much more a verb than a noun: it is the active process of the way in which the self gathers up and holds together all its various elements.

The customary way in which we use the concept of "integration" is to refer to holding things together, even if this holding involves tension. However, in this chapter I have used the term *integration* in a slightly different manner, describing it as an element of transformation, something that always involves both differentiation (or disembedding of the self) and integration (reembedding of the self in a larger context). In more traditional spiritual language, we could also describe it as the alignment of the self around some self-transcendent reference point. Understood in these terms, integration is something that we do more fully at each successive level of self-awakening and self-unfolding.

6. **I am interested to know how your work with the people you describe in this chapter and others has influenced your own journey of awakening.**

> Being able to work with people who seek to become all they can be has been one of the great gifts of my life. This has been particularly true in recent years, as I have shifted my work from psychotherapy to guiding those who seek personal transformation through spiritual openness and awareness. I find that being with people who are open and trusting invites my own deeper opening and trust. Their readiness to settle for nothing less than the freedom of living the truth of their self encourages me to do the same. Being able to accompany people to places where I have not been—or at least in which I do not habitually live—is an awesome privilege and a sacred trust.

APPENDIX I

Dreamwork for Growth and Transformation

Although dreams are usually either ignored or dismissed as illogical and irrelevant—perhaps nothing more than the result of random electrical activity in the brain while we are asleep—they can radically change a person's life. On the night before an important battle late in October 312 CE, just as Constantine was reaching the height of his power as Roman emperor, he had a vision that not only changed him but also changed the world. In this dream, Christ appeared to him and was holding in his hand the Greek letters *chi* and *rho*, the first two letters of "Christ" in Greek. The letters were combined in the form of a cross, and above it was a banner with the words *In hoc signo vinces*, "In/through this sign you shall conquer." Instantly Constantine converted to Christianity and shortly afterward ended three hundred years of persecution of Christians, making the symbol (the Chi-Rho Christogram) that he saw in his dream that of the empire he established, which continued in some form for nearly 1,150 years.

Not all dreams lead to such dramatic consequences, but Constantine was far from alone in having a dream that had an important transformational impact. This is because, as Freud noted, dreams uniquely provide direct access to the unconscious, and the unconscious always plays a central role in transformation. It also has a potentially very important role in our growth, although we can grow along individual lines of development without much attention to the unconscious. Transformation, however, involves a reorganization of consciousness, and this cannot happen apart from the participation of the unconscious.

The Psychospiritual Function of Dreams

Dreams serve at least five important psychological functions, all of which involve the unconscious:

1. Dreams express inner experience. As Daniel, the young captive Hebrew with a reputation for skill in dreamwork, told King Nebuchadnezzar when asked to explain a particularly puzzling and upsetting dream, dreams are given so that we might understand our inmost thoughts (Dan. 2:30). Paying attention to dreams is paying attention to inner realities, and without embracing these realities—which often lie outside awareness—there can be no genuine transformation.
2. Dreams make a contribution to the healing of psychic wounds. This means that they not only identify unresolved conflicts or traumatic experiences but also represent an unconscious effort on the part of the psyche to resolve them.
3. Dreams represent an unconscious effort to creatively generate meaning and coherence for experience. Things that disrupt that meaning need to be woven within the fabric of whatever meaning we have been creating, and dreams make a contribution to this effort.
4. Dreams compensate for imbalances of conscious personality by bringing forth unconscious elements that have been ignored or repressed. They also point to lost parts of personality that need to be reclaimed if we are to be whole.
5. Finally, dreams also provide glimpses of future possibilities and potentialities. They point the conscious self toward wholeness by identifying alternate ways of responding to situations and being in the world.

Wholeness requires a partnership of the conscious and unconscious parts of our self, and dreams offer us a valuable resource in establishing such a partnership. Although dream contents often appear to be opaque and confusing, the purpose of dreams is not to hide but to reveal. They are an attempt to weave together what has been fragmented in our being and to reclaim what has been ignored or lost. They help us know ourselves and therefore are potentially a very important resource in our growth.

However, as noted in chapter 1, before the eighteenth century virtually everyone assumed that dreams also had spiritual significance. This is reflected in a traditional Jewish prayer: "Sovereign of the Universe, I am thine and my dreams are thine. As thou didst turn the curse of the wicked Balaam into a blessing, so turn all my dreams into something beneficial to me." The Bible often presents dreams as the voice of God. Sometimes they are understood as God's foretelling of what is going to happen, as in Joseph's dreams recorded in Genesis 37:5–11. At other times they are taken as God's direct urging of some specific action. An example of this in the Gospel of Matthew is Joseph's dream in which an angel tells him to get up, take the infant Jesus and his mother, and escape into Egypt (2:13).

As on many things, however, the Bible does not offer us a single perspective or teaching on dreams. Sometimes they are viewed with skepticism, as in Ecclesiastes 5:7, which describes attending to dreams as chasing the wind. However, a few verses earlier in that same chapter, we encounter a more psychological view: "Dreaming comes from too much worrying" (5:3). One particularly clear expression of a modern psychological view of dreams is found in Daniel's response to King Nebuchadnezzar's request to interpret the meaning of his dream. Before doing so, Daniel says, "This mystery has been revealed to me, not that I am wiser than any other man, but for this sole purpose: that the king should learn what it means, and that you should understand your innermost thoughts" (Dan. 2:30). Other biblical passages that reflect a similarly modern psychological perspective include Psalm 17:3: "You probe my heart, examine me at night"; and Job 33:14–15: "God speaks first in one way, and then in another, but not one listens. He speaks by dreams, and visions that come in the night, when slumber comes on humankind, and humans are all asleep in bed."

Without going so far as arguing for dreams as the voice of God in the soul, I think we can safely treat them as a vital part of our experience in which we can meet God. If, as I have argued elsewhere, attention to anything can open us to the transcendent,[1] attention to what emerges from our depths surely can do so. This is why dreams have such potential to play an important role in spirituality, growth, and transformation.

Principles of Dreamwork

✢ Rather than interpreting dreams, I recommend attending to them. Think of them as a communication from your depths or, if you will, from the Spirit, something sent for your well-being. A Jewish proverb states that an unexamined dream is like an unopened letter. But not all dreams are of equal value, and so it is not necessary to open each or attend to all equally. The richest dreams usually emerge late in the night, are longer, and have stronger feelings attached to them or contain incongruous or puzzling elements. They are the ones that are most likely to stay with you for a while after awakening; even if you no longer remember all the details, they frequently leave their emotional tone as an aftertaste that lingers as you move into the first moments of the new day. These are the communications from your depths that are most worthy of attention.

✢ Paying attention to a dream is an act of soul hospitality. Don't try to force meaning out of the dream. Simply receive it and hold it lightly. Rather than asking questions of it, listen to the questions it asks of you. A dream of a car out of control and without brakes might be inviting you to ask, "How is my life out of control?" A dream of war might suggest the value of considering, "What inner enemy am I fighting?" Receive these sorts of questions as a gift, something to reflect on or pray about, not a puzzle to be solved.

✢ View the dream as a parable or a Zen koan and avoid taking it too literally. It is a story that makes one basic point, so listen for its overall theme and don't get lost in the details. Don't obsess over the meaning of any one symbol. Keep your focus on the dream as a whole and the overall invitation that it contains. Yet pay particular attention to repetitions over a series of dreams or within a dream. Since dreams are full of redundancies, there is no need to worry if you miss the point of any particular dream. You will get another chance to catch that point if you continue to pay attention to future dreams.

- Consider all dream symbols, including the people who appear in the dream, as representing parts of yourself. Focus on the chief characteristic of people.
- Finally, be prepared to face both the dark and light sides of your inner experience. Both must be engaged if what has been lost or eliminated is to be redeemed. Failing to show hospitality to what is dark, frightening, or confusing increases its power and potential influence. Whoever denies the existence of the inner world does not escape its frightening aspects but renders one's self more vulnerable to them. Denying the reality of the unconscious keeps a person from knowing one's self, and not knowing one's self leads to the risk of being tyrannized by what that person is trying to ignore.

Basic Dreamwork Techniques

1. Immediately upon awakening, write a complete report of any dream on which you wish to work. Note as many details as you can recall, including your feelings. You now have what you will need when you are ready to return to it.
2. When you do return, give the dream a title and identify its major themes. Think of it as a play or a painting. What is it primarily about? How might that relate to your current life situation? Are there any similar feelings, themes, or circumstances?
3. Identify and note your associations to the most important symbols in the dream. For example, in the recurring dream of the shy librarian reported in chapter 1, in which this woman reported seeing herself as a loud-mouthed waitress in a bar with foul-mouthed men, the major symbols would include things like a bar, foul-mouthed men, a loud-mouthed waitress, and playful teasing. Don't be distracted by consulting manuals listing so-called meanings of these symbols. Simply notice your own personal associations, and then allow yourself to ponder them in your head and heart and notice what arises as you do so.
4. Identify and pay particular attention to your dream ego (the person or symbol in the dream with which you most identify). Particularly notice the puzzling or surprising ways in which this character differs from how you normally behave, and consider

whether this offers you the possibility of new ways of being in the world.

5. Pay attention to any gifts or invitations that may be present in the dream. Consider what changes in your waking life you may want to make in response to these gifts and invitations.

Although many other techniques are available, this is the place to begin dreamwork if it is not something you have previously undertaken.

Advanced Dreamwork Techniques

After you have been working with your dreams for a while, you might want to consider some of the many more advanced ways of engaging with dreams that are available:

1. Allow the dream to move forward beyond the point where it ended in your sleep. This is the first of a whole range of dream techniques involving what is usually called the active imagination, or active dreaming. It is quite amazing how simple and powerful this really is. To start, simply make yourself comfortable in a place where you can be free from interruption and express your willingness to allow the dream in question to unfold within you. Now, rather than thinking back to the dream, you will be able to observe it as it unfolds—and interact with that unfolding. The dream may or may not seem to take the same form as what you remember. That is not important. Pay particular attention to the ways in which it differs. Reflect on why you ended the dream where you did in the original dream, and notice how any further development of the dream changes the tone or significance of the whole.

2. Conduct an imaginary conversation with the most important elements of the dream. This should not take the form of an interrogation in which you demand the dream symbol to reveal its secrets to you. Rather, make it a gentle expression of a hospitable dialogue in which you seek to get to know better each important element of the dream. Be sure to include your dream ego (the person or symbol in the dream with which you most identify) in this conversation since it often is the element

that can most easily be engaged by means of this sort of soul hospitality.

3. Consider how each person in the dream might represent some aspect of your self. If you dreamed of a spouse or friend, don't be quick to assume that this is actually a representation of them somehow appearing in your dream. The dream may be pointing you to notice important relational dynamics related to specific people in your external life; but a safer starting point is to assume that each character (or even object) in the dream represents some part of you. When your boss appears in your dream, start by assuming that it might be giving you an opportunity to get to know the bossy part of yourself. Someone of the other sex may be giving you an opportunity to encounter your animus or anima. Watch particularly for strongly attractive or repulsive characters, and consider how they may point toward lost parts of your own self that need integration. Consider how the dream might be pointing to unfinished business from your past and how it may point toward new possibilities for addressing these.

4. Learn about symbols by doing some reading on them—not to acquire a list of what each major symbol means but to begin to better understand the symbolic nature of the language of the unconscious. Notice how animals in dreams often represent emotions or traits. Dogs and other pets often are understood to represent the domestication of our instincts, although they may also stand for loyalty, friendliness, and the intuitive dimension of life. Horses often represent our instinctual and sexual life, which carries us when we are in a good relationship with it, but which tosses us around when we fear our instincts and libido. Birds often represent transcendence, although they are often also thought to represent intuition. Birth and death usually seem to represent a transition to something new. Children are usually a symbol of vitality, while clothes tell us something about how we wish to be seen (persona) or what we fear (running around in underwear or less). Houses are one of the most universal dream symbols and are usually thought to represent the self. Particularly observe the state of repair. If a house appears in a series of dreams, note the progression of houses. But again, be careful to not take any of this too literally. Just notice major symbols, and over time explore further the meanings that they often carry.

✛ One category of symbols that deserves special attention is what Jung called the archetypes. These are symbols that tend to appear repeatedly in all cultures of the world and seem to emerge, not simply from one's personal unconscious, but also from what Jung called the collective unconscious. The exact form in which they appear will be shaped by the dreamer's personal culture, yet being aware of archetypal dreams can often help by allowing you to recognize that you are dreaming something related not simply to your personal story, but also to the human story.

✛ Dreams of a journey are a common example of archetypal dreams. The journey they draw to our attention is not an upcoming business trip or vacation, but the human journey of awakening and unfolding. Notice the condition of the road and where you are on it. And pay attention to what lies ahead as you see farther down that road (or in your dream, watch the journey unfold). Birds, often present in archetypal dreams of a journey, are frequently thought to symbolize the possibility of transcendence. Watch also for expressions of deep love for another person since they often symbolize an urge toward union and transcendence, passion that goes beyond the natural measure of love and ultimately points us toward the mystery of wholeness.

✛ The shadow, another very important archetype, will usually appear as a person of the same sex in a threatening, night-marish role. Sometimes it will take the form of someone who is pursuing us relentlessly but is impervious to blows and bullets (because it can never be totally eliminated). Qualities that differ most strikingly from the dreamer often, in the dream, suddenly disappear or change. This dream element will display qualities that are not a part of the conscious life of the dreamer: they will usually appear to be quite alien to the personality of the dreamer. But remember, the shadow is merely primitive, not evil in itself. This is why it is frighten-ing. Yet it is a part of you that needs to be welcomed into the family of self if it is to no longer function as an internal saboteur.

✛ The animus and anima (belonging either to a female or male respectively, but once again, being unrecognized parts of self) are also very common elements in dreams that represent very important archetypes. Medicine men, shamans, witches, and priestesses often represent an anima element in the dream of a male and are important invitations for the man to take seriously as a way of learning to attend to feelings, moods, fantasies, and other "feminine" modes of knowing and relating. Animus dreams in women will often appear as the handsome male stranger, a romantic but outlaw or otherwise dangerous male. Once again, the animus is a symbolic invitation to consider other ways of being—particularly those who might involve more risk, boldness, or assertiveness.

✛ These are far from the only archetypal characters that may turn up in dreams. Others include the wise old man (magician, doctor, professor, priest, or other authority figure that embodies spiritual wisdom), the trickster (the clown or buffoon who represents a mocking of the self-pretensions of the ego but who disrupts our schemes and often turns up when the ego is facing a situation made dangerous by vanity, overarching ambition, or bad judgment), the persona (the way we present ourselves to outside world), or the divine child (a baby or infant that represents the regenerative force leading toward transformation). Learning to work with these and other archetypal elements of dreams can seldom (if ever) be mastered by reading books. They require the accompaniment of someone who is directly familiar with the deep parts of the self from which these archetypal symbols emerge.

Although some dreams will forever remain opaque to us when we approach them alone and need to be shared with someone familiar with dreamwork, many dreams will reveal their secret gifts to the dreamer who is willing to attend to them. Remember, a dream is not a cryptogram that needs to be decoded by a glossary of symbol meanings. It is an integral and personal expression of your unconscious. This is why understanding dreams is an individual business that can never be adequately accomplished by following some cookbook approach to dream interpretation. Yet it can be beneficially undertaken by anyone who is prepared to offer hospitality to one's own depths.

Appendix 2

Meditation, Prayer, and Awakening

Lao-tzu is often quoted as having said that a journey of a thousand miles begins with a single step. Chinese friends tell me that this isn't the best translation of his actual words. What he actually said was something closer to "Even the longest journey must begin where you stand." Rather than emphasizing either the first step or the distance involved in the whole journey, he was emphasizing that action arises most naturally from stillness, this being quite central to his philosophy and to Taoism.

This reminds us that the journey of awakenings is based not on action but on attention and openness. Awakenings happen within a reflective context. This is the reason why the contemplative dimensions of the spiritual life are so essential to awakening. The absence of stillness results in the absence of transformation because, as Lao-tzu correctly realized, stillness is the birthplace of awareness, and awareness the birthplace of awakening.

Thoughts and Awakening

Awakening always involves the mind. The mind is so fundamental to human existence that it forms a part of all levels and states of consciousness. It is never left behind in psychological or spiritual development. It is, however, transformed as we move through body-, mind-, and soul-centered levels of consciousness.

But because mental activity remains present in all states of human consciousness—even sleep (where dreams remind us that the body may be somewhat dormant but the mind continues to be active)—the mind is also a potential trap in which we can very easily get stuck. Thoughts form the core of this trap. We might think of them as the quicksand of consciousness. This is why so many spiritual traditions emphasize the importance of releasing our attachment to our thoughts. One way of understanding Jesus's teaching about the necessity of losing our self if we are to truly find it is that in order to find our true self we must release the false centers of self in which we so easily settle. Regardless of whether they are body-, mind-, or soul-centered, thoughts remain at the core of these penultimate and therefore ultimately false centers of our being. Thoughts form the background of consciousness organized around body, mind, and soul. They are the static that keeps us distracted and yet at the same time lulls us back asleep whenever we manage to awaken.

The spirit-centered life is not devoid of thoughts. But in it, our attachment to thoughts is softened, and consequently they come and go without dragging us around with them.Eventually we may be able to recognize that our thoughts are not us; they are simply things that arise within us and that we can release. Learning to release thoughts is the route to stillness and the goal of meditation.

Forms of Meditation

Meditation (sometimes called contemplation) is the spiritual practice of stillness in openness and trust. Most spiritual traditions encourage meditation in one form or another, and most hold it to be an important resource for expanding awareness and facilitating transformation. Although all major forms of Eastern religious meditation have corresponding expressions in Christian meditation, this is not to deny significant differences in practice and understanding of meditation both between and within religions. Much of what is called meditation in Christian spirituality would better be described as reflection. Meditating on Scriptures, for example, is based on conscious thought and is quite different from practices more appropriately called meditation. In Christian spirituality these practices are often called contemplation.

However, despite these semantic confusions, meditative practices generally fall into three basic groups, with expressions of each of these to be found in Christian, non-Christian, and nonreligious approaches to meditation.

Concentrative methods rely on focusing attention. Here the mind is given a simple task (such as counting breaths or reciting a simple mantra) so that the deeper waters of one's being can be gathered together in stillness. A second group of meditative practices relies on awareness. Here one aligns one's self with an inner observer and simply watches the flow of energy as thoughts and emotions ebb and flood. The final cluster of meditative approaches is based on surrender. Here there is no need to watch thoughts or emotions. As they or any other things arise in consciousness, you simply release them.

However, beneath the differences between these three approaches lies the shared transformational potential of meditation. In its essence, meditation seeks to accomplish two things: inner stillness and expanded awareness. It is the increased awareness that is transformational; inner stillness is not so much the goal as the method. In the Judeo-Christian tradition, stillness is the place of encounter with the Divine. Psalm 46:10 invites us to be still so that we might know God. But this encounter with the Divine happens in the midst of an equally important encounter that occurs when we are still: an encounter with our selves. Then the question becomes, what are we to do with the thoughts, memories, and aspects of self that stillness seems to catalyze? The answer offered by all three meditative traditions is to simply release them.

Release of what we encounter in meditation is the route to stillness. This is the essence of detachment and the core of surrender. Meditation is not the time to think about what arises in consciousness. It is, rather, the time to release whatever may arise within consciousness. Even thoughts of God are to be released. The most basic rule of meditation is to let go of whatever comes into consciousness. It is this act of release, offered in stillness and presence to self and to God, that makes meditation such a powerful engine of transformation. It is also in this context of stillness, presence, and letting go of whatever arises in consciousness that awareness develops. We become aware of deeper realities when we release our attachment to the more superficial things that normally fill consciousness.

Thoughts are the primary content of consciousness, which we release in meditation. The goal should not be to eliminate thoughts but simply to release them. And as we do so, we become aware that we are more than our thoughts. It is our thoughts that most keep us from awakening. As we release them, we are then able to move beyond them and to know things that could never be squeezed through the filters of rationality or conceptual thought.

Letting go opens up space within the self that is essential to stillness and awakening. Awakening grows out of emptiness, not fullness. Our attachments become our preoccupations and keep us asleep. Opening space within our self through meditation allows the four major levels of our being—body, mind, soul, and spirit—to align with and respond to the flow of Spirit into the depths of our being. Meditation connects us to our body and will bring into consciousness things going on within our body. Attention to breathing, which forms an important part of many meditative traditions, is particularly helpful in grounding meditation in our bodies. But as we let go of body awareness, even awareness of our breath, meditation then connects us to our mind. Once again, as we release our thoughts and other mental contents, we then move into the more spacious reflective place of soul. But meditation once more encourages us to notice and then release the meaning of experiences that now come to consciousness; as we do so, we move into the even more spacious realm of spirit.

Meditation is a discipline that takes practice. In the beginning it will always feel frustrating and difficult. But if continued, over time it will begin to yield its benefits of inner stillness, presence, and expanding awareness. Consciousness will be transformed as our attachment to those things with which we most closely identify is softened. New and larger horizons will emerge, and our small ego-self will be replaced by a self that is larger and more inclusive. But it is not just our consciousness and identity that are being transformed. Our very being is being transformed. We are becoming more than we were, more of who we most truly and deeply are.

Meditation can be practiced both alone and with others. It is best undertaken within a specific tradition rather than practiced in some generic manner. It is, after all, a spiritual practice, and spirituality is best cultivated within a spiritual tradition that gives it shape and meaning and that gives the individual a community of reference and belonging. The Christian tradition offers two major meditative paths: (1) centering prayer, associated primarily with the work of Basil Pennington, Thomas Keating, and Cynthia Bourgeault; and (2) Christian meditation, associated with the work of John Main. Either can be an extremely rich practice for Christians who seek to make meditation part of their own spiritual practice.

Meditation and Transformation

Most of us live most our life on the periphery of our being, not from our depths. Although I have spoken of transformation as an expansion of consciousness, when we begin to think about our connection to our depths, it is also helpful to think of this as a deepening of consciousness. Awakening and transforming involve movement from the circumference to the center of our being. But we are unable to find our own way into that center. As Richard Rohr states, we do not find it, it finds us.[1] We cannot think our way to it, but we can open ourselves to new ways of thinking that come from releasing old ways associated with life at the circumference.

Meditation is a doorway to our center. Or, using more psychological language, meditation opens the possibility of accessing our unconscious and, therefore, to living with a stronger alliance between the conscious and unconscious dimensions of our being. Meditation is a path from ordinary awareness to spiritual awareness, from a knowing about things to a knowing of them. This means that meditation is far more than a way of trying to still ourselves. It is a way of opening our self so that we can be found by our center—by the Spirit of God—and therein truly find our self.

Meditation and Prayer

The Christian forms of meditation bring us, however, to the question of the relationship between meditation and prayer. This is an important question because I think there are limits to what meditation can, in itself, accomplish that are overcome when meditation is placed within a context of prayer. Ken Wilber states that meditation does not directly engage the shadow and can even exacerbate the shadow.[2] I think he is correct in this judgment, and it draws our attention to something very important. It means that, as powerfully transformational as meditation can be, it does not lead directly to the integration of one's shadow—a dimension of the soul work that we discussed in chapter 8 and that must be undertaken apart from times of meditation. Meditation may bring our shadow issues to our awareness, but our work on these issues is not a part of meditation—at least as it is practiced apart from prayer.

I am convinced, however, that the contemplative forms of prayer do offer the Spirit unique access to our unconscious depths and allow a reworking of the unconscious that can lead to an integration of the shadow. Contemplative prayer is more relational than meditation in a context apart from prayer. Although contemplative prayer and meditation may share many features, contemplative prayer is wordless openness to God. Hence it involves a relationship. It is this intentional openness to God while setting aside thoughts that makes contemplative prayer so deeply transformational.

Contemplative prayer always requires hospitality to your deep self, to the deep parts of your self. It demands the openness to receive whatever might arise in you and then gently release it into God's hands. But in prayer you are not alone as you open yourself to whatever might emerge. You do so in a relationship that provides safety and support in holding whatever emerges. That which arises might come with a flood of emotional intensity. Sometimes being still before self and God releases a torrent of emotions. Tears may be intermixed with joy and sadness as repressed memories and fragments of past experience burst into consciousness. But whatever emerges in silence and stillness before God emerges in the place within you in which you are held within God. It emerges, therefore, within the context of prayer, whether or not you are thinking of God or talking to God. Your openness to God makes it prayer.

Thomas Keating describes what happens in stillness and silence before God in unworded presence as divine therapy.[3] It may involve an unloading of the unconscious, but this is only the visible face of the invisible process of reworking your unconscious, a process that is going on as you sit in stillness before God and yourself. This can be very frightening. But you do not need to do more than remain open in faith to the Spirit, who is working in your depths. This isn't the time to try to understand the things that float to the surface of your consciousness. Instead, it is the time to simply note them and then release them to God. But as you recognize their presence, you become aware of what exists within you, and you have an opportunity to peek at the deep hidden work of healing and transformation that God is doing in your soul. This is the transformational way in which contemplative prayer works.[4]

Notes

Preface

1. *The Book of Alternative Services of the Anglican Church of Canada* (Toronto: Anglican Book Centre, 1985), 352.

Chapter 1 Human Awakening

1. Frederick S. Perls, *Ego, Hunger, and Aggression: The Beginning of Gestalt Therapy* (New York: Vintage, 1969).

2. *Anthony De Mello: Writings*, selected and introduced by William Dyceh, SJ (Maryknoll, NY: Orbis, 1999), 50.

3. Eckhart Tolle, *The Power of Now: A Guide to Spiritual Enlightenment* (Vancouver: Namaste, 1997).

4. Douglas Steere, *Prayer in the Contemporary World* (Wallingford, PA: Pendle Hill, 1990), 4.

5. Pim van Lommel et al., "Near-Death Experience in Survivors of Cardiac Arrest: A Prospective Study in the Netherlands," *The Lancet* 358, no. 9298 (2001): 2039–45, http://profezie3m.altervista.org/archivio/TheLancet_NDE.htm.

6. For a fuller discussion of the psychology of Paul, see Edward V. Stein, "The Conversion of Paul," *Pastoral Psychology* 44, no. 6 (1996): 385–93; James Beck, *The Psychology of Paul* (Grand Rapids: Kregel, 2002); James E. Loder, *The Transforming Moment*, 2nd ed. (Colorado Springs: Helmers & Howard, 1989); Krister Stendahl, "The Apostle Paul and the Introspective Conscience of the West," in *Paul among Jews and Gentiles* (Philadelphia: Fortress, 1976), 78–96.

7. For further discussion of the role of attention to breath in Christian prayer, see David G. Benner, *Opening to God: Lectio Divina and Life as Prayer* (Downers Grove, IL: InterVarsity, 2010). For a discussion of the importance of breath as the meeting point of body, soul, and spirit, also see, *Soulful Spirituality: Becoming Fully Alive and Deeply Human* (Grand Rapids: Brazos, 2011), chap. 8.

8. Quoted in Joan Chittister, *The Gift of Years* (Toronto: Novalis, 2008), 13.

9. John Welwood, *Journey of the Heart: The Path of Conscious Love* (New York: HarperCollins, 1990).

10. Ibid., 13.

11. Cynthia Bourgeault, *The Meaning of Mary Magdalene: Discovering the Woman at the Heart of Christianity* (Boston: Shambhala, 2010), 115.

12. Ken Wilber, *Grace and Grit* (Boston: Shambhala, 1991), 405.

13. I particularly thank Dr. Johan Geyser and others who offered helpful questions in responding to my lectures on the topic of this book at the Mosaiek Community, Johannesburg, S.A., in September 2010. My colleague Dr. Jackie Stinton was also once again most helpful in asking probing questions that helped me unpack my thinking, and I extend my appreciation to her for this help.

Chapter 2 Mapping the Unfolding Self

1. Ken Wilber, *Integral Spirituality* (Boston: Integral Books, 2007).

2. For further discussion of this way of understanding soul, see David G. Benner, *Soulful Spirituality: Becoming Fully Alive and Deeply Human* (Grand Rapids: Brazos, 2011). James Hillman's *Re-Visioning Psychology* (New York: Harper & Row, 1975) also presents an excellent discussion of a similar view of the soul.

3. Quoted by Wilber, *Integral Spirituality*, 214.

4. Lloyd P. Gerson, *Plotinus* (New York: Routledge, 1994).

5. For further discussion of this point, see Wilber, *Integral Spirituality*, "Appendix 1: From the Great Chain of Being to Postmodernism in 3 Easy Steps."

6. Ibid., 216.

7. Ibid., 217.

8. Leo Frabenius, *Unknown Africa* (Vienna: Phaidon, 1933), 47; quoted by Ulrich Mohrhoff, "Evolution of Consciousness according to Jean Gebser," *AntiMatters* 2, no. 3 (2008): 54.

9. Both the labels and interpretation of these worldviews are my own. Cultural historians would shudder to read the simplicity of what I sketch here. Jean Gebser (*The Ever-Present Origin* [Athens: Ohio University Press, 1985]) identifies five major worldviews; Duane Elgin (*The Awakening Earth: Exploring the Evolution of Human Culture and Consciousness* [New York: W. Morrow, 1993]) suggests eight. Since my purposes are illustrative, I have offered a simplified account of this most interesting perspective on human unfolding, which can be found in more detail in either of these sources.

10. Quoted by Gebser, *Ever-Present Origin*, 5–6.

Chapter 3 Growth and the Lines of Development

1. Ken Wilber, *Integral Spirituality* (Boston: Integral Books, 2007), 60.

2. Howard Gardner, *Multiple Intelligences* (New York: Basic Books, 1993).

3. James Fowler, *Stages of Faith: The Psychology of Human Development* (New York: HarperCollins, 1995).

4. James Fowler, *Becoming Adult, Becoming Christian: Adult Development and Christian Faith* (New York: Harper & Row, 1984), 55.

5. As Karen Armstrong points out in *The Case for God* (New York: Alfred A. Knopf, 2009), fundamentalism is defined not by the content of belief but by the failure to hold *mythos* and *logos* together, allowing each to enrich the other. When *logos* (the contents of beliefs) become separated from *mythos* (the great stories that carry *logos* in a way that helps us know its larger- and deeper-than-literal truth), the result is something that is no longer truly believable. This, from Armstrong's perspective, is the soil out of which both atheism and fundamentalism arise and flourish.

6. James Fowler, *Faith Development and Pastoral Care* (Philadelphia: Fortress, 1987), 93.

7. Fowler, *Stages of Faith*, 200.

8. Ernest G. Schachtel, *Metamorphosis* (New York: Basic Books, 1959).

9. Robert Kegan, *The Evolving Self: Problems and Processes in Human Development* (Cambridge, MA: Harvard University Press, 1982).

Chapter 4 Transformation and the Levels of Development

1. Ken Wilber, *Integral Spirituality* (Boston: Integral Books, 2007), 50–71.

2. Ibid., 66.

3. As I have described it, consciousness sounds like a human property. This is how it is treated in most of contemporary neuroscience, where it is then even further reduced to being a property not just of human life but specifically of the brain. However, this sort of materialistic, reductionistic, and anthropocentric way of thinking is not the only way to approach an understanding of consciousness. Hindu and Buddhist philosophers have long argued that consciousness pervades the universe and all of its elements, a view that has also been central to such Western philosophers as Bertrand Russell, Alfred North Whitehead, and Gottfried Leibniz. We encounter something similar in Carl Jung's concept of the collective unconscious, which he posited as a sort of divine energy that exists everywhere and is accessed through dreams, intuition, and imagination. The Jesuit priest and paleontologist Teilhard de Chardin coined the term "noosphere" to describe what he called the thinking envelope of the earth. Consciousness, he argued, should be understood as a psychic force that combines but transcends the power of mind and spirit and, above all, the power of love. Although treated with disdain by most neuroscientists, this understanding of consciousness as a property of creation at large receives significant support from modern physics and becomes foundational to the evolutionary theology of such people as Diarmuid Ó'Murchú (e.g., see his *Evolutionary Faith* [Maryknoll, NY: Orbis, 2002]), who considers consciousness to be the all-pervading energy of creation, to be understood not as a onetime event but as an ongoing outflowing of life. In such an understanding, human consciousness is participation in this larger cosmic force, which from a faith perspective is seen to be the outflowing life of God. Our participation in this human consciousness takes the form of inwardness, depth, and wisdom. But consciousness itself is the animating and awakening energy that lies behind all unfolding and becoming. Human consciousness is possible because we are the progeny of a conscious universe.

4. Murray Stein, *Transformation: Emergence of the Self* (College Station: Texas A&M University Press, 1998), 15.

5. Richard Rohr, *The Naked Now: Learning to See as the Mystics See* (New York: Crossroad, 2009), 53.

6. Robert Kegan, *The Evolving Self: Problems and Processes in Human Development* (Cambridge, MA: Harvard University Press, 1982), 44.

7. Nevertheless, I recently spent some time in the slums of Calcutta and was struck by the fact that life circumstances do not necessarily shape identity. While visiting impoverished regions of countries, I have become familiar with the way in which the poorest of the poor tend to look down when they encounter a stranger, never looking the other in the eye and instead communicating the shame they feel in relation to someone obviously of a higher social standing. So what struck me in Calcutta (and other places in India) was the dignity that the poorest of the poor displayed when I encountered them. Rather than shame, what I typically saw in their faces was dignity. Most often they looked me in the eye and carried themselves with dignity that was astounding, given their social status. That sense of dignity came from knowing who they were and what was expected from them—one of the positive consequences of the caste system that certainly does not balance out the negative but does make an important point: identity is not inevitably shaped by life circumstances.

8. Kegan, *The Evolving Self*, 44.

9. I am thankful to Richard Rohr (*The Naked Now*) for his very helpful discussion of faith's central role in transformation. His focus on the mystics' contributions to understanding the transformation of consciousness complements exceptionally well what I am presenting in this book.

10. David G. Benner, *Opening to God: Lectio Divina and Life as Prayer* (Downers Grove, IL: InterVarsity, 2010).

11. Rohr, *The Naked Now*, 52.

12. Dag Hammarskjöld, *Markings* (New York: Ballantine, 1985), 180.

13. This poem is widely attributed to the French poet Guillaume Apollinaire (1880–1918) but is actually by the British poet Christopher Logue (b. 1926), written in 1968 to introduce an exhibition of Apollinaire's work on the fiftieth anniversary of his death and to celebrate his daring spirit. On the displayed poster the poem's title was "Apollinaire Said." See *Guillaume Apollinaire, 1880–1918: A Celebration, 1968* (London: Institute of Contemporary Arts, 1968), an exhibition catalog; Christopher Logue, "Come to the Edge," in *New Numbers* (London: Jonathan Cape, 1969), 65–66; http://en.wikiquote.org/wiki/Christopher_Logue; http://poemof-theday.blogspot.com/2010/04/come-to-edge-christopher-logue.html.

14. Kathy Helmers, personal communication, December 6, 2010.

15. Teresa of Avila, *Complete Works of St. Teresa of Avila*, vol. 1 (New York: Continuum International, 2002).

16. Thomas Keating, "The Four You's," *Contemplative Outreach* 23, no. 2 (June 2008): 1–2.

Chapter 5 Learning from the Christian Mystics

1. Thomas Merton, *The Ascent to Truth* (New York: Harcourt, Brace, 1981), 53.

2. Peter N. Borys Jr., *Transforming Heart and Mind: Learning from the Mystics* (Mahwah, NJ: Paulist Press, 2006), 7.

3. Margaret Cropper, *The Life of Evelyn Underhill* (Woodstock, VT: Skylight Paths, 2003), 5–6.

4. Ibid., 17.

5. Evelyn Underhill, *Mysticism: A Study of the Nature and Development of Spiritual Consciousness* (New York: Dutton, 1911).

6. Evelyn Underhill, *The Ways of the Spirit* (New York: Crossroad Classic, 1993), 142.

7. Underhill, *Mysticism*, 81–94.

8. St. John of the Cross, *The Dark Night of the Soul* (London: Hodder & Stoughton, 1988).

9. The posthumous publication of sixty-six years of correspondence of Mother Teresa with her confessors and spiritual superiors (*Mother Teresa: Come Be My Light; The Private Writings of the "Saint of Calcutta,"* ed. Brian Kolodiejchuk [New York: Doubleday, 2007]) reveals that despite a period in 1946–47 when she experienced a profound sense of union with God, soon after she began her work with the destitute and dying in Calcutta and lasting nearly a half century until her death, she felt no presence of God whatsoever. Far from being a God-intoxicated saint who spent her days in ecstatic mystic union, Mother Teresa learned to deal with her protracted dark night of the soul by converting her feelings of abandonment by God into a life of abandonment to God.

10. Julian of Norwich, *Revelation of Love*, trans. John Skinner (New York: Image, 1996), 24.

11. Thomas Merton, *Thoughts in Solitude* (Boston: Shambhala, 1993), 89.

12. Blaise Pascal, *Pensées* (New York: E. P. Dutton, 1958), 78.

13. David G. Benner, *The Gift of Being Yourself: The Sacred Call to Self-Discovery* (Downers Grove, IL: InterVarsity, 2004).

14. Thomas Merton, *New Seeds of Contemplation* (New York: New Directions, 1961), 36.

15. Thomas Keating, *Open Mind, Open Heart* (New York: Continuum, 1986); Cynthia Bourgeault, *Centering Prayer and Inner Awakening* (Cambridge, MA: Cowley, 2004).

16. For further discussion about the mystical roots of this modern psychological insight, see Borys, *Transforming Heart and Mind*.

17. Richard Rohr, *The Naked Now: Learning to See as the Mystics See* (New York: Crossroad, 2009), 29–30.

18. Ibid., 34.

19. This framework is a slight adaption of that offered by the Great Nest of Existence (which we discussed in chap. 2) that emerged as I sought to find a way to map the unfolding of the awakening self I witnessed in people whose transformation I have observed. I have omitted the first level of existence suggested by the Great Nest because, while philosophers, theologians, and scientists have often asserted that matter may involve consciousness (see, e.g., David J. Chalmers, *The Conscious Mind* [New York: Oxford University Press, 1996] and Dairmuid O'Murchu, *Evolutionary Faith* [Maryknoll, NY: Orbis, 2002], it does not seem meaningful to think of it as possessing identity. I have also changed the second—life as described by the Great Nest of Existence—to body, this being the context within which life is first and most fundamentally experienced in human consciousness.

20. Rohr, *The Naked Now*.

Chapter 6 The Body-Centered Self

1. An identity and consciousness built around being at one with everything that is forms both the foundation and pinnacle of human development. The journey of human awakening begins with differentiation from this sea of nondifferentiation but, as we move toward the highest levels of consciousness and identity organized around spirit, returns us once again to a sense of oneness with all that is. Yet the differences between these two stages of earliest infancy and greatest possible human development are very significant in that, as we shall see, a spirit-centered consciousness retains differentiation as it recovers the sense of oneness. Jesus experienced oneness with the Father and a profound sense of solidarity with all humans, yet there are no signs to suggest that he failed to recognize his own individuality.

2. James Finley, *Merton's Palace of Nowhere: A Search for God through Awareness of the True Self* (Notre Dame, IN: Ave Marie Press, 1978), 35.

3. Eckhart Tolle, *The Power of Now: A Guide to Spiritual Enlightenment* (Vancouver: Namaste, 1997).

Chapter 7 The Mind-Centered Self

1. Here I am making an important distinction between ego and self, a distinction central to analytical (Jungian) psychology, although my own use of the terms differs somewhat from Jung's usage. In brief, without ego (the executive functions of personality) there can be no self (the overall person I experience as "me"). For a more complete discussion of this distinction between the ego and the self, as well as the important role each must play in spirituality, see David G. Benner, *Soulful Spirituality: Becoming Fully Alive and Deeply Human* (Grand Rapids: Brazos, 2011), chap. 5.

2. Richard M. Gula, *The Good Life: Where Morality and Spirituality Converge* (Mahwah, NJ: Paulist Press, 1999).

3. Sigmund Freud, *Civilization and Its Discontents*, trans. James Strackey (New York: Norton, 1989).

4. E. Mansell Pattison, "Ego Morality: An Emerging Psychotherapeutic Concept," *Psychoanalytic Review* 55 (1968): 187–222.

5. The best available current maps of the overall contours of moral development can be found in the work of Lawrence Kohlberg (*The Psychology of Moral Development: The Nature and Validity of Moral Stages; Essays on Moral Development*, vol. 2 [New York:

HarperCollins, 1984]; and Carol Gilligan (*In a Different Voice: Psychological Theory and Women's Development* [Cambridge, MA: Harvard University Press, 1993]).

6. Michael Cox, *The Meaning of Night* (Toronto: McClelland & Stewart, 2006), 294.

7. Although people commonly associate this sort of pressure to conform with religiously based communities, the same pressure to maintain orthodoxy and orthopraxy exists in many other communities that are built on a shared ideology. A classic example is the psychoanalytic community. The earliest signs of resistance to heterodoxy in this tradition go back to Freud. When Carl Jung began to show insufficient attachment to certain core Freudian doctrines (principally the assumption of the universality of the oedipal complex) and to exhibit a dangerous entertainment of radically unorthodox ideas (such as those associated with the collective unconscious), his close personal friendship with Freud was terminated. Freud also saw to it that Jung's credentials as a psychoanalyst were so tarnished that he and his followers were forced to use the name "analytical psychology" for their system of psychology and psychotherapy, to distinguish it from the psychoanalytical system associated with Freud. To this day the psychoanalytic community still has true believers who preserve the core of slowly evolving understandings associated with classical Freudian drive theory, as well as those who stand outside this realm of orthodoxy and practice, research, and theorize in a more heterodox manner.

8. Thomas Merton, *New Seeds of Contemplation* (New York: New Directions, 1961), 36.

9. Several years after being given this simple formula for the levels of self as understood by Asians who are Chinese, I met a Chinese professor of Marxist political philosophy from Zhejiang University in China at a Christian center for dialogue with Taoists and Buddhists in Hong Kong. He was a Taoist who had taken a sabbatical to spend several months in dialogue with Christians. I was there for dialogue with Taoists and Buddhists. After asking about his own spiritual framework, I asked him about his interest in Christianity. I was surprised when he said it wasn't personal, at least not primarily. He went on to tell me that he felt that China needed a social philosophy or religion to help them take the next step in their cultural evolution, and he wished to explore whether Christianity might be good for his country. I further asked about his personal interest in it, a question he would have found strange if he had not studied in the West and been quite familiar with our individualistic approach to life. His answer was that if Christianity was good for his country, it would be good for him; but his primary concern was whether Christianity could take his nation to the next stage of where they needed to go better than the Marxist-Leninist philosophy that had, in his mind, served them well but was quickly outliving its usefulness.

10. Thomas Keating, *Invitation to Love: The Way of Christian Contemplation* (New York: Continuum, 1994), 148.

Chapter 8 The Soul-Centered Self

1. James Hillman, *Re-Visioning Psychology* (New York: Harper & Row, 1975); see also idem, *The Soul's Code* (New York: Warner Books, 1997).

2. For a fuller discussion of ways of living soulfully that nurture and ground our spirituality while at the same time facilitating our becoming more than we are, see David G. Benner, *Soulful Spirituality: Becoming Fully Alive and Deeply Human* (Grand Rapids: Brazos, 2011).

3. Carl G. Jung, *Psychology and Religion* (New Haven: Yale University Press, 1960), 131.

4. Richard Rohr notes that Francis of Assisi considered the kissing of a leper to be the moment of his conversion, suggesting that the deep significance of this act was that the kiss represented for St. Francis his acceptance of his shadow and his forgiveness of himself for being human. Richard Rohr, *On the Threshold of Transformation: Daily Meditations for Men* (Chicago: Loyola Press, 2010), 201.

5. Søren Kierkegaard, *Purity of Heart Is to Will One Thing* (New York: Harper Collins, 1956).

6. Thomas Merton, *New Seeds of Contemplation* (New York: New Directions, 1961).

7. Abraham Maslow, *Religious Aspects of Peak-Experiences* (New York: Harper & Row, 1970).

Chapter 9 The Spirit-Centered Self

1. Robert Kegan, *The Evolving Self: Problem and Process in Human Development* (Cambridge, MA: Harvard University Press, 1982).

2. Daniel Ladinsky, *I Heard God Laughing: Renderings of Hafiz* (Walnut Creek, CA: Sufism Reoriented, 1996), 113.

3. St. Bonaventure and Cardinal Manning, *The Life of St. Francis of Assisi* (Rockford, IL: TAN Books, 1988), 85.

4. Cynthia Bourgeault, *Centering Prayer and Inner Awakening* (Cambridge, MA: Cowley, 2004), 13.

5. William Ralph Inge, *Light, Life and Love: Selections from the German Mystics of the Middle Ages* (London: Methuen, 1904), Kindle e-book, published by Project Gutenberg, location 562–65.

6. Ibid., location 1768–71.

7. Ibid., location 156–57.

8. Raimon Panikkar, *Christophany* (Maryknoll, NY: Orbis, 2005), 115.

9. Hildegard of Bingen, *Scivias*, Classics of Western Spirituality (Mahwah, NJ: Paulist Press, 1990).

10. Ibid., back cover.

11. Pierre Teilhard de Chardin, http://www.amazon.com/Divine-Milieu-Perennial -Classics/dp/0060937254/ref=pd_sim_b_1, *The Divine Milieu*, Perennial Classics (New York: Perennial, 2001).

12. Matthew Fox, *The Coming of the Cosmic Christ: The Healing of Mother Earth and the Birth of a Global Renaissance* (New York: Harper & Row, 1988).

13. Hafiz, *The Gift: Poems by the Great Sufi Master*, trans. Daniel James Ladinsky (New York: Penguin Compass, 1999), 32.

14. *Anthony De Mello: Writings*, selected and introduced by William Dych, SJ (Maryknoll, NY: Orbis, 2008), 105.

15. Thomas Merton, *The Modern Man* (Toronto: Bantam, 1961), para 70, 66.

16. Quoted in Philip Endean, *Karl Rahner and Ignatian Spirituality* (Oxford: Oxford University Press, 2001), 63.

Chapter 10 Spirituality and Awakening

1. It is not just children raised in religious homes who think about God or have images of God. When child psychoanalyst Dr. Ana-Maria Riuzzuto asked young children from religious and secular homes to draw an image of God, none had any difficulty in doing so. Although Freud postulated that belief in God is based on a child's idea of one's father, Rizzuto argues that the God representation draws from a variety of sources and is a major element in the fabric of one's view of self, others, and the world. She describes her research and its theoretical implications in Ana-Maria Ruizzuto, *The Birth of the Living God* (Chicago: University of Chicago Press, 1981).

2. Ken Wilber, *Integral Spirituality* (Boston: Integral Books, 2007), 129.

3. *The Simone Weil Reader*, ed. George Panichas (New York: David McKay, 1977), 11.

4. *Anthony De Mello: Writings*, selected and introduced by William Dych, SJ (Maryknoll, NY: Orbis, 2008), 106.

5. Ernest Becker, *The Denial of Death* (New York: Free Press, 1997).

6. De Mello, *Writings*, 74.

7. David G. Benner, *Opening to God: Lectio Divina and Life as Prayer* (Downers Grove, IL: InterVarsity, 2010).

8. William Ralph Inge, *Light, Life and Love: Selections from the German Mystics of the Middle Ages* (London: Methuen, 1904), Kindle e-book, published by Project Gutenberg, location 138–44.

9. The way in which I have described this contemplative stillness reflects my own understanding and practice as it has been shaped by centering prayer. For a fuller discussion of this contemplative dimension of prayer and its transformational possibilities, see Benner, *Opening to God*, chap. 7.

10. Daniel Helminiak, *Spiritual Development: An Interdisciplinary Study* (Chicago: Loyola Press, 1987), xii.

11. Ibid.

12. Wilber, *Integral Spirituality*, 193.

13. Ibid., 197.

14. Helminiak, *Spiritual Development*, 166.

Chapter 11 The Communal Context of Transformation

1. Carl G. Jung, *The Practice of Psychotherapy*, in *The Collected Works of C. G. Jung*, vol. 16, 2nd ed. (Princeton: Princeton University Press, 1966), 94.

2. Donald Woods Winnicott, *Maturational Processes and the Facilitating Environment: Studies in the Theory of Emotional Development* (London: Karnac, 1995).

3. Robert Kegan, *The Evolving Self: Problem and Process in Human Development* (Cambridge, MA: Harvard University Press, 1982), 116.

4. Ibid.

5. H. Richard Niebuhr, *The Meaning of Revelation* (New York: Macmillan, 1941), 81.

6. Kegan, *The Evolving Self*, 129.

7. Ibid., 258.

8. Ibid., 260–61.

9. Ibid., 261.

Chapter 12 Transformation and Transcendence

1. See David G. Benner, *Opening to God: Lectio Divina and Life as Prayer* (Downers Grove, IL: InterVarsity, 2010), esp. chap. 3, on *lectio divina*, and chap. 7, on centering prayer.

2. Margaret Silf, *Compass Points* (Chicago: Loyola Press, 2009), 224–25.

Appendix 1 Dreamwork for Growth and Transformation

1. David G. Benner, *Soulful Spirituality: Becoming Fully Alive and Deeply Human* (Grand Rapids: Brazos, 2011), 95–105.

Appendix 2 Meditation, Prayer, and Awakening

1. Richard Rohr, *Everything Belongs: The Gift of Contemplative Prayer* (New York: Crossroad, 1999), 20.

2. Ken Wilber, *Integral Spirituality* (Boston: Integral Books, 2007), 126.

3. Thomas Keating, *Open Heart, Open Mind* (New York: Continuum, 2000).

4. For a much fuller discussion of the psychology and theology of this process of transformation through wordless stillness before self and God in prayer, see Cynthia Bourgeault, *Centering Prayer and Inner Awakening* (Cambridge, MA: Cowley, 2004).

Index